CHARLES DICKENS IN AMERICA

CHARLES DICKENS

From a painting made by Francis Alexander in Boston in 1842

CHARLES DICKENS
IN AMERICA

COMPILED AND EDITED BY

WILLIAM GLYDE WILKINS

WITH 41 ILLUSTRATIONS AND PORTRAITS

HASKELL HOUSE PUBLISHERS LTD.
Publishers of Scarce Scholarly Books
NEW YORK. N. Y. 10012
1970

First Published 1911

HASKELL HOUSE PUBLISHERS LTD.
Publishers of Scarce Scholarly Books
280 LAFAYETTE STREET
NEW YORK. N. Y. 10012

Library of Congress Catalog Card Number: 70-120131

Standard Book Number 8383-1092-3

Printed in the United States of America

TO MY FELLOW-MEMBERS

OF

THE DICKENS FELLOWSHIP

FOREWORD

THE writer, on reading *American Notes* and Dickens's
letters from America in the volumes of his collected
letters and his letters to Forster, printed in the latter's
Life of Charles Dickens, has always been struck with
two things: his very severe criticism of the American
newspapers in 1842, and his bitterness on the subject
of International Copyright. In order to satisfy himself
as to the justness of Dickens's opinions at the time
the book and letters were written, he has collected
extracts from the newspapers of nearly every city which
the Author visited during his first trip to the United
States. These were so interesting, as giving the Press-
writers' accounts of the visit, and their opinions of the
Author personally, that the collection was further extended to include anything that could be found in print,
by American writers, relating to the visit—some written
during the time of the visit and some later.

Mr. Philip Hone, who was one of the committee which
entertained Dickens in New York, kept a diary from 1828
to 1850, which was published in 1889 by Bodd, Mead &
Co., New York; and "Four Months with Charles Dickens
during his First Visit to America: By his Secretary,"
published in the *Atlantic Monthly* shortly after Dickens's
death—both contain much interesting matter relating
to Dickens's first visit. One or two private diaries have
been discovered containing references to Dickens which
have never been published. All this material, much of
which has been buried in the files of old newspapers for
nearly seventy years, and in other places for a shorter
time, has proved so interesting to the writer that he has
ventured to arrange it in the order in which Dickens

made his first American tour; and he hopes those who have read Dickens's own account of the trip will be equally interested in reading another account written by American writers. He has allowed these American writers to tell the story, with a few words here and there of his own to make the account a connected one. He has also collected a large number of contemporary engravings of the places mentioned in *American Notes*, and of hotels in which he lodged, which he believes are of equal interest with the text, many of which are reproduced.

The readers can draw their own conclusions as to the justice of Dickens's opinions and criticisms of the Press and people of the United States in 1842.

The account of the dinner given to Dickens by the Press of the United States, in New York in 1868, has also been included, as it contains so many beautiful tributes to the author by such famous editors and writers of the time as Horace Greeley, George William Curtis, Henry J. Raymond, William Henry Hurlbert and others, most of whom have passed away. These speeches have never been printed except in the newspapers immediately after the dinner, and the writer believes they should be preserved in more permanent and accessible form, which is the reason for their being included in this book.

WILLIAM GLYDE WILKINS.

PITTSBURGH (PA.), U.S.A.,
     August, 1911.

CONTENTS

LIST OF ILLUSTRATIONS

CHARLES DICKENS IN AMERICA

CHAPTER I

INTRODUCTORY

THERE can be no doubt in the minds of those who have read *The Life of Charles Dickens*, by his friend Forster, as to what was the prime object of the author's second visit to the United States in 1868. It was, to paraphrase Shakespeare, "to put money in his purse"; in fact, he frankly wrote Forster, who disapproved of the project, "Have no fear that anything will induce me to make the experiment if I do not see the most forcible reason for believing that what I could get by it, added to what I have got, would leave me with a sufficient future."

No fault can be found with him for this reason, as Dickens had a large family, his living expenses were heavy, and he desired to be able to leave his children provided for after his death.

Just what were the reasons which prompted his first visit in 1842 are not so well known. There were to be no readings, and the journey was a tedious, uncomfortable and expensive one to make in those days. Some have thought that the object of the trip was to procure the subject matter for his *American Notes*, published after his return. This, however, was not the principal reason, but was simply the means which he took to provide the necessary funds for his expenses, and, in fact, he had made arrangements with Chapman & Hall for the publication of the book before he left England. Others have thought that the object of the trip was to inaugurate

B

a campaign for international copyright, but Forster has
said that Dickens went to America with no intention of
starting the question in any way, and Dickens himself
has denied that this was the object. What was then the
real object? This question is best answered by a quotation from a paper in the *Journal of the Illinois State
Historical Society*, by Dr. J. F. Snyder, entitled,
"Charles Dickens in Illinois." Dr. Snyder writes—

"To see Cairo was really the main object of his
journey to America. In 1837 one Darius B. Holbrook,
a shrewd Boston Yankee, organized the Cairo City and
Canal Company, a scheme as audaciously illusive as
the John Laws Bubble in 1718; and going to Europe he
plastered the walls everywhere with flaming lithographs
of a grand city at the junction of the Mississippi and
Ohio rivers—in fact, as mythical as the fabled Quivira
of Coronado's search. In London was the banking
house of John Wright & Co., the same that in 1839
confidenced the Illinois Fund Commissioners, Gov.
Reynolds, Senator Young, General Rawlings and
Colonel Oakley, into depositing with them $1,000,000
of Illinois Bonds, resulting in a loss to the State of half
their value. Through John Wright & Company, Holbrook actually sold bonds of his Cairo Company to the
amount of $2,000,000. Among his numerous victims
was Mr. Dickens, who, it is asserted, invested in them
a large part of his slender means."

It will be noticed that this occurred while Dickens
was writing *The Pickwick Papers*, and Dickens may at
that time have had in mind the trip to America and his
American Notes, for, in chapter xliv, Tony Weller
says to Sam, "Have a passage taken ready for 'Merrika
. . . and then let him come back and write a book about
the 'Merrikans as'll pay all his expenses and more, if he
blows 'em up enough."

It may be that Dickens had forgotten the advice of
Mr. Weller, and it may be only a coincidence that he
took the advice and went to 'Merrika, and that he wrote,
not one, but two books referring to that country, but he
certainly did in these two books, in the opinion of many
Americans, "blow 'em up enough."

Many of those whose feelings were personally hurt, and who thought he had not treated America and Americans fairly, were those who were members of self-appointed reception and entertainment committees, and whose vanity had prompted them to hope that when the author returned home and wrote his book especial mention would be made of them, and that the reception or banquet which they had helped to arrange in his honour would be the one affair which he might single out as the most important one of his trip. In this they were disappointed, for Dickens did not mention these affairs at all, as the *American Notes* consists almost entirely of descriptions and criticisms of such public institutions as blind asylums, prisons and slavery, with brief references to some of the cities visited.

Every one who has read *American Notes* and *Martin Chuzzlewit* knows what Dickens's opinions were of America, American newspapers and the American people in 1842, the year in which he first visited the United States. It seemed to the writer, in view of the revival of interest in the author and his writings, due to the fact that 1912 is the centenary of his birth, that it might be interesting to learn what were the views of the press and people of the United States in 1842 as to the author himself. With this idea in mind the writer has obtained extracts relating to Dickens from newspapers in various cities which he visited in that year. Some of these are editorials and others are evidently written by reporters or news-writers who could make their mark with some of the so-called yellow newspapers of the present day. As to the latter, as will be seen later, we can hardly blame Dickens for what he says in his *American Notes* regarding the American Press of that period. The only fault we can find with him is that he did not differentiate sufficiently between the good and the bad, and that with few exceptions he puts all the American newspapers in the class now called "yellow."

Perhaps one of the reasons Dickens had for disliking the American newspaper was that some of their descriptions of his personality and his attire offended

B 2

his vanity. It is no great disparagement of him to say, what every one now concedes, that Dickens was vain of his appearance and that he was fond of gay waistcoats, massive gold watch-chains, large scarf-pins and his wavy locks. It is an axiom that the more vain a man is, the less he wants to be told of his vanity.

While Dickens was not favourably impressed with the Press of the United States, he wrote in the highest terms of most of the hotels at which he stopped, as the following extracts from *American Notes* will show. Of the Richmond Hotel (The Exchange) he wrote, "A very large and elegant establishment, and we were as well entertained as travellers need desire to be;" of the hotel at Baltimore, "The most complete of all the hotels of which I have had any experience in the United States, and they were not a few, is Barnum's in that city, where the English traveller will find curtains to his bed for the first and last time in America;" of the Harrisburg Hotel (Buehler's), "We were soon established in a very snug hotel, which, though smaller and far less splendid than many we put up at, is raised above them all by having for its landlord the most obliging, considerate and gentlemanly person I have ever had to deal with;" of the Pittsburgh Hotel (Exchange), "A most excellent hotel, and we were most admirably served;" of the hotel at Louisville, "We slept at the Galt House, a splendid hotel, and we were as handsomely lodged as though we had been in Paris, rather than hundreds of miles beyond the Alleghanies;" of the Planter's House at St. Louis, "An excellent house, and the proprietors have most beautiful notions of providing the creature comforts."

A comparison of Dickens's letters to Forster, as given in the latter's *Life of Charles Dickens*, with his *American Notes* will show that Dickens's opinion of America and the American people seems to have undergone considerable modification between the time of writing his first letters and the book. The first letters generally are very much more moderate in tone than his later letters and the book, but whether the author really modified his opinions by reason of the opposition to an international

copyright law by some of the American public, prin-
cipally the publishers who had been reproducing his
works, and his financial loss in Cairo (Eden) bonds, or
whether he believed that criticisms rather than praise of
the institutions of the United States would be more
acceptable for English consumption or not, is a question. The writer can hardly believe that this great
author would prostitute his pen in such a manner, and
prefers to believe that the loss of the money he had
invested in "Eden" had soured his pen.

As will be seen by the newspaper accounts of the
dinners and receptions given in Dickens's honour, no
foreigner, be he statesman, warrior or prince, was ever,
up to that time, given such a hearty welcome, or such
pæans of praise as this thirty-year-old author; in fact,
some of the praise was so fulsome that it is a wonder
it did not pall upon its recipient, used as he was to the
adulations of his own countrymen. In a letter to his
friend Mr. Thomas Mitten, dated January 31, he
summed up in the following words exactly what his
own ideas were of the welcome and treatment he had
received up to that time—

"I can give you no conception of my welcome. There
never was a King or Emperor upon the earth so cheered
and followed by crowds, and entertained at splendid
balls and dinners and waited upon by public bodies of
all kinds. I have had one from the far West, a journey
of two thousand miles! If I go out in a carriage, the
crowd surrounds it and escorts me home; if I go to the
theatre, the whole house (crowded to the roof) rises as
one man, and the timbers ring again. You cannot
imagine what it is. I have five public dinners on hand
at this moment, and invitations from every town and
village and city in the United States."

It is a wonder it did not completely turn his head,
and it is not surprising that some of the newspapers
and some of the people thought that perhaps they might
be overdoing it.

In a chapter written for *American Notes*, entitled

"Introductory and Necessary to be Read," and which, by the advice of Forster, was not printed in the book, Dickens wrote—

"Neither does it contain, nor have I intended that it should contain, any lengthened and minute account of my personal reception in the United States; not because I am, or ever was, insensible to that spontaneous effusion of affection and generosity of heart, in a most affectionate and generous-hearted people; but because I conceive that it would ill become me to flourish matter necessarily involving so much of my own praises in the eyes of my unhappy readers."

While Dickens did not give in *American Notes* his own opinions regarding his personal reception in the United States, he did express himself very freely in his letters to Forster, and it is interesting to compare his own account with those that are given in this book. These accounts are all by American writers of the time, most of them being by newspaper writers, and some of them taken from private diaries, which, when written, were not intended for publication, so that, taken together, they give a pretty good idea of the impressions made by Dickens on the Press and people of the United States. These accounts cover his personal doings and experiences in the United States for nearly every day, from the time he landed in Boston on Saturday, January 22, till he embarked at New York on Tuesday, June 7, after a journey lasting nearly five months, and covering, including the United States and Canada, about 5000 miles.

CHAPTER II

BOSTON

THE first information given to the American public that Charles Dickens intended visiting the United States was through a letter dated September 28, 1841, which he wrote to Mr. L. Gaylord Clark, editor of the *Knickerbocker Magazine*, which information Mr. Clark gave to the newspapers. Dickens said in this letter—

"On the 4th of next January, if it please God, I am coming with my wife on a three or four months' visit to America. The British and North American packet will bring me, I hope, to Boston, and enable me, in the third week of the New Year, to set my foot upon the soil I have trodden in my daydreams many times, and whose sons (and daughters) I yearn to know and be among."

Dickens evidently wrote Mr. Clark a second letter, for in *The Evening Post* (New York), January 4, 1842, we find the following—

"*Mr. Dickens.*—This distinguished author, accompanied by his lady, leaves England this day for the United States. We learn from a letter received by the last steamer, from Mr. Dickens, by our old friend Mr. Clark, of the *Knickerbocker*, that it is his intention of passing six months in the United States. After spending a few days in Boston, he will visit New York, where he will tarry some days. 'My design is,' he writes, 'to spend but little time in those two cities, but to proceed to the south as far as Charleston. Our stay will be six months, during which time I must see as much as can be seen in such a space of the country and the people.'

"Mr. Dickens speaks of his visit with the utmost enthusiasm. 'You make me very proud and happy,' he writes, 'by anticipation in thinking of the number of friends I shall find, but I cannot describe to you the glow into which I rise, when I think of the wonders that await us and all the interest I am sure I shall have in your mighty land.'"

Dickens sailed from Liverpool on the *Britannia* on January 4, and arrived in Boston eighteen days later, his arrival being chronicled in one of the Boston papers as follows—

"*Arrival of the ' Britannia.'*—The steamer *Britannia* arrived in Boston on Saturday (Jan. 22nd) afternoon last, after a rather boisterous passage of eighteen days and a detention of ten hours by the fog. She brings intelligence eighteen days late, having Liverpool papers to the 4th instant and London to the evening of the 3rd.

"Among the passengers is Charles Dickens, Esq., the famous ' Boz ' of English literature; he is accompanied by his lady. Earl Mulgrave is also a passenger."

Dickens himself has told us through one of his letters to Forster how he was met on the steamer as she was moored to the wharf, not by newsboys but by EDITORS, and that "there was one among them, though, who was really of use, a Doctor S., editor of the . . . He ran off here (two miles at least) and ordered rooms and dinner." The hotel where the rooms were ordered was the Tremont House, and is no longer standing. This hotel, which at the time of Dickens's arrival, and for many years after, was considered by Americans as one of the best hotels in the country, did not strike him as favourably as some of the other hotels which he visited later in other cities, although he wrote in *American Notes*, "The hotel is an excellent one." He expressed himself, however, regarding it more freely in a letter to Forster, in which he wrote—

"This hotel is a trifle smaller than Finsbury Square; and it is made so hot (I use the expression advisedly) by means of a furnace with pipes running through the passages, that we can hardly bear it. There are no curtains to the beds, or to the bedroom windows. I am sure there never are, hardly, all through America. The bedrooms are indeed very bare of furniture. Ours is hardly as large as your great room, and has a wardrobe in it of painted wood, not larger (I appeal to K.) than an English match-box. I slept in this room two nights, quite satisfied with the belief that it was a shower bath."

He also wrote in this letter—

"I have a secretary whom I take on with me. He is a young man by the name of Q; was strongly recommended to me; is most modest, obliging, silent and willing, and does his work *well*. He boards and lodges at my expense when we travel, and his salary is ten dollars per month, about two pounds five of our English money."

The young man whom Dickens calls "Q" was a young artist of Salem, by the name of George W. Putnam, who at the time of Dickens's arrival was then in Boston as a pupil of Mr. Francis Alexander, a well-known and highly-esteemed artist of that city. In 1870, shortly after Dickens's death, Mr. Putnam wrote a couple of papers which were published in the *Atlantic Monthly*, entitled, "Four Months with Charles Dickens, during his First Visit to America, by his Secretary."

It will be noticed that the "Secretary" does not sign the papers by his name, which is probably accounted for by the fact that in *American Notes* Dickens only mentions him as "my Boston friend." The following extract from these *Atlantic Monthly* papers is interesting, telling, as it does, how "Q" came to be made Mr. Dickens's secretary, and how the Alexander portrait of Dickens came to be painted and how the Dexter bust was modelled.

"Early in the winter of 1841 it had been announced that Charles Dickens would shortly visit this country, and Mr. Alexander wrote to him at London, inviting him to sit for his picture on his arrival. The next steamer brought a prompt answer from Mr. Dickens, accepting the invitation. I was quite glad of this arrangement, for, having read all he had written, and sharing largely in the general enthusiasm for the author and his works, I looked forward with pleasure to the honour of an introduction, through my friend Alexander.'

"Mr. Dickens had appointed ten o'clock on the Tuesday morning succeeding his arrival, for his first sitting to Alexander. The artist's rooms were at No. 41 Tremont Row, not far from the Tremont House. The newspapers had announced the fact, and, long before the appointed hour, a crowd of people were around the hotel and arranged along the sidewalk to see him pass. The doorway and stairs leading to the painter's studio were thronged with ladies and gentlemen, eagerly awaiting his appearance, and as he passed, they were to the last degree silent and respectful. It was no vulgar curiosity to see a great and famous man, but an earnest, intelligent and commendable desire to look upon the author whose writings—already enlisted in the great cause of humanity—had won their dear respect, and endeared him to their hearts. He pleasantly acknowledged the compliment their presence paid him, bowing slightly as he passed, his bright, dark eyes glancing through and through the crowd, searching every face, and reading character with wonderful quickness, while the arch smiles played over his handsome face.

"On arriving at the anteroom Mr. Dickens found a large number of the personal friends of the artist awaiting the honour of an introduction, and he passed from group to group in a most kind and pleasant way. It was here that I received my own introduction, and I remember that after Mr. Dickens had passed around the room, he came again to me and exchanged some pleasant words about my name, slightly referring to the American hero of the Revolution who had borne it.

"The crowd waited till the sitting was over, and saw him back again to the Tremont; and this was repeated every morning while he was sitting for his picture.

"The engravings in his books which had then been issued either in England or America were *very little* like him. Alexander chose an attitude highly original, but very characteristic. Dickens is represented at his table writing. His left hand rests upon the paper. The pen in his right hand seems to have been stopped for a moment, while he looks up at you as if you had just addressed him. His long brown hair, slightly curling, sweeps his shoulder, the bright eyes glance, and that inexpressible look of kindly mirth plays around his mouth and shows itself in the arched brow. Alexander caught much of that singular *lighting up of the face*, which Dickens had, beyond any one I ever saw, and the picture is very like the original, and will convey to those who wish to know how ' Boz ' looked at thirty years of age, an excellent idea of the man.

"I saw the picture daily as it progressed, and, being in the artist's room on the Thursday following the first sitting, Mr. Alexander told me that he had ' just made a disposal of my services.' I did not know what he meant. He then told me that Mr. Dickens and his wife had been at his house that forenoon, and Mr. Dickens said—

"' Mr. Alexander, I have been in the country but a few days, and my table is already heaped high with unanswered letters! I have a great number of engagements already. I did not expect a correspondence like this, and I must have a secretary. Can you find me one?' And Mr. Alexander at once mentioned me. I felt very diffident in regard to it, for I did not feel qualified for such a position, with such a man, however great the pleasure I knew I should derive from it. But my friend would take no excuses, insisted that I was the man for the place, and while we were talking a note came from Mr. Dickens, requesting that he would bring me to the Tremont House. So I went with Mr. Alexander, and was received with great cordiality and kindness by Mr. Dickens and his wife, and made an appointment to commence my duties on the following morning.

"On Friday morning I was there at nine o'clock, the time appointed. Mr. and Mrs. Dickens had their meals in their own rooms and the table was spread for breakfast. Soon they came in and, after a cheerful greeting, I took my place at a side table and wrote as he ate breakfast, and meanwhile conversed with Mrs. Dickens, opened his letters and dictated the answers to me.

"In one corner of the room, Dexter the sculptor was earnestly at work modelling a bust of Mr. Dickens. Several others of the most eminent artists of our country had urgently requested Mr. Dickens to sit to them for his picture and bust, but, having consented to do so to Alexander and Dexter, he was obliged to refuse all others for want of time.

"While Mr. Dickens ate his breakfast, read his letters and dictated the answers, Dexter was watching with the utmost earnestness the play of every feature, and comparing his model with the original. Often during the meal he would come to Dickens with a solemn, business-like air, stoop down and look at him sideways, pass around and take a look at the other side of his face and then go back to his model and work away for a few minutes; then come again and take another look and go back to his model; soon he would come again with his calipers and measure Dickens's nose, and go and try it on the nose of the model; then come again with the calipers and try the width of the temples, or the distance from the nose to the chin, and back again to his work, eagerly shaping and correcting his model. The whole soul of the artist was engaged in his task, and the result was a splendid bust of the great author. Mr. Dickens was highly pleased with it, and repeatedly alluded to it during his stay, as a very successful work of art."

One friend and admirer whom Dickens made during this first visit to the United States, and who later became his American publisher and friend, and whose friendship lasted till the day of Dickens's death, was Mr. James T. Fields, of the firm of Ticknor & Fields, proprietors of the "Old Corner Bookstore," now no longer standing. Mr. Fields, in *Yesterdays with Authors*, wrote—

"How well I recall the bleak winter evening in 1842 when I first saw the handsome glowing face of the young man who was even then famous over half of the globe. He came bounding into the Tremont House, fresh from the steamer that had brought him to our shores, and his cheery voice rang through the hall, as he gave a quick glance at the new scenes opening upon him in a strange land at a Transatlantic hotel. ' Here we are ! ' he shouted, as the lights burst upon the merry party just entering the hotel, and several gentlemen came forward to meet him. Ah ! How happy and buoyant he was then ! Young, handsome, almost worshipped for his genius, belted round by such troops of friends as rarely ever man had, coming to a new country to make new conquests of fame and honour— surely it was a sight long to be remembered and never wholly to be forgotten ! "

Fields wrote further concerning Dickens's first night in Boston—

"About midnight on that eventful landing, ' Boz ' —everybody called him ' Boz ' in those days—having finished his supper, came down into the office of the hotel, and joining the young Earl of M(ulgrave), his fellow voyager, sallied out for his first look at Boston Streets. It was a stinging night and the moon was at its full. Every object stood out sharp and glittering, and ' Boz,' muffled up in a shaggy fur coat, ran over the shining frozen snow, wisely keeping the middle of the street, for the most part. We boys followed cautiously behind, but near enough not to lose any of the fun. Of course the two gentlemen soon lost their way on emerging into Washington from Tremont Street. Dickens kept up one continual shout of uproarious laughter as he went rapidly forward, reading the signs on the shops and observing the architecture of the new country into which he had dropped as if from the clouds. When the two arrived opposite the

' Old South Church ' Dickens screamed. To this day I cannot tell why. Was it because of its fancied resemblance to St. Paul's or the Abbey? I declare firmly, the mystery of that shout is still a mystery to me."

In the *Boston Transcript* of Monday, January 24, there appeared the following—

"We are requested to state that Charles Dickens will be at the Tremont Theatre this evening. The desire to see this popular young author will, no doubt, attract a large audience. We had an hour's conversation with him last evening, and found him one of the most frank, sociable, noble-hearted gentlemen we ever met with, perfectly free from any haughtiness or apparent self-importance. In fact, he is just such a person as we had supposed him to be, judging from his writings, which have acquired a popularity unprecedented in this country. His lady, too, is most beautiful and accomplished, and appears worthy to be the partner of her distinguished husband."

The *New York Tribune*, commenting on this notice, perhaps from a feeling of jealousy, due to the fact that Dickens had landed at Boston, rather than at the "Commercial Emporium," said in their issue of January 26—

"Charles Dickens, our country's well-beloved visitor, will remain at Boston about a fortnight and then proceed southward. He will, of course, give us a call of two or three weeks here in the commercial emporium, if he is not beslavered and lionized into loathing us. We hope to get a look at him, but begin to despair of it, if he is to be disgusted with such licorice doses as the *Boston Transcript* is giving him."

A Boston correspondent of the *New York Commercial* wrote—

"I conversed with Dickens about half-an-hour. He was exceedingly affable—totally free from any haughtiness or self-importance—but full of life and sociability."

The *Tribune*, commenting on this opinion of the Boston correspondent, said—

"Such compliments to the author of *Pickwick* and *Master Humphrey's Clock!* We would give a trifle for a casual remark thereon from the Junior Mr. Weller. For our country's sake, we trust these darkeyisms will not drive Boz home again on the *Britannia*. Spare him till he is fairly rid of his seasickness, and let him have a chance to see us Yankees as we are—some ninnies among us, of course, for it takes all sorts of people to make a world—but the great mass of us are heartily glad to see him, are disinclined to bore him, and not all surprised to find him a gentleman!"

It will be seen from many of the newspaper extracts, and extracts from private diaries given later on, that there was a suspicion lurking in the minds of not a few that perhaps they were overdoing it, in the manner in which Boz was being lionized, and this suspicion became a certainty in the opinions of many, after they had read *American Notes* and *Martin Chuzzlewit*.

On Monday, January 24, the second day after his arrival in Boston, Dickens made a trip to Springfield to visit the State Legislature, a fact which he does not mention in *American Notes*. The Springfield newspapers, so far as can now be ascertained, made no mention of it. The *New York Express*, January 29, however, has the following brief mention of the visit—

"*Visit from Boz.*—Charles Dickens, Esq., paid a visit to the Massachusetts Legislature on Monday the 24th, in company with T. C. Grattan, Esq., the Earl of Mulgrave and two others. Mr. Dickens was introduced to the Secretary of the Commonwealth, Mr. Bigelow, who accompanied him through the different parts of the Capitol. His appearance in the Senate Chamber created quite a sensation among the members. He was introduced there to Mr. Quincy, the President of the Senate, and expressed himself as much pleased with the visit."

While the Springfield papers made no mention of the visit, there is still living in Springfield an old man, who was a boy at the time, who says he remembers the occasion and that Dickens made a speech to the senators.

Shortly after Dickens's arrival, he received a letter from a Dr. R. H. Collyer, a lecturer on animal magnetism, or mesmerism, asking him to attend his lecture in Boston and investigate the subject and witness his experiments. Dickens wrote the doctor a letter which is interesting as showing that he had investigated the subject and was a believer in it.

" Tremont House, January 27, 1842.

"DEAR SIR,

"If we can possibly arrange it, I shall be much interested in seeing your cases, when you come to Boston. With regard to my opinion on the subject of mesmerism, I have no hesitation in saying that I have closely watched Dr. Elliottson's experiments from the first—that I have the utmost reliance in his honour, character and ability, and would trust my life in his hands at any time—and that after what I have seen with my own eyes, and observed with my own senses, I should be untrue to myself if I shrunk for a moment from saying that I am a believer, and that I became so against all my preconceived opinions and impressions.

"Faithfully yours,
"CHARLES DICKENS.

"To Dr. Collyer."

That Dickens was not only a believer in mesmerism, but also an amateur practitioner, is proved by one of his letters to Forster, in which he relates how in Pittsburgh he practised on Mrs. Dickens, and how "in six minutes, I magnetized her into hysterics, and then into the magnetic sleep . . . I can wake her with perfect ease, but I confess (not being prepared for anything so sudden and complete) I was on the first occasion rather alarmed."

A thorough search of the Boston newspapers fails to disclose any account of how Dickens spent his time between his visit to the Legislature and the dinner which

TREMONT HOUSE, BOSTON

CUSTOM HOUSE AND DOCK, BOSTON
Where Dickens landed in 1842

took place at Papinti's Restaurant on February 1, but we know from *American Notes* that he visited most of the public institutions in and around the city.

The dinner was such a great success, and the tributes paid to Dickens are so eloquent and so lengthy, that a chapter will be devoted to that event.

We find, in the *Boston Evening Transcript,* February 5, the following—

"Mr. Dickens visited Lowell on Thursday the 3rd, and examined the several manufacturing establishments in that city. Yesterday he paid a visit to our venerable alma mater—Harvard University. He will leave town this afternoon for Worcester in company with Governor Davis, where he will remain until Monday, when he will proceed to Springfield, thence to Hartford, where he has accepted an invitation to a dinner to be given there on Tuesday."

While the above item in the *Evening Transcript* is the only one that has been discovered in the Boston newspapers, two of the Lowell newspapers contained brief notices of the visit. The *Courier* of February 5 contained the following—

"*Boz in Lowell.*—This celebrated writer visited Lowell on Thursday. He came on the one o'clock train of cars, in company with Mr. Grattan, the British Consul, and several other gentlemen, and left on the five o'clock train. Consequently his stay has been very short, and thousands of his friends in the city had not an opportunity to see him.

"He was received at the depôt by Mr. Samuel Lawrence, whose guest he continued while in the city. We understand that he visited several of the mills with Mr. Lawrence, and expressed himself as highly gratified with his visit. We hope that ere he returns to England he will visit the city again, and thus give his numerous friends here an opportunity of taking him by the hand."

The very highly complimentary manner in which Dickens described the conditions which he found in the mills of Lowell, and the manner in which the operatives

c

in them lived and dressed, and of their literary contributions to the *Lowell Offering*, shows that he not only expressed his gratification with the visit while in Lowell, but also expressed it in his own written account.

The editor of the *Lowell Advertiser* seems to have been offended because Dickens did not favour him with a personal visit, and thus expressed his feelings—

"Boz was in this city last week. The reason we did not mention it was because he passed our office without calling. He didn't call on the *Courier* or the people either. How in the name of reason can he expect puffs and popular applause?"

Dickens visited the mill hospital and wrote of it in very high terms of commendation. The hospital is still in existence, and is supported by contributions from the mill owners.

MERRIMACK MILLS AND BOARDING-HOUSES, LOWELL

MILL HOSPITAL, LOWELL, MASS.

CHAPTER III

THE BOSTON DINNER

AT the time of Dickens's first visit to the United States, Mr. Pickwick and Sam Weller, Oliver Twist and Fagin, Barnaby Rudge and Dolly Varden, Little Nell and grandfather, and Nicholas Nickleby and Smike, were as well known in the United States as in England, and their creator was as great a favourite of his American readers as he was of their English cousins.

It was no wonder, then, when in the latter part of 1841 the news came to Boston that "Boz" was soon to visit America, and that Boston was to be the first city in the United States to be favoured by his presence, that some of the young men of that city decided that the event should be celebrated in a manner to make it memorable. With that end in view a committee was appointed to invite the young and distinguished author to a dinner to be given in his honour, and the following letter was sent to him before his departure from England—

"To CHARLES DICKENS, ESQ.

"DEAR SIR,

"The Young Men of Boston, in common with the whole American people, hail with delight the news of your intended visit to the New World. They send you a cordial greeting across the sea, and before you leave England, they hasten in imagination, but with heartfelt earnestness, to take you by the hand, and to welcome you to America. You will come into a strange land, but not among strangers; for you have long been a welcome guest at our firesides, and there is not a home in our country which has not been made happier by your presence. We do not address you as a son of our fatherland, for 'genius has no country'; we claim your literary reputation as the property of the human race; but it is more especially for your qualities as a man that we admire and love you; for while we are astonished at a power of observation in you which detects novelty in the most familiar things—a fertility of invention which is inexhaustible, and a truth to nature which stamps fictitious characters with the individuality of real life—our hearts are also irresistibly drawn towards you by that richness of humour which never fails to charm, and more than all, by that sympathy with universal man (the concomitant only of the highest genius), which prompted you to utter the noble sentiment, that 'you were anxious to show that virtue may be found in the by-ways of the world; that it is not incompatible with poverty, or even rags; and that you wished to distil out, if you could, from evil things the soul of goodness which the Creator has put in them.'

"Actuated by these sentiments towards you, a number of the Young Men of Boston, at a meeting held on the evening of the 27th of November, appointed the undersigned a Committee to invite you to a public dinner, or more private entertainment, to take place in honour of your arrival, at such a time and in such a manner as may be most agreeable to yourself; and we all earnestly hope that an invitation which we give with our whole hearts, you will find it compatible with the object of your visit to accept.

"With sentiments of the truest regard and respect,

"We are Y'r Ob't Serv'ts,

"GEO. MINNS.
"CHAS. H. MILLS.
"JAMES R. LOWELL.
"HENRY GARDNER.
"SAMUEL PARKMAN, JR."

Upon Mr. Dickens's arrival on January 22, 1842, the committee visited him, and the evening of February 1 was fixed upon by the guest as the time that would be agreeable to him for the event.   Shortly after his arrival Dickens wrote his friend and future biographer, Forster, saying—

"There is to be a public dinner to me here in Boston next Tuesday, and great dissatisfaction has been given to the many by the high price (three pounds sterling each) of the tickets."

The following are the committees which had the dinner in charge—

President, Josiah Quincy, Jr.; Vice-Presidents: Dr. Oliver Wendell Holmes, George S. Hillard, Edward G. Loring, and J. Thomas Stevenson.

The Committee of Arrangements consisted of: E. H. Eldridge, W. W. Tucker, S. A. Appleton, H. Lee, Jr., and S. E. Guild.

The members of the Invitation Committee were: George T. Bigelow, Nathan Hale, Jr., Jonathan Fay Barrett, Frederick W. Crocker, and William Wetmore Story.

A glance at the *personnel* of these committees may not be uninteresting at the present. Josiah Quincy, Jr., the president, was the grandson of the Josiah Quincy who was a famous Boston lawyer and patriot, very prominent at the opening of the Revolutionary War. He was the son of Josiah Quincy, Sr., who, at the time of the dinner, was the venerable President of Harvard College, and was himself then President of the Massachusetts State Senate, and later Mayor of Boston.

Dr. Oliver Wendell Holmes, the genial "Autocrat of the Breakfast Table," was thirty-three years of age and had not yet become famous as the author of "The Wonderful One Hoss Shay," and at the time of the dinner was a practising physician in Boston.

George Stillman Hillard was thirty-three years of age and was a prominent lawyer of Boston, and was later the author of a Life of General McClellan and a Life of George Ticknor.

Edward G. Loring was a prominent attorney, and later Judge of Probate. In 1854 he was United States Commissioner, and as such he attained great notoriety

from the fact that, as Commissioner under the Fugitive
Slave Law, he remanded Anthony Burns, an escaped
slave, back to his master, Charles F. Suttle, a Virginian
slaveholder.

Richard H. Dana, Jr., appeared as attorney for the
escaped slave, but unsuccessfully. The decision caused
a riot and an attack on the courthouse, but without
result, as Burns was conveyed back to Virginia in a
U.S. revenue cutter.

James Russell Lowell, who was one of the committee which extended the invitation to Dickens, was
only twenty-two years of age, and it was only four years
since his graduation from Harvard College; but he
was even at that age making a reputation as a poet.
He had studied law and been admitted to the bar, but
had just decided to abandon the profession of law and
lead a literary life. No one at that time would ever
have prophesied that this young man would later shine
as the United States Minister at the Courts of Madrid
and St. James.

George Tyler Bigelow, who was in his thirty-second
year, was a young lawyer of Boston, and in 1847, at
thirty-seven years of age, was Judge of the Court of
Common Pleas, in 1850 was Justice of the Supreme
Court of Massachusetts, and in 1860 Chief Justice.

Nathan Hale, Jr., was an elder brother of the Rev.
Edward Everett Hale, the celebrated Boston preacher
and author. He was educated as a lawyer, but for the
greater part of his life was an editor, being at this time
the editor of the *Boston Miscellany*, to which James
Russell Lowell was then a contributor.

Jonathan Fay Barrett was a young lawyer of Con-
cord, but of strong literary tastes and very active as a
Whig politician.

William Wetmore Story, the famous American
sculptor, long resident in Rome, was only twenty-two
years of age and was then a practising lawyer in Boston,
where he remained till 1848, at which time he went to
Italy. He was, previous to this time, the writer of
several books on legal subjects as well as some volumes

JOSIAH QUINCY
President, Massachusetts State Senate, 1842

of prose and poetry. He was a classmate at Harvard
of Lowell and Nathan Hale.

Amongst the prominent guests were Josiah Quincy,
Sr.; Washington Allston, the poet and artist; George
Bancroft, the historian; Richard Henry Dana, Jr., the
author of *Two Years before the Mast;* and many others
eminent in the fields of literature, art and the law. It
was probably as representative a body of eminent men
as could well have been gathered together to welcome
the young author, who was then only thirty years of
age.

The following account of the dinner is reprinted from
the *Boston Advertiser*—

Mr. Dickens was received by a committee of the
young men who invited him, and immediately on his
arrival at the appointed hour of five, a full band in the
gallery of the hall commenced playing "Washington's
March." The invited guests, with the president and
vice-president of the day, and a part of the subscribers,
were in one of the drawing-rooms, and the other was
well filled with the rest of the subscribers. The doors
of the room last mentioned were first opened, and the
subscribers took their places at their pleasure at the
tables arranged in the hall, in such a way that no one
had his back to the invited guests. As soon as all had
found places, and order had followed the confusion
necessarily attending the quick moving of a hundred
and fifty persons, the band struck up "God save the
Queen," and the doors of the other drawing-room being
opened, the guests, and the president and vice-presidents, entered, and were shown to the seats reserved
for them.

Before the covers were removed, the Rev. Dr. Parkman asked a blessing on the occasion, in a manner at
once solemn and appropriate.

The dinner then proceeded through various courses,
till, at the appearance of the dessert, the president rose,
and addressed the company in the following manner—

GENTLEMEN,—The occasion that calls us together is

almost unprecedented in the annals of literature. A young man has crossed the ocean with no hereditary title, no military laurels, no princely fortune, and yet his approach is hailed with pleasure by every age and condition, and on his arrival he is welcomed as a long-known and highly-valued friend. How shall we account for this reception? Must we not at the first glance conclude with Falstaff, " If the rascal have not given me medicines, to make me love him, I'll be hanged : it could not be else—I have drunk medicines."

But when reflection leads us to the causes of this universal sentiment, we cannot but be struck by the power which mind exercises over mind, even while we are individually separated by time, space and other conditions of our present being. Why should we not welcome him as a friend? Have we not walked with him in every scene of varied life? Have we not together investigated, with Mr. Pickwick, the theory of Tittle-bats? Have we not ridden together to the "Markis o' Granby," with old Weller on the box, and his son Samuel on the dickey? Have we not been rook-shooting with Mr. Winkle, and courting with Mr. Tupman? Have we not played cribbage with "The Marchioness" and quaffed the rosy with Dick Swiveller? Tell us not of animal magnetism ! We, and thousands of our countrymen, have for years been eating and talking, riding and walking, dancing and sliding, drinking and sleeping, with our distinguished guest, and he never knew of the existence of one of us. Is it wonderful that we are delighted to see him, and to return in a measure his unbounded hospitalities? Boz a stranger ! Well may we again exclaim, with Sir John Falstaff, "D'ye think we didn't know ye?—We knew ye as well as him that made ye."

But a jovial fellow is not always the dearest friend; and although the pleasure of his society would always recommend the great progenitor of Dick Swiveller, "the perpetual grand of the glorious Apollers," in a scene like this, yet the respect of grave doctors and of fair ladies prove that there are higher qualities than those of a pleasant companion to recommend and attach them to our distinguished guest. What is the charm that unites so many suffrages? It is that in the lightest hours, and in the most degraded scenes which he has portrayed, there has been a reforming object and moral tone, not formally thrust forth in the canvas, but infused into the spirit of the picture, with those natural touches whose contemplation never tires.

With what power of delineation have the abuses of his institutions been portrayed? How have the poor-house, the jail, the police courts of justice, passed before his magic mirror, and displayed to us the petty tyranny of the low-minded official, from the magnificent Mr. Bumble, and the hard-hearted Mr. Roker, to the author-itative Justice Fang—the positive Judge Stareleigh! As we contemplate them, how strongly have we realized the time-worn evils of some of the systems they revealed to our eyesight, sharpened to detect the deficiencies and malpractices under our own.

The genius of chivalry, which had walked with such power among men, was exorcised by the pen of Cervantes. He did but clothe it with the name and images of Don Quixote de la Mancha and his faithful squire, and ridicule destroyed what argument could not reach.

This power belongs in an eminent degree to some of the personifications of our guest. A short time ago it was discovered that a petty tyrant had abused the children who had been committed to his care. No long and elaborate discussion was needed to arouse the public mind. He was pronounced a perfect Squeers, and eloquence could go no further. Happy is he who can add a pleasure to the house of childhood—but far happier he who, by fixing the attention of the world on their secret sufferings, can protect or deliver them from their power.

But it is not only as a portrayer of public wrongs that we are indebted to our friend. What reflecting mind can contemplate some of these characters without being made more kind-hearted and charitable? Descend with him into the very sink of vice—contemplate the mistress of the robber—the victim of a murderer—disgraced without—polluted within—and yet, when, in better moments, her natural kindness breaks through the cloud, when she tells you that no word of counsel, no tone of moral teaching, ever fell upon her ear, when she looks forward from a life of misery to a death by suicide—you cannot but feel that there is no condition so degraded as not to be visited by gleams of a higher nature, and rejoice that He alone will judge the sin who knows also the temptation. Again, how strongly are the happiness of virtue and the misery of vice contrasted. The morning scene of Sir Mulberry Hawk and his pupil brings out in strong relief the night scene of Kit Nubbles and his mother. The one in affluence and splendour, trying to find an easier position for his aching head, surrounded with means and trophies of debauchery, and "thinking there would be nothing so snug and comfortable as to die at once." The other in the poorest room, earning a precarious subsistence by her labours at the wash-tub—ugly and ignorant and vulgar, surrounded by poverty, with one child in the cradle, and the other in the clothes basket, "whose great round eyes emphatically declared that he never meant to go to sleep any more, and thus opened a cheerful prospect to his relations and friends," and yet in this situation, with only the comfort that cleanliness and order could impart—kindness of heart and the determination to be talkative and agreeable throw a halo round the scene, and as we contemplate it we cannot but feel that Kit Nubbles has attained to the summit of philosophy, when he discovered "there was nothing in the way in which he was made that called upon him to be a snivelling, solemn, whispering chap—sneaking about as if he could not help it, and expressing himself in a most unpleasant snuffle—but that it was as natural for him to laugh as for a sheep to bleat, a pig to grunt, or a bird to sing." Or take another example, when wealth is attained, though by different means and for different purposes. Ralph Nickleby and Arthur Gride are industrious and successful; like the vulture, they are ever soaring over the field that they may pounce on the weak and unprotected. Their constant employment is grinding the poor, and preying upon the rich. What is the result? Their homes are cold and cheerless, the blessing of him that is ready to perish comes not to them, and they live in wretchedness to die in misery. What a contrast have we in the glorious old twins— Brother Charles and Brother Ned. They have never been to school, they eat with their knives (as the Yankees are said to do), and yet what an elucidation do they present of the truth that it is better to give than to receive! They acquire their wealth in the honourable pursuits of business. They expend it to promote the happiness of every one within their sphere, and their cheerful days and tranquil nights show that wealth is a blessing or a curse, as it ministers to the higher or lower propensities of our nature.

> "He that hath light within his own clear breast,
> May sit i' the centre and enjoy bright day;
> But he that hides a dark soul and foul thoughts,
> Benighted walks under the mid-day sun;
> Himself in his own dungeon."

Such men are powerful preachers of the truth, that universal benevolence is the true panacea of life; and although it was a pleasant fiction of Brother Charles that "Tim Linkinwater was born a hundred and fifty years old, and was gradually coming down to five-and-twenty," yet he who cultivates such a sentiment will, as years roll by, attain more and more to the spirit of a little child; and the hour will come when that principle shall conduct the possessor to immortal happiness and eternal youth.

If, then, our guest is called upon to state what are

> "The drugs, the charms,
> The conjuration and the mighty magic,
> He's won our daughters with"—

well might he reply that, in endeavouring to relieve the oppressed, to elevate the poor, and to instruct and edify those of a happier condition, he had only "held the mirror up to nature." To "show virtue her own form—scorn her own image." That "this was the only witchcraft he used"; and, did he need proof of this, there are many fair girls on both sides of the water who, though they might not repeat the whole of Desdemona's speech to a married man, yet could they tell him—

"That if he had a friend, that loved her,
He should but teach him how to tell his stories,
And that would win her."

I would, gentlemen, it were in my power to present, as on the mirror in the Arabian tale, the various scenes in our extended country, where the master-mind of our guest is at this moment acting. In the empty school-room, the boy at his evening task has dropped his grammar, that he may roam with Oliver or Nell. The traveller has forgotten the fumes of the crowded steamboat, and is far off with our guest, among the green valleys and hoary hills of old England. The trapper, beyond the rocky mountains, has left his lonely tent, and is unroofing the houses in London with the more than Mephistopheles at my elbow. And, perhaps, in some well-lighted hall, the unbidden tear steals from the father's eye, as the exquisite sketch of the poor school-master and his little scholar brings back the form of that gifted boy whose "little hand" worked its wonders under his guidance, and who, in the dawning of intellect and warm affections, was summoned from the school-room and the play-room for ever. Or to some bereaved mother the tender sympathies and womanly devotion, the touching purity of little Nell, may call up the form where dwelt that harmonious soul which, uniting in itself God's best gifts, for a short space shed its celestial light upon her household, and then vanishing, "turned all hope into memory."

But it is not to scenes like these that I would now recall you. I would that my voice could reach the ear of every admirer of our guest throughout the land, that with us they might welcome him on this, his first public appearance to our shores. Like the rushing of many

waters, the response would come to us from the bleak
hills of Canada, from the savannahs of the South, from
the prairies of the West, uniting in an "earthquake
voice" in the cheers with which we welcome CHARLES
DICKENS to this new world.

Mr. Quincy concluded with the following toast—

Health, happiness, and a hearty welcome to Charles
Dickens.

This toast was received with a burst of applause,
and the cheering which greeted Mr. Dickens was loud
and long; as soon as it ceased he responded with the
following address, which he spoke earnestly, and with
apparent feeling—

GENTLEMEN,—If you had given this splendid entertainment to any one else in the whole wide world—if I
were here to-night to exult in the triumph of my dearest
friend—if I stood here upon my defence, to repel any
unjust attack—to appeal as a stranger to your generosity
and kindness as the freest people on the earth—I could,
putting some restraint upon myself, stand among you
as self-possessed and unmoved as I should be alone, in
my own room in England.

But when I have the echoes of your cordial greeting ringing in my ears—when I see your kind faces
beaming a welcome so warm and earnest as never man
had, I feel—it is my nature—so vanquished and subdued that I have hardly fortitude enough to thank you.
If your president, instead of pouring forth that delightful mixture of humour and pathos, which you have just
heard with so much delight, had been but a caustic,
ill-natured man—if he had only been a dull one—if I
could only have doubted or distrusted him or you—I
should have had my wits at my fingers' ends, and,
using them, could have held you at arm's length. But
you have given me no such opportunity; you take
advantage of me in the tenderest point; you give me no
chance of playing at company or holding you at a distance, but flock about me like a host of brothers, and
make this place like home. Indeed, gentlemen, indeed,

if it be natural and allowable for each of us, on his own hearth, to express his thoughts in the most homely. fashion, and to appear in his plainest garb, I have a fair claim upon you to let me do so to-night, for you have made my house an Aladdin's palace. You fold so tenderly within your breasts that common household lamp in which my feeble fire is all enshrined, and at which my flickering torch is lighted up, that straight my household gods take wing and are transported here. And whereas it is written of that fairy structure that it never moved without two shocks—one when it rose, and one when it settled down—I can say of mine that, however sharp a tug it took to pluck it from its native ground, it struck at once an easy, and a deep and lasting root into this soil; and loved it as its own. I can say more of it, and say with truth, that long before it moved, or had a chance of moving, its master—perhaps from some secret sympathy between its timbers and a certain stately tree that has its being hereabout, and spreads its broad branches far and wide—dreamed by day and night, for years, of setting foot upon this shore, and breathing this pure air. And, trust me, gentlemen, that, if I had wandered here, unknowing and unknown, I would—if I know my own heart—have come with all my sympathies clustering as richly about this land and people—with all my sense of justice as keenly alive to their high claims on every man who loves God's image—with all my energies as fully bent on judging for myself, and speaking out, and telling in my sphere the truth, as I do now, when you rain down your welcome on my head.

Your president has alluded to those writings which have been my occupation for some years past; and you have received his allusions in a manner which assures me—if I needed any such assurance—that we are old friends in the spirit, and have been in close communion for a long time.

It is not easy for a man to speak of his own books. I dare say that few persons have been more interested in mine than I; and if it be a general principle in nature

that a lover's love is blind, and that a mother's love is
blind; I believe that it may be said of an author's
attachment to the creatures of his own imagination that
it is a perfect model of constancy and devotion and is
the blindest of all. But the objects and purposes I have
had in view are very plain and simple and may be easily
told. I have always had, and always shall have, an
earnest and true desire to contribute, as far as in me
lies, to the common stock of healthful cheerfulness and
enjoyment. I have always had, and always shall have,
an invincible repugnance to the mole-eyed philosophy
which loved the darkness and winks and scowls in the
light. I believe that virtue shows quite as well in rags
and patches as she does in purple and fine linen. I
believe that she and every beautiful object in external
nature claim some sympathy in the breast of the poorest
man who breaks his scanty loaf of bread. I believe that
she goes barefoot as well as shod. I believe that she
dwells rather oftener in alleys and by-ways than she
does in courts and palaces; and that it is good, and
pleasant, and profitable, to track her out and follow
her. I believe that to lay one's hand upon some of
those rejected ones whom the world has too long forgotten, and too often misused, and to say to the proudest
and most thoughtless : these creatures have the same
elements and capacities of goodness as yourselves;
they are moulded in the same form and made of the
same clay; and though ten times worse than you, may,
in having retained anything of their original nature
amidst the trials and distresses of their condition, be
really ten times better—I believe that to do this is to
pursue a worthy and not useless avocation. Gentlemen,
that you think so too, your fervent greeting sufficiently
assures me. That this feeling is alive in the old world
as well as in the new, no man should know better than
I—I, who have found such wide and ready sympathy
in my own dear land. That in expressing it we are but
treading in the steps of those great master spirits who
have gone before, we know by reference to all the bright
examples in our literature, from Shakespeare downward.

There is one other point connected with the labours (if I may call them so) that you hold in such generous esteem, to which I cannot help adverting. I cannot help expressing the delight, the more than happiness, it was to me to find so strong an interest awakened, on this side of the water, in favour of that little heroine of mine, to whom your president has made allusion, who died in her youth. I had letters about that child in England, from the dwellers in log-houses among the morasses, and swamps, and densest forests, and deepest solitudes, of the Far West. Many a sturdy hand, hard with the axe and spade, and browned with the summer's sun, has taken up the pen and written to me a little history of domestic joy or sorrow, always coupled, I am proud to say, with interest in that little tale, or some comfort or happiness derived from it; and the writer has always addressed me, not as a writer of books for sale, resident some four or five thousand miles away, but as a friend to whom he might freely impart the joys and sorrows of his own fireside. Many a mother—I could reckon them, now, by dozens, not by units—has done the like, and has told me how she lost a child at such a time, and where she lay buried, and how good she was, and how, in this or that respect, she resembled Nell. I do assure you that no circumstance of my life has given me one hundredth part of the gratification I have derived from this source. I was wavering at the time whether or not to wind up my clock, and come and see this country; and this decided me. I felt as if it were a positive duty, as if I were bound to pack up my clothes and come and see my friends. And even now, I have such an odd sensation in connection with these things that you have no chance of spoiling me. I feel as though we were agreeing—as indeed we are, if we substitute for fictitious names the classes from which they are drawn—about third parties in whom we had a common interest. At every new act of kindness on your part, I say it to myself—that's for Oliver—I should not wonder if that were meant for Smike—I have no doubt that is intended for Nell; and so I become a much

happier, certainly, but a more sober and retiring man,
than ever I was before.

Gentlemen! talking of my friends in America brings
me back naturally and of course to you. Coming
back to you, and being thereby reminded of the pleasure
we have in store in hearing the gentlemen who sit
about me, I arrive by the easiest, though not by the
shortest course in the world, at the end of what I have
to say. But before I sit down, there is one topic on
which I am desirous to lay particular stress. It has,
or should have, a strong interest for us all, since to its
literature every country must look for one great means
of refining and improving its people, and one great
source of national pride and honour. You have in
America great writers—great writers who will live in
all time, and are as familiar to our lips as household
words. Deriving (which they all do in a greater or
less degree, in their several walks) their inspiration
from the stupendous country that gave them birth, they
diffuse a better knowledge of it, and a high love for it,
all over the civilized world. I take leave to say, in the
presence of some of those gentlemen, that I hope the
time is not far distant when they, in America, will
receive of right some substantial profit and return in
England from their labours; and when we, in England,
shall receive some substantial profit and return in
America from ours. Pray do not misunderstand me.
Securing to myself from day to day the means of an
honourable subsistence, I would rather have the affectionate regard of my fellow-men than I would have
heaps and mines of gold. But the two things do not
seem to me incompatible. They cannot be, for nothing
good is incompatible with justice. There must be an
international arrangement in this respect; England has
done her part; and I am confident that the time is not
far distant when America will do hers. It becomes the
character of a great country: first, because it is justice;
secondly, because without it you never can have, and
keep, a literature of your own.

Gentlemen, I thank you with feelings of gratitude,

D

such as are not often awakened, and can never be expressed.   As I understand it to be the pleasant custom here to finish with a toast, I would beg to give you—

America and England—and may they never have any division but the Atlantic between them !

It was some time ere the applause and cheering which followed this speech subsided; as soon as silence was obtained, the president said—

It had been said that painters, in portraying pictures of ideal female beauty, unconsciously sketched the features of her who was the dearest to their hearts. If this was as true of the novelist as the painter, how greatly are the admirers of the lovely creations of our friend's genius indebted to her who holds this relation to him !   With his permission, therefore, he proposed—

The health of the lady of our distinguished guest— If she were the model of the pure and elevated females of his works, it might be well said that she was the better half *even* of Charles Dickens.

The toast was drunk with nine cheers, the company all standing.

The president said he would propose one toast more, and for a response to it he should look to the other end of the table.   He then gave—

The Old World and the New—In the beautiful language of our guest, there is one broad sky over all; and whether it be blue or cloudy, there is the same heaven beyond it.

Edward G. Loring, Esq., one of the vice-presidents, responded to this sentiment as follows—

Mr. President,—Your sentiment refers directly to what the sentiment of our guest, your welcome to him, and his English response, must have pressed on the minds of all of us—the peculiar bonds of union between England and America.   There is no one here who would wish them fewer or weaker than they are—a common parentage, a common literature, and common national interests; and yet, stronger and broader.   One common parentage is surely much; yet the relationship of nations

has never proved the strongest of national bonds, nor
withstood the trials of conflicting interests, or the
rivalry for wealth or power; a common literature is
indeed much more, and New England is not the place
in our land where it will be first undervalued. Since
common scholarship began here—and that was the day
and hour the passengers of the *Mayflower* landed on
Plymouth Rock—since then it has been our earnest
New England thanksgiving that we had our birth-
right in English literature, that "the well of English
undefiled" was within the lines of our heritage, and
that we had an inalienable right to draw of its waters,
even under the suspicion that we tinged them as we
drew. It is the blessing we have prized more than any
other, and by which we have profited more than any
other—that we could open the huge volume of English
learning, illumined more brightly than missal ever
shone, that genius had blazoned for a foreign people in
a foreign land, and read its glorious text in the full and
ready apprehension of our own vernacular; but this is
now not peculiar to us—the scholarship of every country
has attained it, and the degree of union that it gives.
Scholars fraternize everywhere, and the Republic of
Letters is as broad as the limits of civilization; but there
is yet another broader and stronger bond than parentage
or literature, which binds not merely the scholars of
England and America, not merely two nations as such,
in their national capacities and relations and interests
—but which binds together the people of the nations of
England and America as one people, and binds them
all the closer as by its own force it excludes the people
of all other nations from the alliance.

The people of other nations are separated from each
other, and have been so, and must remain so, in spite of
all the affinities with which circumstances and civilization have combined to unite them; these are stronger in
modern Europe to-day than between any nations the
world has seen—yet of these nations the people of each
are as distinct from the people of every other as if they
belonged to different epochs of time. This is not

D 2

because of any difference in their degree of civilization —in mental or moral culture—in the schools of their learning, or their systems of philosophy—or in the forms and usages of their social life; in these they are alike— so much alike, that the same classes in the different nations differ less than different classes in the same nation. It is not because their political relations are hostile, for peace is in all their borders; and the wisdom of the statesman is tasked to interweave their political interests. It is not the difference of their forms of government—for in these they resemble each other more than America resembles her mother country; it is not the geographical barriers that separate them from each other—between them no ocean rolls—between many of them neither mountains rise nor rivers run—inhabiting the same continent, the same plain—with a local division so slight that the small grass which fixes its root in one state hangs its blade in the other—with a boundary line as purely mathematical as that of our New England farms, which run from a tree to a stake and stones— yet the people on each side of this line are a distinct people—the governments may league in peace and war —their scholars may consort in literary fellowship, but the people never touch—they are distinct, and are kept distinct, by their different spoken language. This bars their intercourse, and shuts up in each all homelike thoughts and feelings and "their dear familiar words" —they find on each other's tongue the shibboleth of alienation; their different languages mark the line of their insulation, and though that line may be as slight as invisible, yet it is as impassable as the magic circle of a fairy dance—that leaves no impress on the evening dew, yet separates the different beings of different worlds.

So will it be for ever. The difference of language of the nations shall make their people strangers as it has from the beginning. That beginning is recorded in holy writ—the judgment of the plain of Shinar, when Babel fell, has overspread the earth—all time has confirmed it, and the generations of every nation in its variant tongue has repeated it—against it no circumstance or human contrivance has prevailed anything—arts and arms, civilization and conquests, have changed everything else, but of this judgment not one letter is altered—as it was first writ it is now read. Call that record a history or a metaphor, yet the fall of Babel typifies the most pregnant event that marks the course of man; of that event the people of England and America are alone untouched; of Babel's tower not a brick fell between them; from the decree which sundered all other people they alone are exempted, and that decree is their authority, their necessity, to go on together in their great courses, with ideas, thoughts and sentiments in common; and made common by their common utterance. Using not only the same books, but the same spoken words; listening to the same preaching from the desk, to the same teachings of philosophy, to the same discussion of moral and political principles; using the same inventions of art, the same developments of science; applying the same rules of right or wrong to the management of their daily affairs; having the same conventional forms and usages of life, the same table talk, parlour conversation and nursery prattle—all things that go most certainly to fix mental and moral habits, and make first individual and then national character; the people of England and the people of America must be for ever one people—and this is the result of their common spoken language.

This is, sir, a part of what the young men of Boston claim this common spoken language has done for them, and the question comes to their own minds, what have they done for that? Here it is not for them to say; they must repress the impulse to point to their fellow-citizens who are their guests to-day. But, sir, there is one thing they may do, one act of the young men of Boston to which they may refer—for it was the act of their forefathers, when they were the young men of Boston—they founded in their new wilderness HARVARD COLLEGE, and made it its great duty to guard the purity of our English speech. Sir, if we have not profited in that respect by her teachings, it is our own fault; but there is one lesson of hers that we have learned by heart, and would repeat now when we meet her at our own festival—it is, "To give honour to those who in their high office do honour to her.".

When the immense cheering occasioned by this sentiment had subsided, President Quincy, of Harvard University, presented himself before the company, and was received with enthusiastic greeting. He replied to the compliment paid to himself and old Harvard in the following terms—

It is not fair, gentlemen, not quite fair. When I received your invitation, I had many doubts concerning accepting it. I saw very plainly that, if I did, by some hook or crook I should be set up for a speech; and I now feel disposed to give myself the same advice which was once given by Swift. "Sir," said a man to Swift, "I am about to set up for a wit." "Sir," said Swift to the man, "you had better sit down again."

I thought indeed, gentlemen, that I had laid an anchor to the windward, and that I was not to be assailed by either toast or sentiment; that none of that intellectual machinery was applied to me by which it is usual, on such occasions as these, to rasp speeches out of dry and reluctant natures. Why, gentlemen, I belong to a past age. It is no more reasonable to expect a man of threescore years and ten to make a good after-dinner speech than it is to expect he would dance well a hornpipe. Nature is against it. A great many particulars enter into the composition of a good after-dinner speech which it is scarcely possible for an old man to command. Such a speech should at once be witty and wise. It should have sentiment and fancy. There should be a sprinkling of salt—the pure attic; and a large infusion of the essence of roses, provided it be distilled from those which grow on the side of Parnassus. There should be a layer of *utile* and a layer of *dulce* alternately. Sound sense should be at the bottom, and at the top as much sugar work and fancy flummery as the occasion will bear. Now it is next to impossible for a man of my age to collect all these materials at a moment's warning. Besides, there are two essential things in which he is necessarily deficient —memory and fancy. To an old man, Memory is an arrant jade; eternally playing him tricks; and like most of her sex, not at all delicate in letting him know what a preference she has for young men. An old man's fancy can neither run nor walk; much less can it fly, for in its wings there is neither quill nor pin-feather. Besides, gentlemen, it is a rule that, when a man's son has set up in trade, and is carrying it on pretty successfully, it is full time for his father to quit business. Otherwise unpleasant comparisons may occur. It might be said, possibly, that "the father beats the son," which would look unkind and unparental. Or it might be said, which in this case is more likely, that "the son beats the father," which all will agree is quite cruel and unnatural.

The fear of being called up for a speech was not my only difficulty, gentlemen, in accepting your invitation. I reasoned with myself, something in this way. Here is a young man come across the Atlantic, who, ever since he was a man, has been harvesting laurels, and here he is, with his hands full and his head covered with them, and the young men of Boston, with a laudable disposition to do justice to merit, have resolved to place a small twig of Yankee laurel among the great collection he has brought with him from Europe. All this is well, and very proper. But what have I to do with it? I am not a young man. Shall I not be out of place? So I was in great difficulty; for, to tell you the truth, I had an intense desire to be present on the occasion. In this dilemma I said to a judicious friend of mine, "The young men have invited me to the dinner they are to give to Mr. Dickens; do you advise me to go?" "By no means," said my friend; "you will be out of your place, and in their way. Why, you will prevent the young men from cracking their jokes." Now, gentlemen, observe when you will, and you will find that, when a man asks advice, and the advice given thwarts his inclination, instead of acquiescing, he always falls to arguing. And so I did on this occasion. "Why," I replied, "if the jokes they crack are good jokes, I should like to be at their cracking; but if there should be a disposition in any of them to make bad jokes "—a thing, by the way, they never learnt from the writings of the gentleman they desire to honour, for in all his works not a bad joke is to be found—"in such case, should my presence prevent them, it would be useful." So, drawing a reason in favour of accepting the invitation from the very argument adduced against it, I resolved to follow my inclination; threw my judicious friend's advice to the winds, and accepted the invitation.

But my difficulties were not all over, then. Some time elapsed between my acceptance and the dinner, during which my mind was busy with its doubts and conjectures. Shall I be the oldest man in the company? Will there be any one there of my age, or near it? Will there be any but young men there? At length my mind settled down into an intense desire to know how this meeting would be composed; and whether it would be composed wholly of young men. I felt, gentlemen, very much as—I hope what I am going to say will give no offence. Remember, it is not said by way of application or adaptation, but only by way of illustration; I felt then, in regard to the composition of this meeting, very much as Sam Weller did on another occasion. You all know Sam Weller. If any of you do not, I advise you to form an acquaintance with him as soon as possible. He is worth knowing; and quite a classical character. I felt, I say, concerning the composition of this meeting, as Sam Weller did, when invited to dine on a veal pie. "Why," said Sam, "I like the invitation much. A weal pie is a nice thing, a werry nice thing; but then I should like to know, beforehand, how it is composed, and whether there is likely to be found there anything besides— *kittens*."

Gentlemen (continued Mr. Quincy, glancing with

a serious aspect at the reporters), I hope this rambling speech is not to be published, but the presence of those light-fingered gentry in the corner makes me fear that it is.

To be serious, however, gentlemen. At my period of life, and in my position in society, I should not have felt justified in accepting your invitation had I regarded it as a tribute to mere *genius;* had I considered it only as an acknowledgment of allegiance, or as a desire to do honour to that mysterious and wayward power which is creative, but seldom discriminating; which catches and reflects every occurring ray of fancy, utterly regardless whether it be useful or noxious; which we are often compelled to admire at the very moment the associations it introduces into our minds fill us with shame, or pain, or disgust.

In the writings of the gentleman in honour of whom we have now assembled, I saw, indeed, enough of that mysterious and wayward power to satisfy the cravings of that ambition, but I saw also something higher and better than genius. A tone uniformly moral, a purpose always excellent, thoughts deep and brilliant, yet ever transparent with purity; so that it may be truly said of this author, that in all the numerous pages which constitute his writings, there is not one through which the most delicate female mind may not pass "in maiden meditation, fancy free."

These are substantial glories. It speaks well for the age, when a young man can thus write and be popular. It speaks for it more and better, when its young men are willing and anxious to applaud and do honour to the author of such writings.

Gentlemen, I will detain you no longer, but conclude by giving you a toast, if my treacherous memory will so far serve me. I will give you—

Genius—in—— (Here, however, the venerable president's memory did desert him, and after a brief interval spent in vain attempts to summon her to his aid, he looked pleasantly around, and said)—

Gentlemen, a good memory is a great thing, and

I will give you all a piece of advice which it may be useful to you to remember. When you are not certain that you can keep a thing in your mind, be sure to keep it in your pocket. He then, enforcing his example, drew from his own pocket a scrap of paper, and read—

Genius—In its legitimate use, uniting wit with purity; instructing the high in their duties to the low; and by improving the morals, elevating the social condition of man.

During the delivery of his speech, Mr. Quincy was frequently interrupted with bursts of laughter and applause, and the happy sally with which he got over his concluding difficulty set the company in a roar, which continued until the president of the evening, Mr. Quincy, Jr., arose and said that as the president of Harvard University had introduced to them Sam Weller, he would take the liberty to read to them one of the sayings of that distinguished personage—

"If ever I wanted anything of my father (said Sam) I always asked for it in a werry 'spectful and obliging manner. If he didn't give it me, I took it, for fear I should be led to do anything wrong through not having it."

The president then called on one of the vice-presidents at the lower end of the hall, and Geo. S. Hillard, Esq., responded as follows—

Mr. President,—Our meeting together this evening is one of the agreeable results of the sympathy established between two great and distant nations by a common language and common literature. We are paying our cheerful tribute of gratitude and admiration to one who, though heretofore a stranger to us in person, has made his image a familiar presence in innumerable hearts, who has brightened the sunshine of many a happy, and cheered the gloom of many a desponding breast, whose works have been companions to the solitary and a cordial in the sick man's chamber, and whose natural pathos and thoughtful humour, flowing from a genius as healthy as it is inventive, have drawn more

closely the ties which bind man to his brother man, and
have given us a new sense of the wickedness of injustice,
the deformity of selfishness, the beauty of self-sacrifice,
the dignity of humble virtue, and the strength of that
love which is found in "huts where poor men lie." The
new harvest of applause which is gathered by the gifted
minds of England, in a country separated from their
own by three thousand miles of ocean, is a privilege
peculiar to them, and one to which no author, however
rich in golden opinions won at home, can feel himself
indifferent. No brow can be so thickly shaded with
indigenous laurels as not to wear, with emotion, those
which are the growth of a foreign soil. There is no
homage so true and unquestionable as that which the
stranger offers. At home, the popularity of an author
may, during his own life, at least, be greatly increased
by circumstances not at all affecting the intrinsic value
of his writings. The caprice of fashion, the accident of
high rank or distinguished social position, the zeal of
a literary faction or a political party, may invest some
"Cynthia of the minute" with a brief notoriety, which
resembles true fame only as the meteor does the star.
But popularity of this kind is of too flimsy and delicate
a texture to bear transportation. It is only merit of a
solid and durable fabric which can survive a voyage
across the Atlantic. It has been said, with as much
truth as point, that a foreign nation is a sort of contemporaneous posterity. Its judgment resembles the
calm, unbiassed voice of future ages. It has no infusion of personal feeling; it is a serene and unimpas-
sioned verdict, neither won by favour nor withheld from
prejudice. The admiration which comes from afar off
is valuable in the direct ratio of its distance, as there
is the same degree of assurance that it springs from no
secondary cause, but is a spontaneous and unbought
tribute. An English author might see with comparative unconcern his book upon a drawing-room table in
London, but should he chance to meet a well-thumbed
copy of it in a log-house beyond our Western mountains,
would not his heart swell with pride at the thought of

the wide space through which his name was diffused, and his influence felt, and would not his lips almost unconsciously utterly the expression of the wandering Trojan—

"Quae regio in terris nostri non plena laboris ? "

It is also probably true that, in our country, English authors find their warmest and most impassioned admirers. It is as true of the mind as of the eye, that distance lends enchantment to the view. There are no hues so soft and delicate with which the imagination invests that which is unseen or faintly discerned. Remoteness in space has the same idealizing effect as remoteness of time. The voice that comes to us from the dim distance is like that which comes to us from the dim past. We know, but we do not feel, the interval which separates Shakespeare from Scott, Milton from Wordsworth, Hume from Hallam. We know them only by those airy creations of the brain which speak to us through the printed page. Solitude, and silence too, are the nurses of deep and strong feeling. That imaginative element which exalts the love of Dante for Beatrice, and of Burns for his "Mary in Heaven," deepens the fervour of admiration with which the pale, enthusiastic scholar, in some lonely farmhouse in New England, hangs over a favourite author who, though perhaps a living contemporary, is recognized only as an absolute essence of genius, wisdom or truth. The minds of men whom we see face to face appear to shine upon us darkly through the infirmities of a mortal frame. Their faculties are touched by weariness or pain, or some humiliating weakness or unhandsome passion thrusts its eclipsing shadow between us and the light of their genius. Not so with those to whom they speak only through the medium of books. In these we see the products of those golden hours, when all that was low is elevated, when all that was dark is illumined, and all that was earthly is transfigured. Books have no touch of personal infirmity—theirs is undying bloom, immortal youth, perennial fragrance. Age cannot wrinkle, disease cannot blight, death cannot pierce them. The personal image of the author is quite as likely to be a hindrance as a help to his book. The actor who played with Shakespeare in his own *Hamlet* probably did but imperfect justice to that wonderful play, and the next-door neighbour of a popular author will be very likely to read his books with a carping, censorious spirit, unknown to him who has seen his visage only in his mind.

Mr. President, I dwell with pleasure on the considerations to which an occasion like this gives birth. It is good for us to be here. Whatever has a tendency to make two great nations forget those things in which they differ, and remember those only in which they have a common interest, is a benefit to them both. Whatever makes the hearts of two countries beat in unison, makes them more enamoured of harmony, more sensitive to discord. Honour to the men of genius, who made two hemispheres thrill to the same electric touch; who at the same time, and with the same potent spell, are ruling the hearts of men in the mountains of Scotland, the forests of Canada, the hillsides of New England, the prairies of Illinois and the burning plains of India. Their influence, so far as it extends, is a peaceful and a humanizing one. When you have instructed two men with the same wisdom, and charmed them with the same wit, you have established between them a bond of sympathy, however slight, and made it so much the more difficult to set them at variance. When I remember the history of England, how much she has done for law, liberty, virtue and religion—for all that beautifies and dignifies life—when I recollect how much that is most valuable and characteristic in our own institutions is borrowed from her—when I recall our obligations to her matchless literature, I feel a throb of gratitude that "Chatham's language is my mother-tongue," and my heart warms to the land of my fathers. I embrace with peculiar satisfaction every consideration that tends to give us a unity of spirit in the bond of peace—to make us blind to each other's faults, and kind

to each other's virtues. I feel all the force of the fine
lines of one whom we have the honour to receive as a
guest this evening—

> "Though ages long have passed
>   Since our fathers left their home,
> Their pilot in the blast,
>   O'er untravelled seas to roam,
> Yet lives the blood of England in our veins;
>   And shall we not proclaim
>   That blood of honest fame,
> Which no tyranny can tame
>   By its chains?
>
>   .   .   .   .   .   .
>
> "While the manners, while the arts
>   That mould a nation's soul,
> Still cling around our hearts,—
>   Between, let ocean roll,
> Our joint communion breaking with the sun;
>   Yet still from either beach
>   The voice of blood shall reach,
> More audible than speech—
>   We are one."

It is now sixty-seven years since the rapid growth of
our country was sketched by Mr. Burke, in the course
of his speech on conciliation with America, in a passage
whose picturesque beauty has made it one of the
commonplaces of literature, in which he represents the
angel of Lord Bathurst drawing up the curtain of
futurity, unfolding the rising glories of England, and
pointing out to him America, a little speck scarce visible
in the mass of the national interest, yet which was
destined before he tasted of death to show itself equal
to the whole of that commerce which then attracted the
admiration of the world. There are many now living
whose lives extend over the whole of this period—and
during that space, what memorable changes have taken
place in the relations of the two countries! Let us
imagine the angel of that illustrious orator and statesman, when the last words of that profound and beautiful
speech were dying upon the air, withdrawing him from
the congratulations of his friends, and unfolding to him

the future progress of that country, whose growth up to that period he had so felicitously sketched: "There is that America, whose interests you have so well understood and so eloquently maintained, which, at this moment, is taking measures to withdraw from the protection and defy the power of the mother country. But mourn not that this bright jewel is destined to fall from your country's crown. It is in obedience to the same law of Providence which sends the full-fledged bird from the nest, and the man from his father's house. Man shall not be able to sever what the immutable laws of Providence have joined together. The chafing chains of colonial dependence shall be exchanged for ties light as air, yet strong as steel. The peaceful and profitable interchange of commerce — the same language — a common literature—similar laws and kindred institutions shall bind you together with cords which neither cold-blooded policy, nor grasping selfishness, nor fratricidal war shall be able to snap. Discoveries in science and improvements in art shall be constantly contracting the ocean which separates you, and the genius of steam shall link your shores together with a chain of iron and flame. A new heritage of glory shall await your men of genius in those now unpeopled solitudes. The grand and lovely creations of your myriad-minded Shakespeare —the majestic line of Milton—the stately energy of Dryden and the compact elegance of Pope shall form and train the minds of uncounted multitudes yet slumbering in the womb of the future. Her gifted and educated sons shall come over to your shores with a feeling akin to that which sends the Mussulman to Mecca. Your St. Paul's shall kindle their devotion; your Westminster Abbey shall warm their patriotism; your Stratford-on-Avon and Abbotsford shall awaken in their bosoms a depth of emotion in which your own countrymen shall hardly be able to sympathize. Extraordinary physical advantages and the influence of genial institutions shall there give to the human race a rate of increase hitherto unparalleled; but the stream, however much it be widened and prolonged, shall retain the character of the fountain from which it first flowed. Every wave of population that gains upon that vast green wilderness shall bear with it the blood, the speech and the books of England, and aid in transmitting to the generations that come after it, her arts, her literature and her laws." If this had been revealed to him, would it not have required all the glow of his imagination and all the strength of his judgment to believe it? Let us who are seeing the fulfilment of the vision utter the fervent prayer that no sullen clouds of coldness or estrangement may ever obscure these fair relations, and that the madness of man may never mar the benevolent purposes of God.

Mr. Hillard concluded by giving the following toast, which was drunk standing—

The gifted minds of England—Hers by birth; ours by adoption.

The president said he did not know exactly who ought to respond to that sentiment. They had been taught, however, by their guest, that the greatest merit was often found in the byways of life, and he would therefore give—

The adopted authors of England, and the author of "The Highways and Byways of Old Ireland."

Thomas C. Grattan, Esq., in responding to this toast, said—

Mr. President,—Always ready to obey your call, always happy to respond to the voice of my eloquent friend at the other extremity of the table, I cheerfully rise to attempt, as best I may, the task you have assigned to me. Frequently, sir, as it has been my duty to perform a similar task at the public festivities of Boston, the pleasure was never greater, nor did ever I feel the duty lighter, than on this occasion. The many causes for the *pleasure* I need not dilate on; and as to the *task,* it has been almost entirely anticipated, and so ably, by what has been already said in praise of the literature and in honour of the genius of England, that for me to dwell at any length upon the theme would be no better than an ambitious attempt to emulate what I might not hope to equal.

And I might sit down now, sir, but that I am not able to resist the temptation of the position to which you have called me. I cannot avoid saying how proud I feel to have been associated by you with our glorious literature. I say *ours*, sir, emphatically, for it is ours alike, whether we be American, English or Irish. No matter in what country we may have been by accident born; our common language, stronger than claims of birth or parentage, makes that literature our common inheritance, as it is the common bond of union, which has brought us here to-night, and will bind us together for all time. Yes, sir, let what may happen in the chances of the future—let the ties of commercial interests be one by one snapped asunder—let even the charms of social intercourse be torn up by the roots and scattered to the winds by some political tempest, it will be but for a time; for the one link of that language in which we all speak and write and think will be strong enough to hold firm our sympathies, in the safe anchorage of literature, the glory of our respective nations, and a fertile field of delight to millions who labour or who sport within it.

But I must not, Mr. President, indulge further in these desultory remarks, beyond touching on two special reasons for acknowledging the honour of being invited here to-day. The first is, sir, that I was so invited as a simple citizen of that great republic of letters to which so many now present belong—which knows no titles, admits of neither kings nor consuls—and to have been naturalized in which, as one of the humblest of its citizens, is the circumstance of my life to which I look back with the truest and most unalloyed satisfaction. Owing to my connection with literature, the pleasure of witnessing this fine social tribute to one of its brightest ornaments, my pride in all that does it honour is in a double degree gratified by this scene—for he who receives and they who offer such a tribute are alike adding flowers to the wreaths hung up at the shrine of literary fame, at which we are all worshippers.

My second reason, sir, for being particularly pleased at being among you to-day is that it was explicitly

E

and considerately made known to me that I was asked to make one of a company of *young* men—and that no unlucky individual beyond the age of thirty, or thereabouts—a generous latitude—had any chance of being admitted. Before I received this invitation, sir, I confess that I had some serious misgivings, some vague suspicions that I had actually passed the boundary-line between youth and age—a boundary-line which they on its wrong side are as unwilling to acknowledge as the borderers on any other boundary-line whatever. And in truth, sir, I found I could not long deceive myself with the notion to the contrary. But I for a while fondly imagined, sir, that I might possibly succeed in deceiving others as to the sad reality. I first thought of laying some "flattering unction" to my whiskers to change their rather equivocal tints. I next thought of wearing a wig—by hook or by crook endeavouring to make the grey one brown; and so, by deceiving my juvenile friends on this occasion, turning Papinti's Hall into another "Dotheboys Hall."

But, gentlemen, I was spared the necessity of playing any of those fantastic tricks by learning who was to be the president of the feast. Remembering at once the many lively and youthful sallies I had so often listened to from his lips, and that the very head and front of my offending was his as well; and hating, all my life, to fight, and more especially to drink, under false colours, I thought I should be safe in serving under the banner he hung out, and that there could be no *shame* to England, while there was sure to be so much glory to America. I had, moreover, a shrewd notion that spirits of various shades would be mingled here to-night; and finding that I could not claim a right to muster among the black ones, I thought I would be content to range myself among the white.

And I am content, gentlemen—satisfied that it is little matter how soon the head grows grey so long as the heart keeps green, and that mixing in scenes like this is the true method to preserve that verdure of the feelings which makes us indifferent to the march of time, and—for a long time at least—insensible to the approach of age. My countryman, Moore, tells us, in one of his exquisite songs, that

" The best of all ways
To lengthen our days,
Is to steal a few hours from the night."

I hope, Mr. President, that under your victorious auspices we shall carry out that maxim of true philosophy to a large practical extent on this occasion; and I may perhaps be allowed to add, by way of parody or of parallel—and for the special consolation of the venerable gentlemen of thirty *or thereabouts*—that

The best way for old men to spin out life's joys,
Is, as oft as they can, to crack jokes with the boys.

Mr. Grattan concluded by proposing the health of *Richard H. Dana, Jr.*, author of *Two Years before the Mast*.

The president said that, as the gentleman had served so long before the mast, the company would like to see him on the quarter-deck.

On appearing in compliance with the call of the president, Mr. Dana was received with repeated cheers. He said that nothing could have been more unexpected to him, who was among the youngest of those present, than to be called up in the manner in which he had been, and at so early a period in the evening. The president had made an allusion to his service before the mast, but he could assure those who heard him that, whatever of romance might be associated with a sailor's life, in his estimation not two whole years of it could be compared with one moment of the society and approbation of the friends he saw around him. It had been his fortune, he said, to travel in lands little known to the geographer, but it had been the fortune of their guest to travel in new worlds of thought and of imagination. Tracing a parallel between the discoveries of Mr. Dickens in the intellectual world, which were among the greatest events of the ages to which they respectively belonged, Mr. Dana said that their guest had made a new era in literature; and should D'Israeli undertake a continua-

E 2

tion of his curiosities, the most remarkable circumstance among them all would be the fact that a young man, by the mere power of his genius, had in a few brief years so endeared himself to the people of a land not his own as to make a triumphal progress through it. Without detaining the company further, except to thank them for the kind manner in which they had received the compliment which had been given to himself, Mr. Dana said he would conclude by proposing—

The Columbus of modern literature—We welcome him to the new world, who has himself opened new worlds to us.

The president said that after the personal attack which Mr. Grattan had made upon his hair, it was hardly fair for him to make so direct a shot at his young friend, Mr. Dana. It was what Sam Weller would call "addin' insult to injury, as the parrot said ven they not only took him from his native land, but made him talk the English language arterwards." While he was on the subject of Mr. Weller's sayings, he would add that another extract from the works of his young friend (Mr. Dickens) had been handed to him, which he would read: "You've got a pretty voice, a very soft eye, and a very strong memory"—"you know forty-seven songs. Forty-seven's your number. Let me hear one of 'em —the best. Give me a song this minute," Dr. Holmes.

The call of the President was so strongly seconded by the cheers of the assembly that the gentleman pointed at (Dr. O. W. Holmes) could not resist it; and, without a single excuse (thus making himself an exception to all the singers that have gone before him), favoured the company with the following original song—

SONG (*air: Gramachree*)

The stars their early vigils keep,
  The silent hours are near
When drooping eyes forget to weep—
  Yet still we linger here.
And what—the passing churl may ask—
  Can calm such wondrous power,
That Toil forgets his wonted task,
  And Love his promised hour?

The Irish harp no longer thrills,
  Or breathes a fainter tone—
The clarion blast from Scotland's hills,
  Alas! no more is blown;
And passion's burning lip bewails
  Her Harold's wasted fire,
Still lingering o'er the dust that veils
  The Lord of England's lyre.

But grieve not o'er its broken strings,
  Nor think its soul hath died,
While yet the lark at heaven's gate sings,
  As once o'er Avon's side;
While gentle summer sheds her bloom,
  And dewy blossoms wave
Alike o'er Juliet's storied tomb
  And Nelly's nameless grave.

Thou glorious island of the sea!
  Though wide the wasting flood
That parts our distant land from thee—
  We claim thy generous blood;
Nor o'er thy far horizon springs
  One hallowed star of fame,
But kindles, like an angel's wings,
  Our western skies in flame!

The president said that they had been told by the president of Harvard College that it was a very good thing for a man to carry his toast in his pocket, lest his memory might fail. He had so far acted upon that principle as to prepare a toast which he had hoped would draw a speech from His Excellency Governor Davis, but he unfortunately had kept it in his pocket too long, for the Governor had been compelled, on account of indisposition, to retire at an early hour. The toast was—

The political pilots of Old England and of New England—Though their titles may be different, they observe the same luminaries in the literary, and steer by the same stars in the moral, horizon.

For what they had lost in his remissness in not reading the toast before, he said he could only console them by another maxim from Sam Weller's philosophy: "It's all over and can't be helped, and that's one consolation, as they always say in Turkey ven they cuts the wrong man's head off."

The president now gave—

Washington Allston—He who unites the genius of the poet, the pencil of the painter, and the pen of the novelist; his name shall glow for ever upon the eternal canvas.

Mr. Allston arose immediately, and in a low but firm tone, said—

Mr. President—I hope my late illness, from which I have hardly recovered, will be a sufficient apology for my not attempting a speei h. Were I to make one it would be my maiden speech, which can hardly be expected from one at my time of life. I have been lately trying to bottle up some of the healthful spirits of our friend Barnaby, which I had hoped would have served on this occasion; but I found, to my sorrow, that our friend Grip has wickedly uncorked all the bottles. Since, then, I cannot make a speech, I beg leave to propose a toast—

The prophetic raven—who only spoke to posterity, when he cried, "Never say die," to Barnaby Rudge.

Gentlemen, said the president, should you like to hear what Sam Weller has to say in reply to the speech of our friend? It is, "Werry glad to see you, sir, indeed, and hope our acquaintance may be a long one, as the gentleman said to the fi' pun note."

In reply to a sentiment in honour of the merchants of Boston, J. Thomas Stevenson, Esq., one of the vice-presidents, gave the following address—

Mr. President,—Nothing short of your direct call upon me would have induced me to undertake to answer for the merchants here; for I am fully aware that your committee of arrangements honoured me with a seat here to-night, not in expectation that I could contribute to the literary treat of the evening, but from a desirè on their part to show a kind respect to the commercial community. The gentlemen composing that committee know that our figures are not figures of speech—that our notes are not commentaries—that our letters are not belles-lettres—that our stores are not stores of knowledge—and that our folios are rich with nothing, unless perhaps with legendary lore.

But as you have called upon me, I will say one word in obedience alike to that call and to the feelings which the present occasion provokes.

It is a subject of real congratulation that the literary men of the old world are evincing a desire to acquaint themselves by personal observation with the institutions of our country, and with the habits of our people. Nothing could do more to remove any unjust impressions which may exist; and we may say, without subjecting ourselves to the suspicion of vain-boasting, that he who visits us with an open mind, and takes a liberal view of all that is presented to him here, will find much to interest him in the seeming contradictions by which he will be surrounded. Let it be my task to tell our guest of some things which he will find here.

He will find us a very *inviting* people. He will find *hosts* of peculiarities to enjoy, and we will trust that he may enjoy the peculiarities of the *hosts* which he finds.

He will find us full of paradoxes. For he will find the great problem of self-government approaching its solution—the great experiment of democracy, monarch-like, claiming the *crown* for its *issue*.

He will find our army a militia—never in camp, yet always "*intent*" "*upon duty*."

He will find the great cause of temperance advancing with rapid strides, and every drunkard *brandied* with disgrace.

He will find a judiciary respected by all, excepting perhaps at the present moment those who have been in the habit of standing at the *bar*. And if he should go into one of our courts, he will find the bench occupied by a "warring of wits."

He will find our medical schools vieing with the pulpit in delivering us from false *doctoring*. He will find the means of education within the reach of all, through our common schools, while we are boasting all the time that they are uncommon schools.

He will find the religious sentiment developing itself in all its forms, from the rough madness of mormonism to the polished insanity of transcendentalism—good in all, with a *prior* right in none.

He will find no House of Lords here; but most of us lords of houses and our *commons* amply stored with *provisions* for the support of the *constitution*. He will find all men peers and then may wonder how it is so many of our dames are *peerless*.

He will find want purely mechanical—pinching only through the *instrumentality* of some *vice*. He will find no pillory here, but a great variety of *stocks;* and will see whole states setting examples of self-sacrifice, by turning a deaf ear to the demands of *interest;* and if he go into our non-specie-paying states, he will find no "coigne of vantage" there. And if it be not too far-fetched, he may go to Carolina to study the *rice* of this great empire, and thence hasten to Niagara to contemplate its tremendous *fall*. And he may be shocked by the ungrammatical assurance of those of us who are here to-night, that the present time is pastime, and that we ought to *parse* the bottle without *declining* it.

These are things, sir, which every man may find. But if he be one who has recalled literature from mysterious wanderings in the clouds, to deal with and adorn the realities of life—if he be one whose works will not follow him simply because they have preceded him here—if he be one who has touched the spring of human action and sounded the very depths of the soul—if he be one whose genuine wit has made us laugh till we have cried, while his real pathos has wrung out the unwilling tears until their very sources were dry—if he be one who has exposed to us the enormities of obscure vice, while he has cleared away the rubbish from the brilliants of humble virtue, he will find here a welcome and a home.

And, Mr. President, if you will allow to me only time to offer a toast, he shall find how soon, in this country of rapid growths, the unpractised talker can become a *finished* speaker.

Mr. President,—I see a friend from whom I wish to hear, and so will propose—

The U.S. District Attorney—The right hand of the law is raised for no sinister purpose.

To this play upon his name, Franklin Dexter, Esq., replied—

Mr. President,—Being but little given to utter dinner speeches, I hardly know how to answer the punning attack upon my name from my friend at the lower end of the table. While I thank him for the kind but unmerited compliment it conveys, I should feel tempted, since his own name will not admit of any but an equivocal expression of my respect, to attempt a return in kind upon that of our distinguished guest, which is not safe from a very bad pun, when we ask him how he has been able thus to excite all this enthusiasm in a strange people. But as I doubt not he has heretofore suffered in that way, I forbear; and being myself a man more punned against than punning, I will only take the occasion seriously to express my participation in the general joy of the whole table.

Our satisfaction at this meeting is not the mere gratification of curiosity; though we might well be curious to know one who has himself known so much of the various conditions and humours of life. But, in addition to the pleasure of his personal acquaintance, we have that of believing that the interchange of visits between the distinguished literary men of the two countries must have a beneficial effect upon their most important relations. No class of men have so much influence over the feelings and opinions of their countrymen as popular authors. It is within our recent recollection that the most unkind feelings towards England have been produced here by the wanton attacks of some of our distinguished authors upon the character of her whole population and institutions; and it is by no means certain that our political relations with her have not been materially affected by so very inadequate a cause. In this view it is a source of great satisfaction to see those who lead the popular sentiment in the two countries becoming better acquainted and more closely united; and let me offer you as a toast—

The Universal Brotherhood of Literature—a pacificator of the nations.

The president here read the following letter from the author of *Ferdinand and Isabella*—

Bedford Street, January 21, 1842.

GENTLEMEN,

I beg leave to acknowledge my sense of the honour you have done me in inviting me to be present at your proposed dinner to Mr. Dickens. Be assured it would give me sincere pleasure to join with you in this homage to this distinguished foreigner, whose writings have secured him such deserved consideration in the Republic of Letters. But the irritable state of my eyes, which would be sure to suffer from the excitement and heat of such an occasion, compels me to forgo the pleasure I should otherwise have had, of sharing in your festivities. My spirit, however, will be with you—and if you will allow me, I will propose the following sentiment—

The Alchymy of Genius—which can extract truth from fiction, wisdom from folly, and pure morality from vice itself.

With much respect, gentlemen,

Believe me, your obliged and obedient servant,

WM. H. PRESCOTT.

To G. T. Bigelow, Esq.; N. Hale, Jr., Esq.; Jona. F. Barrett, Esq.; Fred. W. Crocker, Esq.; W. W. Story, Esq., Committee of Invitation.

The president now gave the following toast—

The Historian of America—He who has portrayed the discovery, and he who has illustrated the progress of our native land.

George Bancroft, Esq., being thus alluded to, rose and delivered a very eloquent and soul-stirring address, in the course of which he said he recognized the young men of the country as the highest tribunal before which aspirants for honour could plead. They are to take our places, and make up the judgment on our labours. Their regard, their good opinion, their generous sympathy was the best reward. He recalled rapidly the names of many, who in early life gained highest distinction; and paid a warm tribute to the guest of the day, who had put so much heart into all that he did, as to make himself, while a young man, not only world renowned, but world beloved.

The occasion, too, was auspicious as a tribute generally to letters. To two men who had come up to Paris possessed of no other power than that of writing French well, France had paid the tribute of highest stations; the purpose to-day was to do honour to one who rested his right to public respect solely on his genius, and the noble use he had made of it.

Yet, Mr. Bancroft observed, the regard manifested for the guest was a homage also to the spirit of popular liberty. The great tendency of modern civilization was everywhere towards the increase of the power of the people, the recognition of the claims of every man to franchises and a share of authority. The movement in the world of letters corresponded; a writer who joined the rare gifts of humour, pathos and creative power, had made fiction the vehicle of a defence of the rights of the humblest, and by the force of his talent compelled the world to follow humanity even to the poor-house, and acknowledge that it could be redeemed even from the haunts of infamy.

Then, too, the occasion was a symbol of a kind of union among the many millions who have the English for their mother-tongue. Mr. Bancroft repelled the idea that England was to make its power recognized by the sound of its martial airs following the sun in its course; yet he exulted in the thought that in every zone the English is the united tongue of nations ripening for freedom; that under every meridian its literature is the delight of the gay and the solace of the sad.

Nor was this union confined to language only. Mr. Bancroft pointed out the common right of America to a large part of English literature. He observed how many of their greatest minds had expressed the heartiest interest in the New World, and had been most able defenders of the principles on which our institutions are founded.

In particular, allusion was made to Lord Byron. The purpose he so often expressed of visiting this country, the political aspect of his writings, his scoffing at the vices of false civilization, his zeal for the overthrow of abuses and the progress of reform; his hearty sympathy with this country as shown in his giving a place in his writings to the backwoodsman as well as to Washington.

Mr. Bancroft, in conclusion, compared the enthusiasm with which Byron's works had been welcomed all the world over, with the tribute paid to genius now, and gave—

The memory of Lord Byron—Light lie the turf on the ashes of the poet who was ever the adversary of tyranny over mind.

The speech and sentiment of Mr. Bancroft were received with enthusiastic applause.

When silence was restored, the president inquired if gentlemen remembered the excursion made by Mr. Pickwick and his companions, Snodgrass and Winkle, to Dingley Dell, and the particulars of that melancholy ride? Presuming that they did, he would not detain them with a narration of them, but would merely read the pathetic words of Mr. Pickwick, in reference to the horse which he could not get rid of on that occasion—

"'It's like a dream,' ejaculated Mr. Pickwick, 'a hideous dream. The idea of a man's walking about all day with a dreadful horse that he can't get rid of.'"

Gentlemen (continued the president), I will give you— the mayor—

The horse that Mr. Pickwick could not get rid of, and the mayor that nobody even wants to get rid of.

This toast called up the Hon. Jonathan Chapman, the mayor, who made the following humorous reply—

More than tongue can tell, sir, even if it had ages to wag in, am I obliged for the very complimentary character of the sentiment you have just announced. It was so disinterested—such a spontaneous, irrepressible tribute on your part, to unmitigated merit on mine, that from very considerably deeper down than the bottom of my heart, I thank you. But no, sir, I am not quite as green as that. The plain English, as I judge from what has preceded, or, to speak more properly, the familiar Latin of the whole matter is this : *"Expectatur,"* —I will not say, *"oratio,"* for that is too pretending a title, but *"dissertatio in lingua vernacula a Chapman."*

You will be disappointed, however, sir. With whatever authority another individual whose name you bear might utter these cabalistic words, I recognize no such authority in you. I shall attempt no dissertation, and that for two of Mr. Weller senior's reasons : first, because I can't, and second, because I won't.

I am aware that I am indebted to the office which I hold, and not to any personal claims of my own, for the privilege of participating in this beautiful scene. Yes, sir, one of the beautiful amongst human things— the spontaneous, heartfelt tribute of the young men of one country, not to the rank and wealth, but to the mingled intellect and soul of one who, though yet young, has communed with and touched more hearts than ages of common life would permit, and who, in whatever land he may have been born, will find a welcome and a home wherever there is a heart to beat, or where a spark of humanity lingers.

I say that I owe to my office the privilege of being here. Permit me, therefore, to draw on my office for all that I have to say to-night. And let me just premise that it is one of its principal duties to receive complaints, for this is a complaining world, and the quarter in which we live is by no means an exception.

As I was seated in my chair this morning—not asleep, and therefore it could not have been a dream— there entered two persons, evidently strangers. The one was an elderly gentleman, with a mild and beaming countenance; the other much younger, and evidently one of those peculiar personages, half companion, half servant, whom you always find attending upon good old gentlemen. Though I had never seen them before in person, they seemed like old acquaintances. They interested me at once, and I have no doubt they will this whole assembly, when I say that one of them was no less a personage than the honourable Samuel Pickwick and the other by no means dishonourable Mr. Samuel Weller.

Yes, sir, there stood in the mayor's office, in this city, to-day, the great and good Mr. Pickwick—with his bald head so glossy that, if he could turn his own eyes upon it, he would need no looking-glass to make his toilet—with the same "circular spectacles" which he always wore, only that one glass had been knocked out in the immense rush to embrace him immediately upon his landing—clothed in those immortal tights and gaiters which are proof positive of the modern transcendental doctrine that a man is nothing without his tailor —there stood, in short, that illustrious individual whom no description can describe one half so well as the simple epithet, "Mr. Pickwick." And just in the rear, yet so nearly by his side as to seem to say, "almost your equal, but not quite," stood honest, funny Samuel Weller, grasping his hat so closely under his arm that he seemed to be holding on upon himself—as if he feared he were in a land of kidnappers.

I was about to approach these distinguished visitors, when Mr. Pickwick advanced, evidently charged with a speech which would brook no delay in the delivery, and placing himself in his peculiar attitude, "with his left hand gracefully concealed behind his coat-tails, and his right gracefully raised in the air to aid his flowing declamation," at once commenced. With your permission, I will endeavour to repeat what he said—

"Mr. Mayor," said he, "the love of one's friend is natural to man, and of one's benefactors, most particularly natural. You love yours, and I cannot deny that I am influenced by the same tender feelings. There has come to this country, and is now in your city, the youthful but learned editor of the Transactions of the Pickwick Club, of which I have the honour to be the General Chairman, as will appear by the letters G.C.M.P.C. upon my card, which I have the honour to hand you. I stand in a peculiar relation to this man, one never known before; indeed, a truly Pickwickian relation, namely, that he first created me, and then I made him. He is, too, the choice spirit of our club. I love him. Mr. Winkle loves him. Mr. Tupman loves him. Mr. Snodgrass loves him. All love him. Indeed, we never should have consented that he should visit this strange country unless some of us had been secretly sent to take care of him. For we have learned that you are a curious people here—that, as it has been said, whom the gods love die young, so whom the Americans love they utterly kill with kindness."

"Yes," interrupted Mr. Weller, unable longer to repress his feelings, "it is currently reported in our circles that, when the Americans fancies a stranger, they makes him into *weal* pie, and dewours him."

"Hush, Samuel," said Mr. Pickwick; "don't use hard words. Never get into a passion, particularly in foreign countries, where you don't know the customs. But, Mr. Mayor, this is my source of trouble, and I come to complain that your people seem determined to extinguish our editor. I have been trying to get at him for a week, but have not dared to trust my gaiters amidst the crowds that surround him. I tremble when I hear of two dinners in one day, and four suppers in one night. I fear you have designs upon his life, nay, that you mean to eat him up."

"Sir," interrupted I, "do I understand you aright? Do you mean to insinuate that the American people are cannibals? Do you use your words in their common sense?"

"O no, sir," replied Mr. Pickwick, resuming his blandest expression. "I respect and honour the American people. I mean to say they are cannibals only in a Pickwickian point of view. But, besides my personal attachment, I desire this man's life to be spared, for the sake of science, and for the cause of humanity, and of the club. Think not that the club has been sleeping, whilst its editor has been visiting the poor-houses and hovels, touching your hearts and making you better men, by his truthful descriptions. We have been gathering materials, and are doing so still. Even your own country may furnish some of these materials;— not, however, I assure you, for the purposes of bold and coarse personalities, either of praise or of censure,— but for the delicate and beautiful touches of character, —those life-like and soul-stirring descriptions—those pictures of humanity, which show that, behind the drapery of human forms and distinctions, the true element of a man is a warm and beating heart. These are the purposes for which we are at work—purposes, sir, for which, though I, Samuel Pickwick, say it, the editor of the Pickwick Club has no superior upon the face of the earth.

"I pray you therefore," said he, rising to a pitch of enthusiasm which almost choked his utterance, "I pray you to protect him. Let him not be overrun. Let him not be devoured. Spare him to return again to the halls of the club. Spare him, sir, and the blessings of Winkle, Tupman, Snodgrass, Pickwick and the whole race of Pickwickians, shall be on you and yours."

Having thus uttered himself, and leaving his respects for you, sir, and for this assembly, he took his leave.

Feeling myself most particularly honoured by this interview, I give you as a sentiment—

The Hon. Samuel Pickwick, and the Pickwick Club, and its editor—"May they never say die."

> " And when they next do ride abroad,
> May we be there to see."

Mr. J. T. Stevenson, in relation to the fears expressed by Mr. Pickwick, as reported by the mayor, that the editor of the *Pickwick Papers* would be extinguished in America, hoped that at any rate he would not be *put out* by anything that might take place on the present occasion.

Mr. J. M. Field ("Straw") being called upon for a song, he gave the following original and characteristic production, to a popular air—

THE WERY LAST OBSERWATIONS OF WELLER, SENIOR

Remember vot I says, Boz—
  You're going to cross the sea;
A blessed vay avays, Boz,
  To vild Amerikey;
A blessed set of savages,
  As books of travels tells;
No guv'ner's eye to watch you, Boz,
  Nor even Samivel's.

They've 'stablished a steam line, Boz,
  A wi'lent innowation;
It's nothing but a trap to 'tice
  Our *floatin'* population.
A set of blessed cannibals—
  My warnin' I repeats—
For ev'ry vun they catches, Boz,
  Vithout ado they *eats*.

They'll *eat* you, Boz, in Boston! and
  They'll eat you in New York!
Wherever caught, they'll play a bles-
  sed game of knife and fork!
There's prayers in Boston now that Cu-
  nard's biler may not burst;
Because their savage hope it is,
  Dear Boz, to *eat* you first.

They lately caught a *prince*, Boz,
  A livin' vun, from France;
And all the blessed nation, Boz,
  Assembles for a *dance!*
They spares him thro' the ev'nin', Boz,
  But vith a hungry stare,
Contrives a early *supper*, tho',
  And then they *eats* him there!

Just think of all of yours, Boz,
  Devoured by them already;
Avoid their greedy lures, Boz,
  Their appetites is steady;
For years they've been a feastin', Boz
  Nor *paid* for their repast;
And von't they make a blessed feast
  Ven they catches you at last!

F

Lord! how they gobbled "Pickwick"—fate
Which "Oliver" befel!
And watering mouths met "Nic" and "Smike,'
And watering eyes as well!
Poor "Nell" was not too tender, Boz,
Nor ugly "Quilp" too tough;
And "Barnaby"—I'm blest if e'er
I thinks they'll have enough!

I'll tell you what you does, Boz,
Since go it seems you vill;
If you would not expose, Boz,
Yourself their maws to fill;
Just "Marryatt" or "Trollope," Boz,
Vithin your pocket hem;
For blow me if I ever thinks
They'll ever *swallow* them!

This song excited peals of laughter at every line, and at the conclusion there was a spontaneous outburst, which proved how universal was the sentiment expressed in the last stanza, in relation to two of the most amiable individuals who have honoured this country with a visit. The president complimented the author by another draft upon the sage observations of Mr. Weller—

"'Ah,' said the little man, 'you're a wag, ain't you?'"

"'My eldest brother was troubled with that complaint,' said Sam; 'it may be catching; I used to sleep with him.'"

The president here read the following letter from Washington Irving—

Sunnyside, January 25, 1842.

Gentlemen,

I have this moment received your letter of the 17th instant, which has probably been detained in New York. I regret extremely that circumstances put it out of my power to accept your very obliging invitation to the dinner about to be given to Mr. Dickens.

Accept, gentlemen, my best thanks for this very flattering mark of good-will, and believe me,

Very respectfully,

Your obliged and humble servant,

WASHINGTON IRVING.

Messrs. George Tyler Bigelow, Nathan Hale, Jr., Jonathan Fay Barrett, Frederick W. Crocker, W. W. Story, Committee of Invitation.

The following toast was then proposed—

Geoffrey Crayon—May he who has exhibited the *sunny side* of Old England long live on the "Sunny-side" of America.

The president next gave—

Richard H. Dana, Sr.—The glory of fathers is their children, and the glory of children is their fathers.

Mr. Dana, in acknowledging this compliment, spoke of the sacred nature of the allusions which induced him to rise, and added that, like many others, he felt a degree of gratitude to the distinguished guest of the evening. From his writings he had derived joy, hour after hour; and even more than that, in reading many of his passages he had felt a sorrow that was dearer than joy. He then referred to some of the lighter characteristics of the productions of Mr. Dickens, and concluded by humorously observing that as talking was rather dry work, he would take the liberty of tendering to Mr. Dickens Bob Sawyer's invitation in Bob Sawyer's words —of asking him "if he would take something to drink."

The president here read the following letters from Drs. Channing and Stuart—

GENTLEMEN,

I thank you for your invitation to the dinner to be given to Mr. Dickens. I have many sympathies with you and with the gentlemen whom you represent, in regard to this distinguished writer, but it will not be in my power to accept your invitation.

Very truly yours,

WILLIAM E. CHANNING.

To the Committee of Invitation.

F 2

Andover, January 22, 1842.

GENTLEMEN,

Your note of the 17th inst. reached me yesterday. I thank you most sincerely for the kind invitation which it contains. Most gladly would I accept it if circumstances permitted. Mr. Dickens's works have been a favourite source of resort for me, when I wished to relax from graver study. There is so much in them to excite the imagination, to interest the feelings, and to make man kinder and more beneficent to his fellow-man, that I have come to entertain a high regard for the author, and a lively interest in his success and future usefulness. Most eagerly would I embrace any proper occasion to make acquaintance with him, and to do him honour.

I doubt not that you will enjoy "the feast of reason and the flow of soul." But my present engagements, and the state of my health, forbid me to accept your friendly proposal. In spirit I shall be present with you, and with my whole soul give a most hearty welcome to Mr. Dickens on his entrance into a new world. We have material enough here for him to construct several new edifices, perhaps some with which he may rear a temple that will perpetuate his name among us.

I never write toasts, much less do I *drink* them. But if I could be present with you, I should be greatly tempted to volunteer the following—

The Star from the East, which has thrilled so many hearts with joy by its radiance, and scattered light over so many dark places filled with the habitation of cruelty —May equal splendour attend its remaining course, and its setting be in a heaven of unclouded glory !

I am, gentlemen, with much respect,

Your obedient servant,

MOSES STUART.

Messrs. G. T. Bigelow, N. Hale, Jr., and others.

The president gave—

The Clergy of New England—There may be among them differences of faith in religion, but no difference

of feeling concerning the great interests of humanity;—
and called on the Rev. Dr. Palfrey, who responded with
great felicity, and in the course of his remarks argued
in favour of the passage of laws in England and
America, securing to the authors of each nation the
profits of their works in both, and concluded with the
following sentiment—

Mutual justice between nations, extending to the
mutual protection of the fabrics of the mind.

The president, after alluding to the ingenious ex-
pedient practised by that most noted "sawbones," Dr.
Robert Sawyer, to attract the public attention when just
entering upon his professional life—the leaving of an
empty bottle at all the houses in his neighbourhood, "by
mistake"—gave—

The medical profession—They have left off the
practice of sending around empty bottles for their own
profit, and are doing all in their power to prevent other
people from sending round full ones for their comfort.

Dr. Bigelow being called on, responded to this toast
as follows—

Mr. Chairman—I confess that I do not perceive in the
present exigency any very urgent occasion for calling
in the services of the medical profession. It seems to
me that we are surrounded by good looks and good
spirits, and, as far as we may trust appearances, there
has been no especial lack of good appetites. And if I
were permitted to extend a little further my medical
report on the condition of the present meeting, I should
say that the pulse of this assembly beats with but one
measure, and that the tongues which have been put
forth on this occasion are certainly of the smoothest
description.

I might proceed further with my professional remarks,
but find myself forestalled by the chairman, who, in his
introductory speech, has informed the meeting that a
foreign practitioner has arrived among us, and that he
"has been giving us medicines." If it be so, sir, my
occupation is gone. Nevertheless, I shall not exhibit
any professional jealousy, nor shall I favour the pro-

position which has been made this evening, to deliver over the new visitor to be "eaten by cannibals." The worst I wish him is that, when he is again invited to dine, he may not have to "eat his own words" upon quite so large a scale as he has done this evening.

The chairman has not enlightened us upon the character of the newly-discovered medicine, whether it be poppy or mandragora, or some more potent drug. But if I may risk a conjecture, he must mean a certain foreign composition, which has lately been imported in the form of papers, bearing the stamp and label of Pickwick & Co. This is a very good medicine, sir, and has many things to recommend it. In the first place, it is very accessible, being placarded in all our shop windows, and kept in every man's house. It is also economical, for a little of it goes a long way, and it is acknowledged by all to be "very filling for the price." Furthermore, sir, it is very convenient, for it does not require the old prudential precaution, "when taken to be well shaken," for those who take it are very sure to shake themselves.

But, sir, like all other agreeable stimulants, its use requires caution. It is found that those who resort to it are very apt to fall into an habitual indulgence. The victims of this practice are not unfrequently confined to their houses; they grow indifferent to objects around them; the muscles of their faces are affected by spasmodic movements; and, finally, they fall into convulsions. And the worst of it is, sir, that we have no remedy for the evil, nor efficient means of preventing it. My excellent friend at the other end of the table has talked about temperance measures, but if we propose a total abstinence society, nobody will sign the pledge. And if we look around at those who are sipping at this fountain in hopes to influence the moderate drinkers, they will tell us there are no such persons to be found. And when we threaten them with the serious consequences which must follow their infatuation, they tell us that, whatever the consequences may be, they are certainly anything but serious.

In short, Mr. Chairman, I fear there is no such thing as resisting this tide of popular sentiment. For how can we expect to influence an excited multitude, with scarce a sober man among them. Despairing, therefore, to produce reform among so incorrigible a set, or even to effect any considerable diversion in our favour, when the author of the mischief has made all the diversion himself, it only remains for us to succumb with as much dignity as we may, and I shall only stipulate for your permission to deliver a parting opinion in the form of a toast.

The readers of Pickwick—Always certain to have their own way, for they are always certain to be the majority.

The president said that as he had taken the liberty to allude to a distinguished member of the medical profession, he could not incur the responsibility of neglecting Sampson Brass, Esq., "an honourable member of the legal profession—the first profession in this country, sir, or in any other country, or in any of the planets that shine above us at night, and are supposed to be inhabited." And, speaking of the law, he said the peculiar position of his friend at the lower end of the hall (Mr. Loring, vice-president, who had Judge Warren on one side and W. H. Gardiner, Esq., on the other) brought to his mind another of Mr. Weller's observations.

"Battledore and Shuttlecock's a very good game, when you ain't the shuttlecock, and two lawyers the battledores, in which case it gets too excitin' to be pleasant."

Mr. Loring, for the purpose of calling up one of the gentlemen alluded to, gave—

Our old colony—She has given us the best laws, the best venison, and the best *judges* of both.

(We have no report of Judge Warren's remarks, except the following sketch.)

Judge Warren said that he had a right to complain of this personal attack upon him by the president and vice-president, as he had good reason to believe that he should be permitted to enjoy this occasion in peace, and without being called upon to travel out of the path which his profession and office prescribed to him; but the connection between law and venison was not very apparent, though it was true that they were both *dear*, and both the better when well *digested;* and it might be that this and other resemblances had given fraternity to those legal veterans *John Doe* and *Richard Roe.*

He then adverted to the difficulties which any one must encounter in attempting to speak upon any subject here; in discoursing upon fine arts in the presence of Washington Allison; upon novels and romance when Mr. Grattan has presumed to come among *us* young men; upon history where Mr. Bancroft happened to be; or upon any literary and scientific topic under the eye of the President of the University. He could therefore content himself with the sweeping and time-honoured declaration that he had made diligent preparation for a speech, but had been anticipated and plagiarized by those who had preceded him.

He then said that while engaged in his legal studies the case of Bardell *v.* Pickwick (3 Dickens's Reports, 245, one of the best reported cases to be found in the books) had not escaped his notice. He there found that Mr. Justice Stareleigh was described as "*a most particularly short judge,*" from which he inferred that *brevity* was regarded as a great excellence in judges, and that any great degree of length would, on this occasion, lead to a repetition of the pathetic inquiry of Mr. Weller, Senior, "Vy worn't there a alibi?"

He concluded by offering, as he said, a toast, which had as much connection with what he had said as would be expected between an impromptu speech and a prepared sentiment.

The injustice of America—She denies to England the right to search American ships, but insists, as among her dearest privileges, upon her right of searching in British books.

It having been suggested that the other battledore remained, W. H. Gardiner, Esq., arose and addressed the company at some length, and in an eloquent manner. He spoke of the relations existing between America and England, and denied that there was any ground to appre-

hend any rupture between the two countries. He treated
with scorn the gasconading of silly, vile and prejudiced
people on the borders of the neighbouring British pro-
vinces. He said that the Peel administration had taken
a cordial step towards an amicable termination of the
Boundary question, and he had no doubt it would be
met in the same spirit by the Webster administration.
He gave as a toast—

The Anglo-Saxon race—Though politically divided,
essentially united; its union is prized above all price,
save one, the price of honour.

The president gave—

The patent Boz medicines—They ought not to be
administered in homœopathic doses.

Dr. O. W. Holmes, on being called on for a toast,
spoke of having been anticipated in the remarks he had
expected to offer (as a toast to the editor of the *North
American Review*).

As he saw a gentleman near him from whom he
should like to hear, he would propose as a sentiment—

The Clergy—Welcome and useful wherever honest
men should be. It is not the steeple that makes the
church, the pulpit that makes the sermon, nor the cloth
that makes the preacher.

This toast called up the Rev. Caleb Stetson, who
addressed the company as follows—

Mr. President, when a man is called upon to speak
and has nothing to say, it may be well that he should
not feel himself called upon to say anything. Much
that I would like to say has already been better said by
others. I will not sit down, however, without expressing my deep joy at seeing, face to face, one with whom
I, in common with my fellow-citizens, have long held
spiritual communion.

The profession which I unworthily represent ought
to feel a deep interest in our guest as a fellow-labourer
in the cause of humanity. We cannot but regard him
as a great preacher of righteousness; for he is a preacher
of truth, of reality. He deals not in fiction; there is no
sham about him.

Mr. President, some philosophers are of opinion that genius does not *invent* but *discover;* it penetrates the veil between us and the spiritual world, and becomes acquainted with glorious forms of beauty and life hitherto unknown. The poet is an inspired seer, who ranges over the mystic dreamland to *find* what exists, to reveal what is hidden.

Accordingly, we find more truth in the creations of the man of genius than in the details of the man of fact. Poetry tells the truth, where history lies. Who does not feel that there is more living reality in those persons whom genius has made immortal than in the long lines of kings who strut in dim procession through the pages of history? Tell me not that Shakespeare's men and women are "unreal mockeries," mere fictions of his imagination. No, he looked quite through the world-shadows which surround us into the realms of invisible beings and *found* them there, immortal as his own genius. Is Bardolph a fiction? is Poins, is Pistol, is Dame Quickly a fiction? Is not the inimitable Jack Falstaff as much a reality as the President of the United States? Who at this moment doubts the actual existence of Imogen, Desdemona, Jaques, or Hamlet?

And our distinguished guest, who made us all love him as a friend before we saw his face, has he not introduced us to a whole crowd of new acquaintances, which are living realities as much as himself? Tell me not that these people are "figments of his brain." We know better. Why, sir, I have myself had a peep into the interior of "Dotheboys Hall." I know Mr. Squeers well. He is still at the head of a literary institution, and thrives, I hear, even more than his pupils. At the time of my acquaintance with him he was not married. He had no Mrs. Squeers then to aid him in promoting the ends of good learning by the ministration of sulphur and of birch.

I was riding with a friend one day, several months ago, when a forlorn-looking boy, standing at the junction of two roads, inquired which of them led to Boston. I pointed out the way and he turned to depart; but something about him interested me. I said to my friend, "Do you see that boy? Do you observe the multiform, many-coloured patches upon his garments, revealing the work of no ordinary hand? He is a desolate orphan, with none to care for him. It is, it must be, Oliver Twist. He has strayed away from Mr. Bumble's dominions, beyond the reach of Mrs. Corney's providence." Now I loved little Oliver with an exceeding affection, and I could not bear that he should wander alone into the unknown tumults or vast solitudes of the great city. Pure, elemental spirit as he was, without flesh enough for corruption to work in, I yet feared that he might fall into the hands of his persecutors, be clutched by old Fagin the Jew, or be entrapped and warped from his integrity by the Artful Dodger. I called the poor boy to me, and inquired into his prospects. He had no prospects, no parents, no friends, no home. He was seeking "*a living*." I told him if he did not find it to come to me. And he went his way. Four days later he came to my house, weary, sad, disappointed. He had not obtained the *living*. In the city he found no rest for the sole of his foot; no place to lay his head but a stable, and out of that a cruel ostler drove him ignominiously with a broom. I took him in, and went to procure a place for him; while gentle hands administered to his urgent necessities, supplying, for the sake of Boz, food and raiment and means of ablution. And—but it is a long story; the rest need not be told.

Mr. President, the mayor of your city has informed us of the arrival of Mr. Pickwick, in search of his friend and editor. I have reason to believe, sir, that I have the honour to be related to Mr. Pickwick myself. I am descended from English ancestors; I am, as you may have observed, a somewhat large man, and am said to bear a family resemblance to that gentleman. About two years ago, I was walking in a street in New Bedford, when a little maiden, looking out of a window and seeing me pass, exclaimed, with infinite delight, "O mother, mother, isn't that Mr. Pickwick?"

But it is time to be serious. Our friend, whom we so

love and honour "for his work's sake," has carried the torch of genius into those "dark places which are full of the habitations of cruelty," wretchedness and crime. He has himself the largest, most generous feeling of the brotherhood of all men, and he has taught us to feel a deeper sympathy with all men. What revelations has he made of the mysteries of guilt and remorse! The agony of Sikes, fleeing from the ghastly spectre of his murdered victim, and still carrying the curse with him—his bosom sin, his bosom misery—is worth a hundred sermons. There is a reality which the heart acknowledges in all his pictures of humble, guilty and passionate life. And we feel that here is one able and willing to do justice to poor fallen humanity. He has shown us a great heart, full of living affections, beating and throbbing under its veins. Our distinguished friend has taught us never to hate or scorn a wandering, guilty man, for he is our brother—all human conditions, all human experiences, are interesting to us. We are bound up, for weal or woe, with the destinies and hopes of humanity. We are taught to discern in every man something that lies deeper than his folly and sin; for under the moral ruins lie buried the rudiments of a great soul—buried, but not dead—alive, redeemable. Melancholy indeed is the wreck of an immortal man; but more venerable still in his fallen grandeur than the ruins of an ancient temple, upon whose defaced and broken columns the traveller gazes with mournful admiration.

This writer has indeed introduced us into new regions of most interesting reality. To use his own words, he has added, by some of his representations, to the stock of human cheerfulness—by others, to the stock of human sympathy.

Mr. Stetson gave the following toast—

Our guest—We might be disposed to pay him distant homage as "a bright particular star" among the serene lights of the firmament, but that he interests us more as a friend, because he is the friend and brother of all men. Out of the abodes of want and sorrow and crime he has preached forth a living gospel of humanity.

By Mr. Clifford, of New Bedford—

The venerable Mr. Pickwick—He has become to us this night, if never before, a *great* reality.

In the course of some by-play, Mr. Grattan remarked that the president's four *vices* were equal to the four cardinal virtues of any other man.

In reply to Mr. Grattan, Edw. G. Loring, Esq., vice-president, said : Mr. President, every man's "vices" speak for themselves—I would speak for your "four vices"; your guests on either hand (Mr. Dickens and Mr. Grattan) make us regret that, like a most virtuous gentleman, you have "put your vices far from you"; to which Geo. S. Hillard, Esq., replied from the other end of the table, that that might well be, as they were opposite to so much that was *good*.

The president read the following letter from Judge Story—

Washington, January 21, 1842.

GENTLEMEN,

It would afford me very sincere gratification to be able to attend the public dinner to Charles Dickens, Esq., according to your kind invitation. But my necessary attendance at the Supreme Court interposes an insuperable bar to my enjoyment of such a pleasure. I look upon Mr. Dickens as among the most distinguished authors of our day, for genius, originality, variety of talent, and mastery of all the workings of the human passions. To him may be applied with singular truth and felicity the line of Lord Byron descriptive of Crabbe the poet—

"Though Nature's sternest painter, yet the best."

I have the honour to remain, with great respect,

Your obliged friend and servant,

JOSEPH STORY.

Messrs. Geo. Tyler Bigelow and others, Committee, etc.

The president here observed, "We have heard of the good things of the *Warren;* we should now like to hear the good things of the *Park*."

John C. Park, Esq., in reply to this call, said—

I regret, Mr. President, that it was not my good
fortune to have had an opportunity to say the little I
am desirous of saying somewhat earlier in the evening.
There is a certain stage in a dinner party in which
sentiment is obliged to give place to sparkling wit, and
each successive dish is expected to have a stronger
seasoning of attic salt. Of such wit I profess to have
none. But there are peculiar associations connected with
the event of the evening, which perhaps press upon my
mind with more force and vividness than upon the mind
of any other person present. There have been scenes
described by our distinguished guest which rise upon my
recollection with startling reality; and if the company
in the midst of their hilarity can spare me a moment, I
will give my feelings utterance.

I can easily understand, Mr. President, why it is that
the heart of every person is attracted with sympathetic
feeling towards the writings of our distinguished guest,
as he describes with minute truth the singularities and
peculiarities of character out of which society is formed.
He has given to the lives of each of us a new zest. I
walk abroad into life almost with new faculties and perceptions. I seize upon new and fresh and interesting
traits of character in my fellow-men which I should not
have detected or appreciated if it were not for the perceptions awakened by his magic pencil. These are the
causes which have endeared him to all of us.

But it has been my fate, from the peculiar circumstances of my professional engagements, to see more,
perhaps, than others present of that class of life from
which our friend has drawn many a sad moral, and
conjured much of his deepest interest. I mean the
criminal—the felon—the convict! Beauties of graphic
description which others can scarcely realize are to me
bold sketches of scenes which I have myself studied;
and I can testify to the life-like portraits which spring
up before my vision when I peruse those thrilling pages
which describe such scenes as the trial and last hours of
Fagin the Jew. I have seen the inanity of mind crushed
by the weight of surrounding peril when, like that

felon's, it pauses in the midst of the solemn warnings of the judge to count the iron spike-points that surround his dock, and wonder if they will repair the broken one or let it be as it is. I can realize, as a thing of life, the morbid curiosity which fills up the horrid moment while the jury have retired, who are to decide on his life, by wondering if the portrait of himself which the man in the gallery is sketching be or be not a correct likeness. It is from contemplating such scenes that I have best learned the depth of the writer's observation, and been taught to look forward with ardent desire to the moment when I could see the man who had marked these startling scenes—scenes which had made so deep an impression upon my own mind.

Your first vice-president, sir, was proud to claim for England and America some exclusive property in the mind and genius of our highly-gifted guest, based upon the ground that we speak a common language. I rejoice as he does in this fact, for it has made his works as familiar to my countrymen's hands and hearts as their household gods. But it is in vain for us to hope for success in this self-appropriation. No, sir, the language he speaks is not the language of one nation or one clime. It is the language which is understood by the poor widow on the banks of the Ganges, who gives to the world and to her god the best proof of her devotion as she mounts the funeral pyre of her husband. It is felt by the Indian mother on the Western prairie as she covers over her little one to shield it from destruction. It comes in soft whisperings to the child of want and neglect as it rests in holy reliance upon the arm of its God. It requires no tongue—it needs no alphabet—it is the universal language—it is the language of the heart!

But, sir, there is one other point to which I desire to call the attention of the company. I am aware that, though somewhat past the limited age which entitles one to mingle with the young men, I am in the midst of them, and possibly they cannot yet realize my feelings. Still, it is but a few years since we were all

children. Those past years are hallowed in the very
souls of each of us by the recollections of a mother's
love—a mother's teaching—as at her knee we learned
to lisp the first outpourings of a child's fond heart. I
feel, then—I see by your looks that I have your sympathies, and I proceed. The scenes of childhood—of
infant purity—of youthful suffering—of early and premature death—how they have been portrayed around all
of us! To me personally the tie has been that of the
nearest and dearest brotherhood. And let me say to
you, sir (addressing Mr. Dickens), that there are now,
within the limits of this one city, where you this day
stand the stranger-guest, hundreds of mothers who,
with tears of happiness and consolation, have blessed
the man who has painted to life their own lost and loved
one in the saint-like death of little Nell. It is in
obedience to such a mother's wish that I now stand
here; and though I feared that perhaps my feelings
would ill accord with the festivities of this evening, still
I came that I might look upon *that man*, and tell her if
he realized in form the soul that breathed within. Sir,
I rejoice that I have been here. There has, throughout
our evening's enjoyments, flowed an undercurrent of
deep and glowing sensibility which has encouraged
me to give utterance to the thoughts that burn within
me. I feel sure our guest will pardon me. And now
let me give a sentiment, perhaps unusual at the festive
board—yet one which I feel confident will meet a ready
response in every heart—

Little children—They are flowers which bloom on
every land—and though they utter no sound, they speak
a universal language—the language of the heart.

After some observations upon the late mildness of
the weather, the president gave—

The fair days of this winter—Our distinguished
guest, in every clime, carries his own sunshine about
him.

Geo. Minns, Esq., being called upon for a sentiment,
said: I have been much interested in the touching
speech just delivered, especially as I know of instances

of parents under similar bereavements deriving consolation from the beautiful sentiments with which the
author concludes his account of the death of Nell. They
are indeed "beautiful garlands concealing the sculptured
horrors of the tomb." But, not to dwell too long upon
a pathetic topic, especially so near the close of the evening, I wish to refer to that thrill of delight which went
through every heart at the first announcement of Mr.
Dickens's intended visit to this country. It was as if a
brother, who had been long absent in a far distant land,
had sent us news that he was about to return home.
With such feelings we hastened to meet him upon his
arrival. I well recollect the feeling of anxiety (so natural
at such a moment) which possessed me just before my
introduction to him—a feeling of blended hope and fear
—of confidence that I could not be disappointed, and of
fear lest, as too often happens, the anticipation might
surpass the reality. Shall I find in him, I asked myself,
all the qualities of those genial characters which he so
finely describes, and whose delineations are treasured in
our hearts? When, however, I had the pleasure of
seeing him, when I felt the clasp of his hand, cordial
as that of my dearest friend, when I enjoyed his frank
and hearty conversation, I felt the idleness of all doubt,
and that he was all his delightful conceptions combined
in one glorious whole.

I have said that his exquisite delineations of character
are stamped upon all our hearts. How true it is that
the heart is the memory! Whatever is imprinted upon
that never dies.

Some philosophers, historians, mathematicians, etc.,
are said to be immortal; but they are not so in any
true sense of the word. They are not totally forgotten,
but they are hardly ever remembered. There is as much
difference between that immortality which is connected
with the mere intellect and that which is associated with
the affections, as there is between dry and sour old age
and that which is green with all the blooming joys of
youth. Mr. Dickens is sure of a true immortality,
because he has written his works upon the hearts of
all—the uneducated as well as the intellectual, the poor

G

as well as the rich—the obscure as well as the famous—
and there they will remain for ever embalmed in pleasant
recollections.

Mr. President, I sympathize in all that has been said
of Old England. I admire England for all that she
has done for the great mind of the world. I have a
still stronger affection for Ireland (which country has
been so ably represented here this evening) and am as
susceptible as a female to Irish blarney. But I love my
own country more than all, because she values the man
for himself alone, and pays no regard to mere adven-
titious circumstances. The proudest nobleman in
Europe might travel through this country, and he would,
if unendowed with talent, receive but very little attention, and that little from those whose good opinion
would be worthless. But our guest will meet with a
far different reception. I am proud of my country that
such is the case, and I believe that nowhere are his
works more universally appreciated than in America.
Thousands and tens of thousands all over the land are
at this moment looking forward with eagerness to the
time when they may tell him how glad they are to see
him in America. But it is not alone among those who
may see him—that appears to be almost a hopeless
endeavour from the numbers who are crowding around
him to express their kindly feelings—but everywhere,
in many a lowly dwelling in the city—in many a farmhouse in the country—and in many a solitary log-cabin
in the forest, miles distant from any other habitation—is
he frequently thought of with the most enthusiastic love.
Many sumptuous entertainments and splendid balls may
be given him; but more than all, and infinitely above all,
and what I am sure he will *prize* infinitely above all, the
great heart of this whole people beats towards him with
the warmest feelings of attachment. It rushes to meet
him, not with adulation—no, that it despises—but with
that right, true, hearty and manly fervour which a noble
mind like his richly deserves, and which a noble mind
like his delights to reciprocate. The whole people will
unite as one man to do honour to that creative and

benevolent genius which brightens winter nights and shortens summer days—which strikes the stoniest heart and melts it to water—which is the fire upon our hearthstone, making home cheerful; and in some faint measure to express this feeling which America has to every true man, I will propose as a sentiment—

America welcomes to her shores every man whose eye is single and whose heart is true.

The president here announced that he had received the following letters from gentlemen who had not been able to attend the dinner—

Portland, January 22, 1842.

GENTLEMEN,

My engagements are of such a nature that I dare not promise to be with you, much as I desire it; and my respect for the occasion, for the committee, and for Mr. Dickens, myself, oblige me to decline your very obliging invitation. At such a board there must be no empty chairs.

Please accept my thanks, gentlemen, and my best wishes for your happiness severally, and for that of your guest, the *reformer*, not only of the particular occasion you have in view, but for the rest of your lives. Were I with you, I should offer a toast to Old England, as the mother of New England, or as the grandmother of nations—New England being the mother of nations, at least in the new world, and she the mother of New England. I should thank her for sending forth her herald of reformation in literature, as hitherto in science, and politics and religion; and your guest for picturing the old English humours, in all their heartiness, faithfulness and simplicity, and better still, in the old English tongue.

Respectfully, gentlemen, I am, etc.,

JOHN NEAL.

Messrs. Geo. Tyler Bigelow, and others, Committee.

G 2

Boston, January 21, 1842.

GENTLEMEN,

I respectfully offer you my grateful acknowledgments of your flattering invitation to the proposed dinner to Mr. Dickens.

I should be proud and gratified to join you in this honourable duty—honourable alike to yourselves and your distinguished guest—but untoward circumstances of a personal character oblige me, very reluctantly, to relinquish the pleasure of uniting with you.

Let me repeat my sincere acknowledgments to you for your politeness, and believe me to be,

Gentlemen, your grateful servant,

CHAS. SPRAGUE.

Messrs. Bigelow, Hale, Barrett, Crocker and Story, Committee.

Glenmary, January 25, 1842.

DEAR SIR,

Very much to my regret, I am compelled to decline the kind invitation to the Committee of Arrangements to meet Mr. Dickens at dinner. Imperative engagements keep me at home, where, indeed, I hope Mr. Dickens will find me, as I have already written to beg for that pleasure and honour.

I may be permitted, even at this distance, however, to join my fellow-townsmen in proffering the warmest welcome to Mr. Dickens, and to express the lively interest I feel in their promised enjoyment of his visit. It would be a great pleasure to *millions* this side the water to look on his face, but nowhere will he be met with greater, and at the same time more appreciative and discriminating, enthusiasm than in Boston. I congratulate both him and my townspeople on his commencing there the endless harvest of his American laurels.

Enviable as Mr. Dickens's reputation is for its extent, it is much more enviable for its *quality*. He has advanced, *pari passu*, in the admiration and *affection* of the world, and his "progress" through our country will be as much waited on by loving hearts as by admiring heads. I have startled myself too, with asking what class or description of persons will be foremost to welcome him. He is the favourite author of the old, but he is as much the favourite of the young. He is adored by the poor and humble, but his praise is without stint from the intelligent and critical. Those who love to weep over a story, and those who prefer to laugh —those who seek amusement only from an author, and those who exact of him an influence for good—young and old, merry and sad, wise and simple, rich and poor —all love him—all know him—all would go far out of their way to see and welcome him. His fame is strangely universal—enviably, most enviably, warm and genial.

I could have wished that Mr. Dickens had first travelled incognito in this country. It will be difficult to express to him *viva voce* how his genius is felt among us. More than any living author, his laurels brighten when his face is turned from them. If prodigality and sincerity in our praises can gratify him, however, he will not lack gratification.

Renewing my regrets that I cannot be present at your kind invitation, and with many thanks to the committee for the honour they have done me, permit me to subjoin a sentiment and subscribe myself.

Yours very truly,
N. P. WILLIS.

W. W. Story, Esq.

Master Humphrey's Clock—Wound up to run with the stars. It will keep Time (or Time will keep *it*) till the world run down.

New York, January 31, 1842.

GENTLEMEN,

I greatly regret that I cannot be with you to-day, as I had anticipated, to join you in doing honour to one of the greatest genuises of this age; but finding myself unexpectedly in a business maelstrom, made up of little currents of avocation which have provokingly converged upon me at this moment, I am compelled to forgo the high enjoyment I had promised myself.

If distant "*sentiments*," however, are admissible, I will ask you to oblige me by offering the following. I hope it will not be considered as going out of the way; and if it *should* be, I can only interpose the excuse, that if the subject (who has never, as I learn, during a *long* life [I wish I hadn't said *that*] been twenty miles from his beloved city) would ever come away from *home* to be toasted, there should be no occasion to send so far to honour him on his own ground. I give you, Mr. Chairman—

The Health of Charles Sprague, our Poet of the Heart, who amid the cares and turmoil of active life, keeps his holier affections and better thoughts "unspotted from the world."

Wishing you, what you *must* have—a delightful "night of it."

I am, your obliged,
L. GAYLORD CLARK.

To the Committee of the Dinner to Mr. Charles Dickens.

The president said he had received the following volunteer sentiment—

Dickens—A great name—it has not been used for centuries, without having the article before it.

It now being near one o'clock, the president announced his intention of leaving the chair, and gave as a parting sentiment—

A speedy return to Charles Dickens.

He then withdrew with Mr. Dickens and other guests, leaving Mr. Stevenson in the chair, and after a few songs and volunteer sentiments the company broke up, perfectly delighted with their guest and their entertainment.

Jas. T. Fields, in *Yesterdays with Authors*, writing in 1871 of this dinner, says—

"It is idle to attempt much talk about the banquet given on that night in February, twenty-nine years ago. It was a glorious episode in all our lives, and whoever was not there has suffered a loss not easy to estimate. We younger members of the dinner-party sat in the seventh heaven of happiness and were translated to other spheres. Was there ever such a night before in our staid city? Did ever mortal preside with such felicitous success as did Mr. Quincy? And how admirably he closed his speech of welcome, calling upon the young author amid a perfect volley of applause! Health! Happiness! and a hearty Welcome to Charles Dickens! And when Dickens stood up at last to answer for himself, so fresh and so handsome with his beautiful eyes moist with feeling and his whole frame aglow with excitement, how we did hurrah, we young fellows. Trust me it was a great night, and we must have made a great noise at our end of the table, for I remember frequent messages came down to us from the 'Chair' begging that we hold up a little and moderate if possible the rapture of our applause."

CHAPTER IV

WORCESTER—HARTFORD—NEW HAVEN

DICKENS left Boston on Saturday, February 5, for Worcester, which he described as "a pretty New England town, where we had arranged to remain under the hospitable roof of the Governor of the State, until Monday morning."

Two of the Worcester papers contained very brief notices of his visit to the town, which are here given—

"Boz, the author of *Pickwick*, etc., with his lady, came up from Boston on Saturday the 5th, in the cars, with Governor Davis, and passed the Sabbath with him. The Governor introduced his *general* friends to his guest, Saturday evening, and his *particular* friends on Sunday evening. Boz left town on Monday morning on the cars for Springfield."—*Worcester Palladin*, February 9, 1842.

"Charles Dickens (Boz), the celebrated author, with his lady arrived in town on the evening of the 5th, and left for Hartford via Springfield on the morning of the 7th. While here, many of our inhabitants called upon them at the mansion of Governor Davis, where they stayed during their tarry in town."—*The Massachusetts Spy*, February 9, 1842.

It will be noticed that not only these two, but practically all the American papers, when mentioning Mr. Dickens, says, "Charles Dickens and 'lady,'" some spelling it with a capital L and others with a small one, and they generally mention that he arrived "in the cars."

J. DAVIS
Governor of Massachusetts, 1842

The editor of the *Worcester Egis* evidently believed
that the arrival of the great Boz was an event entitled
to more extended notice than the mere mention of his
arrival in town, and that his readers wanted to know
something of the author's personality, attire and mental
characteristics. He saw Boz at the Governor's mansion,
but whether as one of the Governor's *general* or *particular*
friends the editor does not say, and the result
was the following brilliant effusion, which was copied
in several of the papers of other cities.

"We found a middle-sized person in a brown frock
coat, a red figured vest, somewhat of the flash order,
and a fancy scarf cravat, that concealed the collar and
was fastened to the bosom in rather voluptuous folds
by a double pin and chain. His proportions were well-
sounded, and filled the dress suit he wore. His hair,
which was long and dark, grew low upon the brow, had
a wavy kink where it started from the head, and was
naturally, or artificially, corkscrew, as it fell on either
side of his face. His forehead retreated gradually from
the eyes, without any marked protuberance save at the
outer angle, the upper portion of which formed a prominent ridge, a little within the assigned position of
the organ of ideality. The skin on that portion of the
brow which was not concealed by the hair instead of
being light and smooth, flushed as readily as any part
of the face, and partook of its general character and
flexibility. The whole region about the eyes was prominent with a noticeable development of nerves and
vessels indicating, say the phrenologists, great vigour
in the intellectual organs with which they are connected.
The eyeballs completely filled their sockets. The aper-
ture of the lids was not large, nor the eye uncommonly
clear or bright, but quick, moist and expressive. The
nose was slightly aquiline, the mouth of moderate
dimensions, making no great display of the teeth, the
facial muscles occasionally drawing the upper lip most
strongly on the left side, as the mouth opened in speaking. His features, taken together, were well propor-
tioned, of a glowing and cordial aspect, with more

animation than grace, and more intelligence than beauty.

"We will close this off-hand description without going more minutely into the anatomy of Mr. Dickens, by saying that he wears a gold watchguard over his vest, and a shaggy greatcoat of bear or buffalo skin that would excite the admiration of a Kentucky huntsman. In short, you frequently meet with similar-looking young men at the theatres and other public places, and you would infer that he found his enjoyments in the scenes of actual life, rather than in the retirement of a study, and that he would be likely to be about town, and witness those scenes which he describes with such unrivalled precision and power. We believe that it is well understood that he draws his characters and incidents less from imagination than from memory—depending for its resources less upon reflection and study than upon observation. His writing bears slight evidence of reading, and he seldom if ever quotes from books. His wonderful perceptions, his acute sensibility, and his graphic fancy, furnish the means by which his fame has been created.

"Mr. Dickens was born February 7, 1812. He was therefore thirty years of age on Monday last. The early maturity of his genius and reputation has but few parallels. May he long live to edify and amuse the world, and to receive the reward of praise and emolument which is his just due."

Dickens left Worcester on Monday evening and has told us in *American Notes* how he went by railroad to Springfield, and, without stopping again in that city, embarked in a very small steamboat for a twenty-five mile ride down the Connecticut River for Hartford, where he arrived in the afternoon. He spent four days in the town, during which he visited the State House, Insane Asylum, and the Deaf and Dumb Asylum. The Hartford newspapers did not have anything to say about his visits to these institutions, in fact about the only thing they did print was a very brief account of the dinner given to him at the City Hotel. The following account of

GOVERNOR DAVIS'S HOUSE, WORCESTER, MASS.

ROOM IN GOVERNOR DAVIS'S HOUSE IN WHICH DICKENS
SLEPT, 1842

the dinner is reprinted from the New Haven *Commercial
Herald*, with the exception of Dickens's speech, which
is copied from the *New York Tribune*.

"*Boz at Hartford*—A gentleman from Hartford has
favoured us with the following account of the proceedings at the entertainment given to Mr. Dickens on
Tuesday evening last—

"About seventy persons were at the dinner. William
J. Hammersly, Esq., presided, and made a very good
speech by way of preface to the toast drank in honour
of the distinguished guest. Mr. Dickens made an
excellent speech—

"'Gentlemen, to say that I thank you for the earnest
manner in which you have drunk the toast just now so
eloquently proposed to you—to say that I give you back
your kind wishes and good feelings with more than
compound interest—and that I feel how dumb and power-
less the best acknowledgments would be beside such
genial hospitality as yours—is nothing. To say that in
this winter season flowers have sprung up in every footstep's length of the path which has brought me here—
that no country has ever smiled more pleasantly than
yours has smiled on me—and that I have rarely looked
on a brighter summer prospect than that which lies
before me now—is nothing. (Applause.)

"'But it is something to be no stranger in a strange
place—to feel, sitting at a board for the first time, the
ease and affection of an old guest, and to be at once on
such intimate terms with the family as to have a homely,
genial interest in its every member—it is, I say, something to be in this novel and happy frame of mind—and
as it is of your creation and owes its being to you, I
have no reluctance in urging it as a reason why, in
addressing you, I should not so much consult the form
and fashion of my speech, as I should employ that
universal language of the heart which you, and such as
you, best teach and best can understand. Gentlemen, in
that universal language—common to you in America and
to us in England, as that younger mother tongue, which,

by the means and through the happy union of our two great countries, shall be spoken ages hence by land and sea over the wide surface of the globe—I thank you.

" ' I had occasion, gentlemen, to say the other night in Boston, as I have more than once had occasion to remark before, that it is not easy for an author to speak of his own books. If the task be a difficult one at any time, its difficulty certainly is not diminished when a frequent recurrence to the same thing has left one nothing new to say. Still, I feel that in a company like this, and especially after what has been said by the president, that I ought not to pass lightly over those labours of love, which, if they had no other merit, have been the happy means of bringing us together.

" ' It has been often observed that you cannot judge of an author's personal character from his writings; it may be that you cannot—I think it very likely for many reasons that you cannot—but at least the reader will rise from the perusal of a book with some defined and tangible idea of the writer's moral creed and broad purposes, if he has any at all; and it is probable enough that he may like to have this idea confirmed from the author's lips, or dissipated by his explanation. Gentlemen, my moral creed—which is a very wide and comprehensive one, and includes all sects and parties—is very easily summed up. I have faith, and I wish to diffuse faith in the existence—yes, of beautiful things, even in those conditions of society which are so degenerate, so degraded and forlorn, that at first sight it would seem as though it could not be described but by a strange and terrible reversal of the words of Scripture—God said let there be light, and there was none. I take it that we are born, and that we hold our sympathies, hopes and energies in trust for the Many and not the Few. That we cannot hold in too strong a light of disgust and contempt, that before the view of others, all meanness, falsehood, cruelty and oppression of every grade and kind. Above all, that nothing is high because it is in a high place; and that nothing is low because it is in a low one. (Loud applause.) This is the lesson taught us in the great Book of Nature. This is the lesson which may be read alike in the bright track of the stars, and in the dusty course of the poorest thing that drags its tiny length upon the ground. This is the lesson ever upper-most in the thoughts of that inspired man who tells us that there are

> " Tongues in trees, books in the running brooks,
>   Sermons in stones, and good in everything."

" ' Gentlemen, keeping these objects steadily before me, I am at no loss to refer your favour and your generous hospitality back to the right source. While I know, on the one hand, that if, instead of being what it is, this were a land of tyranny and wrong, I should care very little for your smiles or your frowns, so I am sure upon the other that if, instead of being what I am, I were the greatest genius that ever trod the earth, and had diverted myself for the oppression and degrada-tion of mankind, you would despise and reject me. I hope you will whenever through such means I give you the opportunity. Trust me that whenever you give me the like occasion I will return the compliment with interest.

" ' Gentlemen, as I have no secrets from you, in the spirit of confidence you have engendered between us, and as I have made a kind of compact with myself that I never will while I remain in America omit an oppor-tunity of referring to a topic in which I and all others of my class on both sides of the great water are equally interested—equally interested—there is no difference between us—I would beg leave to whisper in your ear two words—International Copyright. I use them in no sordid sense, believe me; and those who know me best know that. For myself, I would rather that my children coming after me trudged in the mud and knew by the general feeling of society that their father was beloved and was of some use, than I would have them ride in their carriages and know by their bankers' books that he was rich. But I do not see, I confess, why one should be obliged to take the choice, or why fame, besides play-ing that delightful revel for which he is so justly cele-brated, should not blow out of the trumpet a few notes of a different kind from those with which she has hitherto contented herself.

"'It was well observed the other night by a beautiful speaker whose words went to the heart of every man who heard him, that if there had existed any law in this respect, Scott might not have sunk beneath the mighty pressure on his brain, but might have lived to add new creatures to his fancy to the crowd which swarms about you in your summer walks, and gathers round your winter evening hearths.

"'As I listened to his words there came back fresh upon me that touching scene in the great man's life, when he lay upon the couch surrounded by his family, and listened for the last time to the rippling of the river he had so loved over its stony bed. I pictured him to myself, faint, wan, dying, crushed both in mind and body by his honourable struggle; and hovering around him the phantoms of his own imagination—Waverley, Ravenswood, Jeanie Deans, Rob Roy, Caleb Balderstone, Dominie Sampson—all the familiar throng, with Cavaliers, and Puritans, and Highland Chiefs innumerable overflowing the chamber, and fading away in the dim distance beyond. I picture them fresh in traversing the world, and hanging down their heads in shame and sorrow, that from all those lands into which they have carried gladness, instruction and delight for millions, they brought him not one friendly hand to help, to raise him from that sad, sad bed. No, nor brought him from that land in which his own language was spoken, and in every house and hut at which his own books were read in his own tongue, one grateful dollar-piece to buy a garland for his grave. Oh! if every man who goes from here, as many do, to look upon that tomb in Dryburgh Abbey, would but remember this and bring the recollection home.

"'Gentlemen, I thank you again, and once again, and many times to that. You have given me a new reason for remembering this day, which is already one of mark in my calendar, it being my birthday, and you have given those who are nearest and dearest to me a new reason for recollecting it with pride and interest. Heaven knows that, though should I grow ever so grey, I shall need nothing to remind me of this speech in my life. But I am glad to think that from this time you are inseparately connected with every recurrence of this day; and that on its periodical returns I shall always in imagination have the unfading pleasure of entertaining you as my guests in return for the gratification you have afforded me to-night.'

"Several eloquent speeches were made and sentiments given by Governor Ellsworth, John M. Miles, Dr. Brigham, Prof. Stewart, Messrs. Barnard, Dixon, Putnam, Curtis (of Millingford), Green, etc. Bishop Brownell was present, and invoked the blessing before dinner; letters were read from Washington Irving, George Bancroft, etc.

"Mrs. Dickens stood in the hall with several other ladies, listening to the speeches. Her name was given and received with great applause. She is a fine-looking lady, and makes herself very agreeable to those who call upon her. She must have been amused at Mr. Miles's speech to Democratic literature. He commenced with the angels, approximated to the patriarchs, floundered through Republican resolutions, and ended in ' pop'lar literature,' which he said could not be ' monopolated ' by any aristocracy. One of the guests, about the middle of his speech, moved the previous question, which was not seconded, and so the Judge was permitted to proceed. He was rather witty at times. He said that if there was not a lion in his way there was one right before him. The audience could hardly tell whether he referred to Mr. Dickens or Governor Ellsworth, who sat together on the right of the chair. The Judge and the Bishop were on the left.

"Mr. Putnam in his toast referred to ' Grip ' the raven, a favourite bird with the children of Mr. Dickens, who are in London. The first three, I believe, are girls, and the fourth a young ' Boz.' Likenesses of these four youngsters were shown to the company at the table.

"Mr. Dixon read the following complimentary lines to Mr. Dickens on his arrival in Hartford, written by Mrs. Sigourney—

Welcome ! o'er the ocean blue,
   Welcome to the youthful West,
Ardent hearts and spirits true
   Greet thee as a favour'd guest.

Well our Motherhood hath taught us
   How to honour those, whose skill
From the realms of genius brought us
   Various treasures, at their will,
And her children would not be
False to her—or cold to thee.

And that Motherhood hath shown us,
   How the stranger's heart to cheer ;
By her hearth-stone she hath placed us,
   There to learn her lessons dear ;
Of such fair example we
Would not now forgetful be.

On our lips her accents linger,
   In our views her blood doth run,
And a heaven-born faith inspireth,
   Child and parent, both as one ;
So we breathe, with spirit free,
Love to her and love to thee.

"Several songs were sung, which were well received,
amongst which was the following, written for the
occasion by Mr. Hammersly—

I'll sing you a new-made song, but from no aged pate,
Of a fine young English gentleman, whose *mind* is his estate,
And who always keeps it furnished at a bountiful old rate
With sad and sweet, and merry tales, which in books he doth relate,
Like a fine young English gentleman, a type of better times.

His heart so true, the dwelling is, of all that's rich and rare,
The mansion of the beautiful, the noble and the fair ;
No guest so poor, he cannot find a hearty welcome there,
While kindness sits with melting eyes within the old arm-chair :
God bless this fine young gentleman, this type of better times.

He comes across the ocean waste, to see our western land,
Where many a welcome grasp he'll meet, from many a friendly
   hand,
And many a voice will cry to him, " Oh, still maintain your stand,
And on hypocrisy and vice still stamp the burning brand,"
Like a fine young English gentleman, a type of better times.

VIEW ON THE CONNECTICUT RIVER, 1839

HARTFORD, CONN.

96

God speed him on his earthly course, and blessings on him pour,
Grant to him rich and bounteous gifts, from Heaven's exhaustless
  store ;
Make him as life the longer lasts, but love mankind the more.
And may he in a green old age, still flourish at fourscore,
Like a fine *old* English gentleman, a blessing to his times.

"The dinner did great credit to Mr. Judson, of the
City Hotel; over seventy different dishes were mentioned
on the bill of fare. Mr. Dickens is much pleased with
Hartford. He dined last evening with Col. Grant and
received calls this afternoon. Mrs. Sigourney and several
distinguished persons called upon him this afternoon.

"Mr. Dickens is thirty years of age, and appears much
younger. He seems to enjoy himself very much at a
dinner party, and tries to make all around him feel
happy. In conversation yesterday, referring to Marryatt,
Hall, etc., he said that this country had been shamefully
treated. Governor Ellsworth at the dinner expressed a
hope that he would examine our institutions and give a
fair report upon them. He welcomed Mr. Dickens with
much spirit and good-will."

Mr. Henry C. Robinson, of Hartford, one of the leading lawyers of New England, who died some years ago,
used to relate the following incident in connection with
Dickens's visit to Hartford—

"I am sure that at no other time did Dickens speak to
any American boy as he spoke to me. What he said
was not so much, but it was Charles Dickens who said it,
and he said it to me, and that was enough.

"I was then between eleven and twelve years of age
when Dickens came to Hartford in 1842.

"We knew in Hartford the hour at which Dickens
would arrive, and there was a great throng at the steamboat landing waiting to see him. I was not able to be
there, for I was at school at the time he arrived. But I
heard that he was staying at the City Hotel, which at
that time was the leading hotel of the city, and located
only three or four minutes' walk from the old State

H

House. So as soon as I was out of school I went to the hotel, determined to stand in front of it until I had caught a glimpse of Charles Dickens.

"I think I must have stood there about an hour—it may have been a little longer—when, looking up at one of the windows opening upon the room at the side of the main entrance to the hotel, I saw Charles Dickens standing there. I knew him instantly from the photographs I had seen of him. I was attracted by his peculiar waistcoat of very vivid colour, from the pockets of which dangled a very prodigious watch-chain. He alternately tossed the chain in his hands and twisted it around his fingers. I also noticed his eyes, because they were very blue. After a while he put his hands in his pockets and stood looking across the street, not noticing me at first. At last his eyes became fixed on me. He looked at me steadily for I do not know how many minutes. I stared at him steadily in return. I remember that I thought: This is the man who told me about Sam Weller, who was one of the great favourites of my boyhood days.

"I wonder what Dickens thought of me! He certainly looked me through and through. We must have been, in fact, a spectacle, the lad and the famous author staring at each other.

"At last Dickens spoke, and the words have been treasured in my memory ever since. This is what he said, and I heard him distinctly, though he spoke through the window: 'Go away, little boy, go away.' Then he waved his hand gently, smiled upon me, and with that benediction I departed.

"I did not see him again until 1867, when he made his second visit to America. He had changed greatly in physical appearance, excepting that his eyes retained that brilliant blue tint, the bluest eyes I ever saw."

He left Hartford at 5 p.m., Thursday, February 11, by rail for New Haven, where he arrived at 8 p.m., and went to the Tontine Hotel, where he remained that night. The New Haven *Commercial Herald* on the previous Monday contained the following—

"*Boz in Transit.*—The Hartford Committee are to meet the Dickenses at Springfield, from whence he is to be escorted to that City, where a dinner is to take place on Wednesday. Hope the Hartford folk will allow him to pass this way, that the New Haven colony may, at least, have the honour of his footstep. He may tread on classic ground, and amid the pure atmosphere of the sons of light, recover enough of his natural force and elasticity to enable him to bear the fumes and ' nauseous slaves ' of the great emporium. We hope our folks will treat him like a gentleman, and not like a show."

A correspondent of the *Herald* was afraid if Dickens came to New Haven that he might not be given a fitting reception, and therefore wrote a communication to that paper suggesting that he be given a public reception "to secure that pleasure which thousands of our citizens anxiously covet," in other words to give them a chance to get a look at him.

The following is *Suum Quique's* communication—

"Messrs. Editors : No slight gratification followed the announcement in the closing chapter of *Barnaby Rudge* that the author of *Oliver Twist* and *Nicholas Nickleby* had determined to pay a visit to this country. Many hailed with joy that determination, and anxiously anticipated much pleasure, in gazing upon the form and features of him who had contributed so bountifully to the land of mirth. Charles Dickens, we are assured, has landed in Boston, and is now enjoying the courtesies and hospitalities which the inhabitants of that city never fail to extend to the high-minded and deserving. And while the literary men are straining every nerve to render his sojourn pleasant in this country, why should the literati and citizens of this ' City of Elms ' withhold their tribute, and omit paying that respect and deference which genius of the most exalted kind never solicits but always deserves ? Mr. Dickens comes not among us to spy out the nakedness of the land, but to visit the brethren whom he can learn to love, and with whom his

large heart cannot fail to sympathize. Why, then, can
we not receive him with that welcome which is so mani-
festly his due? Surely within the halls of this old
nursery of learning, and among those connected with the
medical and legal departments, there ought to be rever-
ence enough for him who has made such vigorous war-
fare upon our risible faculties, to seek out devices by
which he be assured of the respect and honour entertained towards him by the majority of Americans. Will
they, then, omit to make arrangements to give him a
public reception, and be behindhand in welcoming true
genius to our land?

"These hints are thrown out by the writer in hopes
that the suggestion may not pass by unregarded, but that
measure may be seasonably taken to secure that pleasure
which thousands of our citizens anxiously covet."

A search of the files of the *Commercial Herald* fails
to discover any account of his arrival and brief stay in
the city, other than the following—

"Mr. Charles Dickens and lady arrived here last evening in the cars from Hartford, and departed this morning in a steamboat for New York. There was a great
curiosity to see one so well known through another
medium and the rush to the Tontine for that purpose
was a complete mêlée, without order and very little con-
straint. We hope that we shall have the pleasure of
seeing Mr. Dickens here again, when the fever is abated,
and when he will have an opportunity to see as well as
be seen. He was waited upon by some of our professional gentlemen and others, who tendered him those
public and private attentions which time did not enable
him to enjoy."

Mr. Putnam, in the *Atlantic Monthly* articles previously referred to, gives the following account of a
reception which was forced upon Mr. Dickens, on the
evening after his arrival at the Tontine, and the attention
paid him he very probably did not enjoy—

"From Hartford Mr. Dickens went to New Haven, arriving there in the evening. The news spread rapidly that 'Dickens had come,' and at once the throng of visitors poured in. Before he had been there an hour the hotel was crowded and the street outside filled with people. Citizens of the highest distinction hastened with their friends to pay their respects, for it was understood that his stay in the city would be very short. The Yale students were there in force, and such was the desire to see him that he was urgently requested to receive the throng assembled, and for hours the people filled the reception-room and held the halls and passages of the hotel. As the crowd increased the landlord found it necessary to put two stout porters on the main staircase, who locked their hands across the stairs, and kept the throng somewhat at bay. As fast as those in the reception-room had their introduction, and retired by another way, the two porters on the stairs would raise their arms and suffer another instalment of the crowd to pass; and thus, until nearly eleven o'clock at night, the admirers of 'Boz' pressed around him for a look and an introduction, and all this was evidently from a love and appreciation of the man. It was nearly midnight before Mr. Dickens could retire to his room."

After Dickens's departure for New York, which took place on Saturday evening, there appeared the following items, the first in the *Palladium* and the second in the *Commercial Herald*—

"Mr. Dickens, accompanied by his lady, arrived in the cars last evening and took lodgings at the Tontine. He left in the boat for New York this morning. A large number of our citizens paid their respects to him at his lodgings, and much interest was manifested by all classes to obtain a sight of, or an introduction to, the distinguished stranger. He has been the principal subject of conversation for the last few days, and as much so, perhaps, by those who know nothing of his reputation as an author, as by those to whom his works had become as familiar as household words. We have an anecdote in illustration. ' Fagin,' who was anxiously inquiring in regard to his arrival, and the length of time he would spend in the city, among other questions very earnestly and innocently asked if ' Boz ' and ' Dickens ' would *both* be here at the same time."

"The Dickens has come and gone; he stole in, in the darkness of the night, and stole out, in the fog of the mountain. But, what with the halloing of the boys at Mr. J.'s lecture, the cry of fire, the ringing of bells, and the light of the conflagration, we got up about as pretty a piece of glorification, all for Boz, as the poor man will meet with anywhere in the United States. The sun came out of the fog about 10 o'clock and behold! the Glory had departed."

There was one citizen of New Haven who seemed to have an idea that the American people were overdoing it in the manner in which they received Mr. Dickens, and having this idea in his mind, thought that he should let his fellow-citizens know that such adulation as was shown the author was not befitting good American citizens, and therefore proceeding to ease his mind, he wrote the following communication to the *Commercial Herald*—

"Messrs. Editors : Have you seen the celebrated Mr. Dickens? Well, what do you think of him? In what order of beings do you rank him? Is he human? If so, *qui tanti talem genuere parentes?* Is he not rather one of those mystic beings whom the Learned Black- smith would denominate *a mythological demi-god?* The adulation paid him reminds us of European servility, ill-befitting Americans—much less the descend- ants of the Puritans, who never bowed the knee to any earthly potentate or kissed the toe of any dignitary. Either Mr. Dickens must be a man of sense, or he must not. If he is, he must look upon the Yankees as a set of silly parasites; if he is not, their folly is the more palpable and disgraceful.

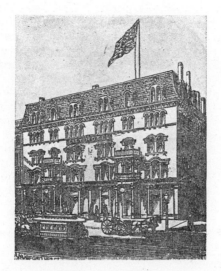

CITY HOTEL, HARTFORD

NEW HAVEN, FROM PERRY HILL

"Query : Would it not be well for some shrewd enterprising Yankee to procure Boz, put him in a cage, and take him about the country for a *show?* I mean nothing disrespectful to Mr. Dickens. I regard him as a man of no ordinary abilities; a benefactor of the race, if you please. Proper respect and deference should be paid him, but this servile homage, this sickening flattery, is doubtless as contemptible in his eyes as it is derogatory to us."

CHAPTER V

NEW YORK

MR. AND MRS. DICKENS arrived in New York Sunday morning, February 13, and went to the Carlton Hotel on Broadway, where they remained until they left for Philadelphia on Sunday, March 6, a week later than was their intention, as their departure was delayed by reason of the illness of Mrs. Dickens.

Most of Dickens's time was spent in visiting the public institutions, such as the Tombs prison, the Penitentiary, Alms House and Lunatic Asylum, the last three being on Blackwell's Island, and not Long Island, where Dickens locates them in *American Notes*. He was entertained privately by some of the leading people of the city, but the principal events of his stay were the "Boz Ball" and the "Dickens Dinner," the former taking place at the Park Theatre the day after his arrival, and the latter at the City Hotel on Friday of the same week. With the exception of very full accounts of these two events, the newspapers did not pay a great deal of attention to the doings of Dickens during the three weeks he remained.

Mr. Philip Hone, a prominent banker and ex-mayor of New York, in an entry in his diary dated January 24, says regarding Dickens's arrival in Boston—

"I signed, three or four days ago, with a number of other persons, a letter to be presented to him on his arrival in the city, giving him a hearty welcome and inviting him to a public dinner, which, from the spirit which seems to prevail on the subject, will be no common affair."

There also appears the two following entries in the diary, referring to the dinner, and also to the ball—

104

"January 27.—In addition to the dinner which it is intended to give Mr. Dickens on his arrival in New York, a grand ball is to be gotten up for him and his lady, at the Park (Theatre), where it is proposed to have *tableaux vivant* and other devices illustrating some of the prominent scenes in his admirable stories. For this object a meeting was held last evening at the Astor House, which was attended by fifty or sixty respectable gentlemen.

"The Mayor presided, and a letter, of which I am selected to be the author, was agreed upon, signed by all present, and entrusted to David C. Colden, to be delivered by him in person to Mr. Dickens, in Boston, inviting him to the fête and requesting him to name the day on which it shall take place. This is all well, but there is danger of overdoing the matter, and making our well-meant hospitalities oppressive to the recipient. We are a people of impulse; when we get fairly mounted upon the back of a *lion*, we are all apt to drive him with might and *mane*, until the ' royal beast ' is fain to escape from the menagerie."

At this meeting, the following resolutions were unanimously adopted—

"*Resolved:* That in the opinion of this meeting, it is proper and becoming in the citizens of New York to unite heartily in these demonstrations of respect and esteem which have been, and will be, everywhere in our land called forth by the visit of Mr. Dickens to America; not because of his talents alone, but in consideration of the noble use he has made of those talents, in indicating the rights and claims and feelings of humanity at large, without distinction of rank or circumstances."

"*Resolved:* That in welcoming Charles Dickens to America, we feel that we are at once paying due homage to genius and fulfilling the demands of gratitude; for as individuals we owe gratitude to the minister of intellectual delight, and also as Republicans we are bound to thank him who has, in his writings, so eloquently maintained the cause of the humble and oppressed, who exhibits, in every line, his own keen sensibility to wrong, and the prevailing spirit of all whose work is a touching illustration of the truth that in the elementary constitution of men there is no difference, whatever difference may have been created."

"*Resolved:* That in the arrangement of a fitting reception for the visitor we delight to honour, regard be had to the participation of the ladies; for we feel assured that our countrymen will look with little favour on any device which excludes them from joining in a festival given in honour of him whose imagination and heart gave birth to ' Little Nell.' "

"*Resolved:* That all gentlemen present, and such others as may be hereafter named, constitute a General Committee."

Mr. Hone's diary contains an entry of February 1, referring to meetings of the committees in charge of arrangements for both the ball and dinner—

"I went to two *Boz* meetings last evening; one at the Carlton House, of the *dinnerites*, at which Chief Justice Jones presided. A committee of arrangement was appointed and the officers of the dinner selected. They consist of Washington Irving, John Duer, John A. King, Judge Betts and myself, and we are to determine on the presiding officer and the names of the vice-presidents. The other was a meeting of the *ballites*, at the Astor House, the Mayor in the chair. A long report from the Committee was adopted. This affair is in a forward state, and promises to eclipse the Lafayette Ball at Castle Garden."

The following is the letter to Mr. Dickens inviting him to the ball, which Mr. Hone was delegated to prepare—

New York, January 26, 1842.

SIR,
The citizens of New York having received the agreeable intelligence of your arrival in the United States, and appreciating the value of your labours in the

cause of humanity, and the eminently successful exercise of your literary talents, are ambitious to be among the foremost in tendering to you and your lady the hearty welcome which they are persuaded is in reserve for you in all parts of our country. With this object in view, we have been appointed a committee in behalf of a large meeting of gentlemen convened for the purpose, to request your attendance at a public ball to be given in this city.

Mr. Colden, one of our members, will have the honour of presenting the invitation, and is charged with the agreeable duty of presenting their congratulations on your arrival. We shall expect, through him, your kind acceptance to this invitation and your designation of the day when it may suit your convenience to attend.

> We are, sir,
> With great respect,
> Yr. Obt. Servants—

Danl. B. Tallmadge.	John W. Francis.
Chas. A. Davis.	J. W. Edmonds.
John C. Cheesman.	Chas. W. Sanford.
Wm. H. Maarwelt.	Geo. P. Morris.
Prosper M. Wetmore.	Wm. Turner.
A. M. Cozens.	A. G. Stout.
John R. Livingstone, Jr.	R. Faynweather.
Wm. B. Darr.	W. R.
James M. Smith, Jr.	Martin Hoffman.
William Granden.	J. Beekman Fish.
Waddell.	James Phalen.
D. S. Gregory.	W. H. Appleton.
Wm. Grimell.	F. W. Edmunds.
Wm. Starr Miller.	S. Draper.
F. A. Tallmadge.	J. S. Bartlett.
Robt. W. Morris.	John Inman.
Philip Hone.	

To Charles Dickens, Esq., etc.

Mr. Colden went to Boston and presented this letter to Dickens, and returned to New York with the following reply—

Tremont House, Boston, January 28, 1842.

MY DEAR SIR,

I beg to convey to the Committee of Gentlemen, whose organ you are, very hearty and cordial thanks for their most kind congratulations; and my glad acceptance of the honour they propose to confer upon me.

I have had the pleasure of seeing your agent, and of explaining my movements and engagements to that gentleman. Rest assured, that I shall be proud and happy to meet you at any time you may appoint, after receiving his explanation of my engagements.

With many thanks to you and the Committee generally,

I am, My dear Sir,
Yours, faithfully and obliged,
CHARLES DICKENS.

Robert Morris, Esq.

The date set by the Committee for the ball after receiving this letter was Monday, February 14, and the place at which it was to be held was the Park Theatre.

As stated, Dickens arrived in New York on Sunday, 13th, and on the next day there appeared in the *Tribune* the following notice of his arrival—

"Charles Dickens with his lady reached our city on Saturday, in the steamboat from New Haven, and was allowed with very little annoyance to proceed to his rooms at the Carlton House. A very miscellaneous, but not large, assemblage had collected on the wharf where he landed, but they were content to gratify their curiosity in silence. We believe he was permitted to spend the evening and the Sabbath in peace undisturbed—to go to church or stay at home as he chose—to eat his dinner undepressed by the brooding horror of a speech to make at the end of it—and to go out and in unannoyed by a spy standing ready to note down his words and caricature his actions. If the facts were otherwise he will at least do our country the justice to satisfy himself that his tormentors are not American. He will this evening attend the grand ball given in honour of his visit at the Park

Theatre, and on Friday evening he will be present at a superb dinner given him by our foremost citizens at the City Hotel. He will leave the city on his progress southward this day fortnight. We understand that he has already promised to attend as many parties, dinners, balls, etc., as will occupy the entire interim, leaving little or no opportunity for unharassed observation. This is to be regretted; since it is not in our fashionable and holiday life that he can find materials for future portraiture and higher intellectual effort. It was not in ballrooms and dinner parties that he learned to stir the heart of universal humanity with the rugged fortunes of Oliver Twist and Nicholas Nickleby, the woes of hapless Smike, and the fortitude and purity of angelic Nell."

The following, from the *Evening Post* of February 4, contains the report of the Committee in charge of the "Boz Ball"—

Boz in New York.—The arrangements for reception to Mr. Dickens in New York are on the most splendid scale. A sub-committee, appointed by the general committee, to suggest a plan of proceeding, made the following report: "That they had considered it advisable to offer Mr. Dickens and his lady a public ball; that, to heighten the effect of the ball, and in compliance with the desire generally expressed, they recommended that the ball-room should be made to represent compartments of the 'Curiosity Shop,' in which the productions of 'Boz' might be illustrated; and, in order to give a novel and agreeable feature to the intended fête, they suggested that a number of tableaux vivant should be formed by competent artists, in the intervals of the dances, 'drawn from the novels, poems, sketches and dramas of Mr. Dickens, and shadowing forth in living pictures the graphic and glowing descriptions of this singularly gifted and original author.'" The Committee further recommended the following sketch of decorations and devices for the ball-room and arrangements for the floor—

1. The inside of the theatre to represent a magnificent saloon hung with chandeliers.

2. The audience part of the house to be ornamented with festoons of flowers, garlands, draperies, and trophies emblematical of the different States of the Union.

3. The floor to extend from the front of the boxes to the back of the building, where, on an elevated stage, arrangements be made for the representation of numerous tableaux vivant from the works of Mr. Dickens, represented by artists, under the direction of the Committee.

4. The stage part of the theatre to be highly embellished with various designs from the writings of "Boz," illustrating many of the striking, original, novel, graphic and familiar scenes.

5. A full and sufficient orchestra, comprising the principal musical talent at present in the city, to be engaged and so arranged as to add to the general effect, without diminishing the space allotted to the company.

6. The ball-room to afford accommodation for upwards of 3,000 persons.

7. The following arrangements are also recommended—

Order of the Dances and Tableaux Vivant.

1. Grand March.
2. Tableaux Vivant : A sketch by Boz.
3. Amile Quadrille.
4. Tableaux Vivant : The Seasons, a poem, music.
5. Quadrille Waltz, Selections.
6. Tableaux Vivant : The Book of Oliver Twist.
7. Quadrille March, Norma.
8. Tableaux Vivant : The Ivy Green.
9. Victoria Waltz.
10. Tableaux Vivant : Little Nell.
11. Basket Quadrille.
12. Tableaux Vivant : The Book of Nicholas Nickleby.
13. March.
14. Tableaux Vivant : A sketch by Boz.
15. Spanish Dance.
16. Tableaux Vivant : Pickwick Papers.
17. Boz Waltz.
18. Tableaux Vivant : Washington Irving in England and Charles Dickens in America.
19. Postillion Quadrille.
20. Tableaux Vivant : Curiosity Shop.
21. March.
22. Tableaux Vivant : The Club.
23. Contra Dance.
24. Tableaux Vivant : The Book of Barnaby Rudge.
25. Gallopade.

On motion, it was resolved, that the chairman appoint a sub-committee of sixteen to carry the foregoing arrange-

NEW YORK BAY

CARLTON HOTEL, NEW YORK

ments into effect. The following gentlemen were then named by the chair—

Philip Hone.	William Starr Miller.
John C. Cheesman.	Charles A. Davis.
Geo. P. Morris.	Martin Hoffman.
J. W. Francis.	Jas. M. Smith, Jr.
Henry Inman.	Prosper M. Wetmore.
W. H. Maxwell.	John W. Edmonds.
John R. Livingstone, Jr.	Daniel B. Tallmadge.
Charles W. Sanford.	

On February 8 the *Evening Post* published the rules and regulations to be observed at the ball, which were as follows—

"The ball to be given to Mr. Charles Dickens and lady under the direction of a committee of citizens of New York will take place at the Park Theatre on Monday, the 14th of February.

The doors to be open at half-past seven, and dancing to commence at nine o'clock.

The Committee to appear in full ball dress, and wear rosettes with appropriate designs.

Military and naval officers to appear in their respective uniforms.

All fancy dresses to be positively excluded except such as are admitted under the direction of the Committee.

An ample supply of refreshments to be provided for the company.

Cloak- and retiring-rooms to be set aside for the accommodation of ladies, and suitable attendants to be in waiting.

An awning to be erected in front of the theatre.

Carriages will come into line with the horses' heads towards Chatham Street, and take up in the opposite direction.

Gentlemen are requested to dismiss their carriages on arriving at the door and to take the one opposite to the entrance on their departure.

The superintendent of carriages will be in attendance

to preserve regularity and to see that no imposition be
practised on the company through carelessness, extra
charges or otherwise.

An efficient police has been engaged to secure order
on the arrival and departure of the company.

No more persons will be admitted to the fête than the
ball-room can conveniently accommodate.

In behalf of the Committee of Citizens,

ROBERT H. MORRIS, *Chairman.*

D. C. COLDEN, ⎱ *Secretaries."*
D. C. PELL,   ⎰

The following description of the ball is taken from the
Evening Post of February 15—

"The fête at the Park Theatre, last evening, is
described as one of the most magnificent that has ever
been given in this city. The gorgeousness of the
decorations and the splendour of the dresses, no less than
the immense throng, glittering with silks and jewels,
contributed to the show and impressiveness of the occasion. It is estimated that nearly three thousand people
were present, all richly dressed and sparkling with animation. The doors of the theatre were thrown open at half-
past seven o'clock, and such was the eagerness to get in
that in less than an hour the whole area of this immense
building was densely crowded. Great pains had been
taken with the decoration of the theatre, and the lobbies,
halls, saloons, boxes and green-rooms were each taste-
fully ornamented with festoons, wreaths, garlands, portraits and statues. The seats of the first tier were covered
with white muslin, trimmed with gold, and the columns
festooned with fine drapery. The second tier was ornamented with a series of medallions, rosettes and silver
stars, representing the works of the distinguished guest
of the evening, the centre ornament being the head of
Mr. Dickens, surmounted by an eagle holding a laurel
wreath. In the middle of the theatre was the orchestra,
containing twenty-five seats, covered with muslin and
gold, and hung with wreaths; while the stage part of the
room represented a large and magnificent chamber of

carved and gilded oak, with deep Gothic windows on
each side, and a lofty, fretted ceiling. The whole
appearance was striking beyond description.

"Mr. Dickens entered the theatre about nine o'clock,
and after proceeding to the back part of the stage, was
introduced by the Mayor to those who wished to speak
with him. 'Mrs. Dickens,' says the reporter of the
Express, ' is a fine-looking Englishwoman, and appeared
much to enjoy the honours given her husband. Soon
after entering, both participated in the dance in the
cotillion in the centre of the room. Mr. Dickens was
dressed in a suit of black, with a gay vest, and Mrs.
Dickens in a white, figured Irish tabinet trimmed with
mazarine blue flowers; a wreath of the same colour round
her head, and with pearl necklace and earrings. Her
hair was curled in long ringlets.'

"Between the different dances the tableaux vivant
were exhibited at the back of the stage. A curtain,
painted like the frontispiece of the *Pickwick Papers*, was
drawn up at the sound of a gong, when the artists procured for the occasion were discovered in attitudes and
positions descriptive of several familiar passages from
Mr. Dickens's works. These were—

1. Mrs. Leo Hunter's dress, *dejeuner.*
2. The middle-aged lady in the double-bedded room.
3. Mrs. Bardell faints in Mr. Pickwick's arms.
4. Mrs. Bardell encounters Mr. Pickwick in prison.
5. The red-nosed man discourseth.
6. Mr. and Mrs. Mantalini in Ralph Nickleby's office.
7. Oliver Twist at Mr. Maylie's door.
8. Little Nell, her grandfather, the military gentleman, and Mr. Slum's unexpected appearance.
9. Little Nell leading her grandfather.
10. The Stranger scrutinizing Barnaby's features in
the widow's cottage.
11. The Pickwick Club.
12. Washington Irving in England and Charles
Dickens in America.

"The festivities, which passed off with much good
feeling, were continued to a late hour in the night."

I

Mr. Hone wrote in his journal, the day after the "Boz Ball"—

"*Feb*. 15.—The agony is over; the 'Boz Ball,' the greatest affair in modern times, the latest compliment ever paid to a little man, the fullest libation ever poured upon the altar of the muses, came off last evening in fine style; everything answered the public expectations, and no untoward circumstances occurred to make anybody sorry he went.

"The author of the *Pickwick Papers* is a small, bright-eyed, intelligent-looking young fellow, thirty years of age, somewhat of a dandy in his dress, with 'rings and things in fine array,' brisk in his manner, and of a lively conversation. If he does not get his head turned by all this, I shall wonder at it. Mrs. Dickens is a little, plump, English-looking woman, of an agreeable countenance, and, I should think, 'a nice person.'"

In *Forty Years in America*, the author, T. L. Nichols, M.D., who attended the "Boz Ball," gives the following account—

"So it was a ball at the Park Theatre—the Old Drury of New York—where the Cookes, the Keans and Kembles had delighted us, that was fixed upon. There was a supper, I believe, and there was a series of tableaux vivant, representing some of the best scenes in the *Pickwick Papers*, and the earlier works of the 'immortal Boz.' I remember the immense crowd of the 'beauty and fashion' of New York that filled the theatre from its dancing-floor, laid over stage and pit, to the gallery. I remember the mixed committee, official, fashionable and literary, and some one who aspired to all these distinctions. I think Irving and Cooper were there—I am sure of Halleck and Bryant. Willis sported his ringlets there, no doubt; and can I ever forget the beaming, rosy, perspiring face of the American Korner, General George P. Morris?

"There was a rush near the door, a flutter through the crowded theatre, a hush of expectation, a burst of 'See the Conquering Hero comes,' and the author of *Pickwick* and the *Uncommercial Traveller*, with all of the honour and pathos that lie between, burst upon our astonished and delighted vision. Then the cheers, then the waving of handkerchiefs from floor to boxes, and all the tiers— and tears, no doubt, of joy and happiness, and bouquets innumerable, gave what was possible to the irrepressible enthusiasm of the hour.

"I remember Mr. Dickens as my eye caught him there, with all that throng around him, and he the cynosure of ten thousand eyes, allowing each person present the usual number. His hair was in the bright gloss of its youthful, silken curls; his face was full, and ruddy with English health—not seamed, as now, with the thought and work of all these years. His dress was, I thought, sufficiently pronounced; but he was, on the whole, eminently satisfactory and sufficiently imposing. It was hard to open a passage where two or three thousand people were crowding to see and be near, if possible, shake hands with him, but with tremendous efforts he was escorted round the room.

"We tried to dance. Mrs. General Morris honoured the thrice-honoured author with her fair hand for a quadrille, but the effort to dance was absurd. I remember being in a set with two young army officers who were afterwards heroes in Mexico, but even their prowess could do little toward carrying their partners through the galop in such a rush. Happily it was before the age of crinoline, and what room there was we made the most of; but it was like dancing in a canebrake, the poor girls clinging to their partners to avoid being swept beyond their power to protect them."

While Dickens wrote Forster that if he dropped a letter in the street it would be related in the newspapers the next day, a careful search of the New York *Evening Post* and New York *Tribune*, with the exception of full accounts of the ball and the dinner, fails to discover much, if any, to which he could take exception, as the only items found of a personal nature were brief notices that he had attended two private dinners, had gone to church on Sunday, had visited the Tombs, and that he had left the city and gone to Philadelphia. In fact, neither of these papers gives any personal mention of his days from February 13 to March 5, a period of three weeks, with the exceptions noted above. Dickens, however, in *American Notes*, tells of his visits to various public institutions, and of his wanderings around the city streets, Broadway, the Bowery, and visits to the theatres. Mr. Putnam wrote concerning his stay in New York—

"Prof. Felton was often with him, and some quiet evening walks were taken about the metropolis by the two, in which they visited some of the fashionable restaurants of the city. Speaking of the oyster suppers, in his *Notes* Mr. Dickens always alludes to his friend as the 'heartiest of Greek professors.'

"Washington Irving came very often, and the meeting of these kindred spirits was such as might have been expected. They were delighted with each other, and at all hours they were admitted. A great ball was given in honour of Mr. Dickens and his lady, a full account of which was given in the papers of that day.

"Besides Irving and Felton, came Bryant, Willis, Halleck, Clark of the *Knickerbocker*, and many others of the stars of the literary firmament; and on one occasion Mr. Dickens had to breakfast with him, Irving, Bryant and Halleck. The clerk of the Carlton was himself a great lover of literature, and remarked to me, 'Good Heaven! to think what the four walls of that room now contain! Washington Irving, William Cullen Bryant, FitzGreene Halleck and Charles Dickens.'"

Mr. Charles Lanman of Georgetown, D.C., who was a friend of both Dickens and Irving, in an article published shortly after Dickens's death, wrote that Irving not only visited Dickens in New York in 1842, but that Dickens visited Irving at his residence at Sunnyside.

Professor Felton, in his remarks on the death of Washington Irving, before the Historical Society of Massachusetts, gave some of his recollections of the intimacy between Dickens and Irving. He said—

"I passed much of the time with Mr. Dickens and

Mr. Irving, and it was delightful to witness the cordial intercourse of the young man, in the flush and glory of his fervent genius, and his older compeer, then in the assured possession of immortal renown. Dickens said in his frank, hearty manner, that from his childhood he had known the works of Irving; and that before he thought of coming to this country, he had received a letter from him, expressing the delight he felt in reading the story of Little Nell."

Dickens in one of his letters to Forster related how Irving broke down in his speech at the Dickens Dinner at the City Hotel, but none of the New York newspapers mentioned the fact.

The *Aurora* of Tuesday, February 15, contained the following notice of the two private dinners which Dickens attended—

"Yesterday, Mr. Dickens and lady dined with Charles A. Davis, Esq., who resides, we believe, at 365, Broadway, and is a merchant on Broad Street. This gentleman is also distinguished in literature as the author of the letters of Major Jack Downing, which appeared in the New York *Daily Advertiser*, much the best of all that have been written under that signature.

"This was a very quiet and excellent affair, and one calculated to give Mr. Dickens a very favourable idea of our society.

"To-day (Tuesday) he will also dine out, and, if we are not misinformed, with Daniel C. Colden, Esq., of 28, Laight Street. It will doubtless be an elegant affair, and the quiet family party, which Mr. Dickens insists upon, will be made up of the *élite* of the ancient régime. Indeed, it is probable that Mr. Dickens was never, in England, admitted into such really good society as since he landed in this country. He has seen and will see more aristocracy in Boston and New York than he has ever seen, and probably ever will see, in his native land."

The *Aurora* is the paper which Dickens referred to in one of his letters to Forster, dated February 17, in which he wrote—

"Another paper, coming after the ball, dwells upon its splendour and brilliancy, hugs itself and its readers upon all that Dickens saw; and winds up by gravely expressing its conviction that Dickens was never in such society in England as he has seen in New York, and that its high and striking tone cannot fail to make an indelible impression on his mind!"

On Sunday, the 20th, Dickens attended St. John's Church with ex-President Van Buren. On Thursday, the 24th, he attended a private dinner at the Astor House, as shown by the following notice from the New York *Express*—

"*Another Dinner to Dickens.*—On Thursday last Mr. Dickens fulfilled his last engagement in this city, when he dined with some fifty gentlemen at the Astor House. The dinner was strictly private, and, feeling this, each one threw off all those formalities he is compelled to assume when he knows every word and action is readily noted to be blazoned forth to the world. Mirth and good humour were the order of the night—the guest delighted the company with two speeches abounding with rich humour and given most inimitably, and charmed every one by his unaffected manners and the spirit with which he entered into the engagements of the evening."

The following extract from the *Tribune* of February 23 is given, for the reason that it contains a letter of Dickens which is not included in the published volumes of his letters—

C. H. Delevan's Lecture.—Notwithstanding the many festive and other birthday celebrations held last evening throughout the city, a Lecture on Temperance delivered by C. H. Delevan, Esq., at the Hall of the New York Society Library, drew a full and respectable audience. He divided the subject into four parts or classifications: economy, health and mental capacity, laws of decorum, and patriotism; which he forcibly illustrated by the retrospective and concurrent effects of intemperance. Previous to the lecture Mr. D—— read the following communication from Charles Dickens, Esq.—

Carlton House, February 16.

DEAR SIR,

I very much regret, and so does Mrs. Dickens, that in consequence of the numerous engagements which we have made, it is not in our power to accept the welcome invitation of the New York Mechanics' Institute.   And I assure you that I regret this the more because I have formed the very highest respect for the object which brings them together on the anniversary of Washington's birthday, and for its great influence upon the most valuable portions of society.

I am, dear sir, yours faithfully and obliged,

CHARLES DICKENS.

Charles H. Delevan, Esq.

Monday, March 2, was the day Dickens visited the "Tombs" prison which he has so graphically described in the *Notes*.   The *Evening Post* mentions the visit in the following brief item—

"Mr. Dickens has not yet left the city, being detained by the serious indisposition of his Lady.   He walked through the Tombs yesterday, incognito, and visited most of the cells."

The following article from the *Evening Post* of February 18 is interesting as giving the editor's idea of the reason for the enthusiasm with which Dickens was received in the United States—

"*The Ovations to Mr. Dickens.*—The French journal of this city, *Le Courier des États Unis*, is endeavouring to account for the enthusiasm which has been manifested toward the author of the *Pickwick Papers*.   It is a curious problem, it says, of the social physiology that deserves to be solved.   Three causes are then assigned to account for what it considers this extraordinary ebullition of feeling.

"The first of these is the instinctive desire which Americans have to refute the accusations of coldness, self-love, money-making, and Puritanic strictness, brought against them by foreigners, and to do this they resort to unusual displays, just as a man charged with avarice will indulge in some splendid extravagance to retrieve his reputation.   The second is that they suppose the author has come to study their character and institutions, and are anxious to conciliate his good opinion, even to the extent of bribing his judgment.   Like a young miss who expects a new lover, they take care to make their toilette with pains.   And the third is that the austerity of our religious tenets and forms, preventing the people from those everyday social amusements to which other nations are accustomed, take these occasions to give vent to their natural love of hilarity and excitement.   Six days are employed in the counting-house, and the seventh in the church.

"We do not think our French critic has gone to the bottom of this matter.   The main cause of the movement to which he refers is the merit of the individual, and an honourable desire on the part of the community to testify their appreciation of it.   Many who take a more active part are, no doubt, prompted by a vain curiosity, or by a paltry ambition to render themselves conspicuous. But the great majority of them, we believe, are sincere admirers of the man and his work.   His more obvious excellences are of that kind which are the more easily understood by all classes—by the stable-boy as well as the statesman.   His intimate knowledge of character, his familiarity with the language and experience of low life, his genuine humour, his narrative power, and the cheerfulness of his philosophy, are traits that impress themselves upon minds of every description.   But besides these, he has many higher traits to interest the higher orders of mind.   They are such as recommend him particularly to Americans.   His sympathies seek out that class with whom American institutions and laws sympathize most strongly.   He has found subjects of thrilling interest in the passions, sufferings and virtues of the mass.   As Dr. Channing has said, ' he shows that life in its rudest form may wear a tragic grandeur; that amidst follies and excesses, provoking laughter or scorn, the moral feelings do not wholly die; and that the haunts

of the blackest crime are sometimes lighted up by the
presence and influence of the noblest souls. His pictures
have a tendency to awaken sympathy with our race, to
change the unfeeling indifference which has prevailed
toward the depressed multitude into a sorrowful and
indignant sensibility to their wrongs and woes.

"Here we have the secrets of the attentions that have
been showered upon Mr. Dickens. That they may have
been carried too far is possible; yet we are disposed to
regard them, even in their excess, with favour. We
have so long been accustomed to seeing the homage of
the multitude paid to men of mere titles or military
chieftains that we have grown tired of it. We are glad
to see the mind asserting its supremacy—to find its
rights generally recognized. We rejoice that a young
man without birth, wealth, title, or a sword, whose only
claims to distinction are in his intellect and heart, is
received with a feeling that was formerly rendered only
to conquerors and kings. It is but a fair return. The
author, by his genius, has contributed happy moments
to the lives of thousands, and it is right that the thousands should recompense the gift. If their enthusiasm
shall be always as discriminating as it is in this instance,
there will be little reason to complain.

"Yet, it must be confessed, there is much truth in
the third position assumed by the writer for the French
journal."

The account of the dinner at the City Hotel has been
reserved for a separate chapter, containing, as it does,
so many interesting speeches, and particularly that of
Mr. Mathews on International Copyright, which gives
the arguments from the standpoint of both the American
and English authors.

CHAPTER VI

THE DINNER AT THE CITY HOTEL, NEW YORK

THE following invitation was sent to Mr. Dickens on his arrival at Boston—

New York, January, 1842.

To CHARLES DICKENS, Esq.

DEAR SIR,
    The undersigned, for themselves, and in behalf of a wide circle of their fellow-citizens, desire to congratulate you on your safe arrival, and tender to you a sincere and hearty welcome.

Though personally unknown, still we can assure you that you will find yourself no stranger among us. That genius with which you have been so singularly gifted, and which your pen has directed with such consummate skill, in delineating every passion and sympathy and peculiarity of the human mind, has secured to you a passport to all hearts; whilst your happy personifications, and apt illustrations pointing at every turn a practical and fruitful moral, have rendered your name as familiar to us as household words.

In testimony of our respect and high regard, as a slight, though thankful tribute to your genius, we request that you will name as early a day as will suit your convenience to meet us in this city, at a public dinner, where, as elsewhere, it will be our pride and pleasure to express to you our gratitude for the many rich intellectual feasts you have so often spread before us.

We are very sincerely and cordially, your friends,

S. Jones.
William T. McCoun.
Saml. R. Betts.
John Duer.
Henry Cary.
Theodore Sedgwick.
Wm. Saml. Johnson.
D. S. Kennedy.
James G. King.
Henry Brevoort.
Charles March.
Anthony Barclay.
J. Prescott Hall.
James Gallatin.
John A. King.
Wm. Kent.
David S. Colden.
G. G. Howland.
James I. Jones.
Jacob R. Leroy.
M. C. Patterson.

Washington Irving.
Philip Hone.
Daniel B. Tallmadge.
David S. Jones.
Martin Hoffman.
Charles King.
Wm. C. Bryant.
Wm. B. Astor.
Maturin Livingston.
Hamilton Fish.
Jas. D. P. Ogden.
M. H. Grinnell.
Wm. H. Aspinwall.
Edward Curtis.
Edward Jones.
Wm. C. Rhinelander.
Abm. Schermerhorn.
Thos. W. Ludlow.
FitzGreene Halleck.
Chas. Augs. Davis.

Mr. Dickens's reply—

Tremont House, Boston,
January 27, 1842

My dear Sirs,

I need not tell you that I accept with inexpressible pride and pleasure the invitation with which you have honoured me, and I cannot tell you how much moved and gratified I have been by the terms in which it is conveyed. Your kind and earnest words have done my heart good— you have made me feel indeed that I am no stranger among you, and I have looked at your names a hundred times, as if they were the faces of old friends.

As nearly as I can guess, I shall be in New York on Saturday, the 12th of February, or it may be a day earlier. Any day toward the latter end of the following week that will suit you, will suit me.

Be assured that you cannot name any time which will not be a bright day in the calendar of my life, and that all hours and seasons will be alike welcome to me.

Believe me, dear sirs, with cordial and affectionate regard, your faithful friend,

CHARLES DICKENS.

To the Committee, etc., etc., New York.

The day fixed for the dinner was Friday, February 18, and the following report of the dinner is reprinted from the New York *Evening Post* of February 19, with the exception of the speech by Mr. Cornelius Mathews, which is taken from the *Tribune*—

Dinner to Mr. Dickens.—A large number of persons were present at the complimentary entertainment given to Mr. Charles Dickens, at the City Hotel, last evening. Washington Irving presided on the occasion, assisted by Judge Betts, Philip Duer, John Hone, Gulian C. Verplanck, John A. King and James de Peyster Ogden, who acted as vice-presidents.

The tables were sumptuously furnished with all the delicacies of the season and the room was elegantly decorated and arranged. Reverend Henry W. Bellows, of the Unitarian Church, asked the benediction, and after the cloth was removed the president rose and said—

I never regretted more than I do at this moment my want of the habit of public speaking. For I feel that I could now wish to give way to the current of my thoughts and feelings. And yet I am like a poor horse-man and must be careful how I get into the saddle or I shall be thrown from my seat. And yet, on further consideration, I do not see much cause to regret this inability of mine to interest you in this way; for I feel that there will be no want of champions ready to take my place. I see so many of them round me at this moment, firmly seated in their saddles, and who find it difficult to rein in their steeds, until the signal is given them to start. So, therefore, I leave the field, and with a few preliminary remarks I will dispose of my part of

CITY HOTEL, NEW YORK
Where the 'Dickens Dinner' was given

PARK THEATRE, NEW YORK
Where 'Boz Ball' took place

124

the subject. I confess I never rose under deeper or more pleasurable excitement or with more feelings of pride as an author, than when I look around on this assembly of my townsmen, met to greet the arrival of an author among them. I never was more proudly conscious of the intellectual character of my countrymen than in witnessing this burst of enthusiasm which has been echoed from city to city, to welcome a mere literary visitor to our land. (Applause.) And this, too, at a time of great public distress, when every mind, more or less, is corroded by care, and the most prosperous among us doubts the foundation of his prosperity.

Gentlemen, this enthusiasm is of the right kind. It speaks well for the people—it speaks well for the nation. We have been accused of being sordid and mercenary—and too much given up to the pursuits of our more worldly interests. But in the present instance our enthusiasm has given the lie to the charge and has spontaneously arisen in one wide scene of homage paid to intellect. (Cheers.) Gentlemen, it is impossible for me to proceed—gentlemen—I'll give you a toast—

Charles Dickens, the literary guest of the nation.

When the applause with which this sentiment was greeted had subsided, Mr. Dickens arose and spoke substantially as follows—

Gentlemen—I don't know how to thank you—I really don't know how. You would naturally suppose that my former experience would have given me this power, and that the difficulties in my way would have been diminished, but I assure you the fact is actually the reverse and I have completely baulked the ancient proverb that "a rolling stone gathers no moss," and in my progress in this city I have collected such a weight of obligations and acknowledgments—I have picked up such an enormous mass of fresh moss at every point, and was so struck with the brilliant scenes of Monday night, that I thought I could never by any possibility grow any bigger. Allow me again: I have made continually new accumulations to such an extent that I am compelled to stand still, and can roll no more!

Gentlemen, we learn from the authorities that when fairy stones, or balls or rolls of thread, stopped of their own accord—which I do not—it presaged some great catastrophe to be near at hand. The precedent holds good in this case. When I have remembered the short time I have before me to spend in this land of mighty interests, and the poor opportunity I can at best have of acquiring a knowledge of, and forming an acquaintance with it, I have felt it almost a duty to decline the honours you so generously heap upon me and pass more quietly among you, for Argus himself, though he had but one mouth for his hundred eyes, would have found the reception of a public entertainment once a week too much for his greatest activity; and as I would lose no scrap of the rich instruction and the delightful knowledge which meet me on every hand, and already I have gleaned a great deal from your hospitals and common jails, I have resolved to take up my staff and go my way rejoicing, and for the future to shake hands with America not at parties, but at home; and therefore, gentlemen, I say to-night with a full heart and an honest purpose and grateful feelings that I bear, and shall ever bear, the deep sense of your kind, your affectionate and your noble greeting—which it is utterly impossible to convey in words. No European sky without and no cheerful home or well-warmed room within shall ever shut out this land from my vision. I shall often hear your words of welcome in my quiet room and oftenest when most quiet; and shall see your faces in the blazing fire. If I should live to grow old, the scenes of this and other evenings will shine as brightly to my dull eyes fifty years hence as now—and the honours you bestow upon me shall be well remembered and paid back in my undying love and honest endeavours for the good of my race.

Gentlemen, one other word with reference to this first person singular, then I shall close. I came here in an open, honest and confiding spirit if ever man did, and because I felt a deep sympathy in your land; had I felt otherwise, I should have kept away. As I came here, and am here, without the least admixture of one hundredth part of one grain of base alloy, without one feeling of unworthy reference to self in any respect, I claim in reference to the past for the last time, my right in reason, in truth and in justice, to approach as I have done on two former occasions, a question of literary interest. I claim that justice be done, and I prefer this claim as one who has a right to speak and be heard. I have only to add that I shall be as true to you as you have been to me. I recognize in your enthusiastic approval of the creatures of my fancy, your enlightened care for the happiness of the many, your tender regard for the afflicted, your sympathy for the downcast, your plans for correcting and improving the bad, and for encouraging the good; and to advance these great objects shall be to the end of my life my earnest endeavour to the extent of my humble ability.

Having said this much with reference to myself, I shall have the pleasure of saying a few words with reference to somebody else.

There is in this city a gentleman who at the reception of one of my books—I well remember it was *The Old Curiosity Shop*—wrote to me in England a letter so generous, so affectionate, and so manly that if I had written the book under every circumstance of disappointment, of discouragement and difficulty, instead of the reverse, I should have found in the receipt of that letter the best and most happy reward. I answered him and he answered me, and so we kept shaking autographically, as if no ocean rolled between us. I came here to this city eager to meet him, and [*laying his hand upon Irving's shoulder*] here he sits ! I need not tell you how happy and delighted I am to see him here to-night in this capacity.

Washington Irving ! Why, gentlemen, I don't go upstairs to bed two nights out of the seven—as a very creditable witness near at hand can testify—I say I do not go to bed two nights out of the seven without taking Washington Irving under my arm.

And when I don't take him, I take his own brother,

Oliver Goldsmith. Washington Irving! Why, of whom but he was I thinking the other day when I came up by Hog's Back, the Frying Pan, Hell Gate and all these places? Why, when not long ago I visited Shakespeare's birthplace, and went beneath the roof where he first saw light, whose name but his was pointed out to me upon the wall? Washington Irving—Knickerbocker—Geoffrey Crayon—why, where can you go that they have not been there before? Is there an English farm—is there an English street, an English city or an English country-seat where they have not been? Is there no Bracebridge Hall in the distance? Has it no ancient shades or quiet streets?

In bygone times, when Irving left that hall, he left sitting in an old oak chair, in a small parlour of the Boar's Head, a little man with a red nose and an oilskin hat. When I came away he was sitting there still! Not a man like him, but the same man—with the nose of immortal redness and the hat of an undying glaze! Crayon, while there, was on terms of intimacy with a certain Radical fellow who used to go about with a hat full of newspapers, woefully out at elbows, and with a coat of great antiquity. Why, gentlemen, I know that man—Tibbles the Elder, and he has not changed a hair. And when I came away he charged me to give his best respects to Washington Irving.

Leaving the town and the rustic life of London, forgetting this man if we can, putting out of mind the Country Churchyard and The Broken Heart, let us cross the water again, and ask who has associated himself most closely with the Italian peasantry and the bandits of the Pyrenees? When the traveller enters his little chamber beyond the Alps, listening to the dim echoes of the long passages and spacious corridors, damp and gloomy and cold—as he hears the tempest beating with fury against his window, and gazes at the curtains, dark and heavy and covered with mould, and when all ghost stories that ever were told come up before him—mid all his thick-coming fancies, whom does he think of? Washington Irving. Go farther still—go to the Moorish fountains, sparking full in the moonlight—

go among the water-carriers and the village gossips, living still as in days of old, and who has travelled among them before you, and peopled the Alhambra, and made eloquent its shadows? Who awakes there a voice from every hill and in every tavern, and bids legends, which for centuries have slept a dreamless sleep or watched unwinkingly, start up and pass before you in all their glory?

But leaving this again, who embarked with Columbus upon his gallant ship—traversed with him the dark and mighty ocean—leaped upon the land and planted there the flag of Spain—but this same man now sitting by my side? And being here at home again, who is a more fit companion for money diggers, and what pen but his has made Rip Van Winkle—playing at ninepins on that thundering afternoon—as much a part and parcel of the Catskill Mountains as any tree or crag that they can boast.

But these are topics familiar from my boyhood, and which I am apt to pursue, and lest I should be tempted now to talk too long about him, I will in conclusion give you a sentiment—most appropriate, I am sure, in the presence of such writers as Bryant, Halleck and—— But I suppose I must not mention the ladies here—

The Literature of America—She well knows how to do honour to her own literature, and to that of other lands, when she chooses Washington Irving for her representative in the country of Cervantes.

Judge Betts, the first vice-president, when called on for a sentiment, after a brief and pertinent address, gave the following—

The Literature of Romance—Its highest powers have been displayed in depicting everyday life, and the language of everyday life.

John Duer, Esq., second vice-president, was called upon. He said: "Mr. President, it is a duty, a most solemn duty, I am called upon to perform, and I shall perform it with a solemnity befitting the occasion. And if any person here is supposing that he will be entertained, or find occasion for jest or unseemly merriment,

K

his hopes will be sadly disappointed. I stand here in the capacity of public prosecutor of one accused of high crimes and misdemeanours. Without further preamble I shall proceed to discharge my duty. You have before you a great criminal, and you, gentlemen, are the jury empanelled to pass on the guilt or innocence of the accused. We have had great difficulty in getting possession of the person of the criminal. He has recently arrived in this country, and was immediately seized by some evil-disposed persons, and while in their hands forced to submit to such treatment that to me it is a wonder and mystery that he was able to survive. He is now here, and we have to pass upon his guilt or innocence, and I have no doubt that he will receive his deserts. This paper which I hold in my hand is an indictment recently found. (Great laughter.) Really, gentlemen, this laughter upon this solemn occasion appears to me very unseemly. This paper, I say, is an indictment recently found by the Grand Jury of the City and County of New York. It is endorsed Washington Irving, Foreman, Charles A. Davis, Secretary— so that its authenticity cannot be doubted. This indictment I shall now proceed to read, and I ask for it your serious attention—

CITY AND COUNTY OF NEW YORK, SS.

The Grand Jurors of the City and County of New York, in the Name and Behalf of the People of the State of New York and of the United States, on their oaths present that one Charles Dickens, otherwise called Boz, now or late of the city of Westminster, in that part of the United Kingdom of Great Britain and Ireland called England, Gent, not having the fear of critics before his eyes, and being thereunto moved and instigated by a certain familiar spirit, and restless genius, heretofore, to wit, on the first day of January, in the year 1836, and on diverse days and times during the said year 1836, and during the year 1837, at the city of Westminster aforesaid, to wit, in the city and county of New York, made, composed, indicted, wrote,

WASHINGTON IRVING

printed and published, or caused and procured to be printed and published, in a succession or series of numbers, and in pamphlet form, diverse papers loosely stitched, called and known by the name, appellation or denomination of *Pickwick Papers;* and that the said Charles Dickens, otherwise called Boz, during the year aforesaid, and on diverse days and times in every subsequent year, to the year 1841 inclusive, by the means, intervention and agency of diverse subordinate persons called editors, publishers and booksellers, to wit, 5000 editors, 10,000 publishers and 10,000 booksellers, caused and procured the said *Pickwick Papers* to be reprinted and re-published in a great variety of shapes and forms, to wit, in newspapers, weekly journals, magazines, pamphlets and books; and that the said Charles Dickens, otherwise called Boz, during the years aforesaid, in addition to the copies sold and distributed in the said United Kingdom of Great Britain and Ireland, and of the continent of Europe, caused and procured, by and through his agents aforesaid, a large number of copies, to wit, 200,000 copies of the said *Pickwick Papers*, so reprinted and republished, to be vended, sold, circulated dispersed and distributed throughout the State of New York aforesaid, and throughout the United States, and in every city, town, village and hamlet thereof :

And the Grand Jurors aforesaid, on their oaths aforesaid, further say that the said *Pickwick Papers* purport to contain a history of the proceedings, actions and discourses of the members of a certain pretended association or club, called the Pickwick Club, and that in the said history, the ingredients of which, humour and pathos, are mixed and compounded with so much skill and art, and the various events, incidents, adventures and scenes therein related are painted, are described, with so much vivacity and force and with such a deep insight into the true springs of human action and thought, and the characters of the persons therein introduced, and rendered throughout so probable and consistent, that the whole narration is made to wear and assume the semblance of truth, nature and reality, so that many thousand persons, not only in the said United

K 2

Kingdom of Great Britain and Ireland, but in the state of New York aforesaid, and throughout the United States, in reading the said *Pickwick Papers*, have not only experienced many strange and violent changes of mood, fear, temper and thought, but the Grand Jurors aforesaid, on their oaths aforesaid, say that a large number of persons in the state of New York aforesaid, to wit, 200,000 persons, and a much larger number of persons in the United States, to wit, 500,000 persons, in reading and studying the said *Pickwick Papers*, have been seduced, deceived, deluded and cheated into the persuasion, conviction and belief that the said pretended Pickwick Club was and had been an actually existing club, and that the scenes, incidents, adventures and events in the said *Pickwick Papers* described had actually taken place, happened and occurred, and that the persons whose actions and discourses in the said papers were, or have been actually true and living persons; whereas the Grand Jurors aforesaid, on their oaths aforesaid, say that the several matters, things, events, incidents, persons and characters in the said *Pickwick Papers* contained, are the sole product of the fancy and imagination and invention, prompted by the observation and judgment of the said Charles Dickens, otherwise called Boz; and that no such club as the pretended Pickwick Club was ever formed or existed, and that no such events, incidents, adventures and scenes as in the said *Papers* are described, ever took place, happened or occurred; and that the persons whose actions and discourses in the said papers are related were not and never have been actual, true and living persons : with the exception of Samuel or Samivel Weller, whom the Grand Jurors aforesaid, on their oaths aforesaid, say they verily believe to be a real person, now living in the city of London, to wit, in the city and county of New York, aforesaid :

And the Grand Jurors aforesaid, on their oaths aforesaid, further say that the said history or narrative in the said *Pickwick Papers* contained, and the events, incidents, adventures, scenes, persons and characters aforesaid, so far from being, as is commonly asserted and believed, real, genuine, authentic and true, are all, each and every one of them, with the exception aforesaid, wholly, absolutely and altogether feigned, fictitious, fabulous and false.

Wherefore the Grand Jurors aforesaid, on their oaths aforesaid, present and charge that the said Charles Dickens, otherwise called Boz, now or late of Westminster aforesaid, in making, composing, inditing, writing and in printing and publishing, or in causing to be published the paper so called the *Pickwick Papers* as aforesaid, and in causing and procuring the same to be reprinted and republished, vended, sold, circulated and distributed as aforesaid with the intent not only to cheat, deceive and delude the subjects of the Queen of the United Kingdom of Great Britain and Ireland, and the subjects of the several kings, princes, potentates and powers on the continent of Europe, but with the further special and wicked intent to cheat, deceive and defraud the good citizens of this state and the United States, has been and·is guilty of high crimes and misdemeanours, contrary to the statute in such case made and provided, and against the peace of the people of the State of New York and their dignity.

Mr. Duer followed up this playful vein by acting as judge and prosecutor, assuming that the truth of these grave charges against Boz was matter of universal notoriety and needed no formal proof, nor could the culprit be allowed to plead to the indictment for fear of his fascinating tongue. A plea of not guilty would be entered for him as not pleading; but the judge would allow no pleading, and he summoned the company present as a jury to give their verdict. "Guilty" was the unanimous response, amidst a tempest of most unjudicial cheers. The judge proceeded to pass sentence upon him that he should not repent, but go on repeating his transgressions—which the jury concurred in most heartily.

Mr. Philip Hone, after a few happy remarks, gave—

A Bill at Sight—Drawn by Cheeryble Brothers in favour of Charles Dickens, on American Hospitality.

Accepted and duly honoured without discount or defalcation.

He was followed by Gulian C. Verplanck, who contrasted the author they were met to welcome with the earlier English authors. He then remarked on the stronger relish with which the productions of the English genius were read in this country, than those of Germany and France, assigning the causes of it, and concluded with this toast—

The health of all who, speaking the rich tongue that Shakespeare spoke, unite with us in awarding to genius its fitting honours.

Hon. John A. King, fifth vice-president, on being called on, spoke as follows—

"If it could be permitted, on such an occasion, to go back to the period which terminated in Europe with the overthrow of that master-spirit which aspired to the empire of the world, and which ended in this country in the establishment of peace between the two kindred nations—if it might also be permitted to contrast that period with the present, and show the influence prolonged peace has had on nations and individuals, it would afford a most remarkable study for the historian and philanthropist. A long war of revolutionary ambition had deluged the eastern continent in blood, and man, with all his energies, was the patient instrument of power, ambition and never-ending conflict; then all the intelligence of the age, its men of Letters, of Science and the Arts, were either seduced to praise or awed into silence by the blandishments or menaces of power. Man was then a slave, for he toiled and bled not for himself, but for others. The mind, then, too, given to be free as the elements, lost its vigour, or at least worked only by command. When peace with her golden wings covered again the earth, the salient springs of knowledge once more gushed forth in every land. The Mind of man, recoiling upon itself, soon taught him the power that was in him, and the great objects to be attained and secured by the uncommon exercise of all his faculties. The Slave became suddenly the Master, and he who lately received the unresisting command of a superior, now bows alone to intelligence and worth. The first was the Age of Iron—thi, the Golden Era. The first saw the human passions freed and millions led to battle at the will of the conqueror—this beholds those passions subdued, and increased millions obedient under equal laws and regulated liberty. Among the nations which have made the greatest advance in all the arts, inventions and humanities of peace, England and America are most distinguished. The common origin, language and laws have mutually encouraged and supported each other in the noble race of emulation. Where liberty dwells and the laws are equal, each one feels their elevating power, and man stands forth in all his varied attributes. The spirit of the age is full of inquiry, and knowledge flows in from every side. Education here at least will spread, draw on our generous minds abroad, and send back in return the free offerings of kindred minds. The age, too, is marked by the varied inventions and productions of genius. The power of steam, the great agent of modern times, has solved both time and space, and multiplied to an unlimited extent the power of man in every branch of art and industry; and quickly and variedly as the human head ever works, this great agent can throw as rapidly upon the printed pages.

Another and perhaps a greater power has also grown up and been strengthened by the peaceful relations of the world during a quarter of a century. This power and influence of mind have been achieved by the press —the ready instrument of the fertile mind—in spreading its riches before millions of thinking and intelligent men. In all branches of knowledge writers of the highest order have flourished. In the popular branches of literature a new and most attractive style has arisen, true in the delineation of individual character and of classes of men—depicting in the most graphic manner their impulses, habits and passions. Among the gifted writers who have thus revealed and illustrated the mysteries of the human heart, describing scenes of the deepest interest in the easiest and most eloquent manner appealing most forcibly to the finest sympathies of our nature, and giving to his varied works the best moral direction, stands the guest whom we here in this western hemisphere this day receive and welcome as a brother and a friend.

Young, but of rare renown, he comes among us who have eagerly sought and read and appreciated each effort of his genius; he has left a great and powerful and kindred people to visit another land, where millions of free men are also ready to greet and grasp him by the hand—who has so often charmed and delighted their leisure hours. Here then he stands in the midst of an intelligent and reading people, ready ever to do honour to genius and talent, belong to whom it may, and above all to those who, writing in their mother tongue, record in such eloquent and glowing colours the sufferings, the wrongs, the patient virtues of those whose lot is cast in the humble walks of life. If in crossing the wide ocean which separates, but which would never divide, us, he has changed his native skies to those less genial, perhaps, because not his own, may the mind and genius, alike the pride of either shore, know no friendly change, but return in all its pristine vigour to observe, describe and illustrate the good and the evil, wisdom and folly, as each in its turn, or in mingled action, shall rise up before him. He had found us a true, intelligent and wholly a generous and confiding people; and he may accept here the general wish that he may find health and all that he deserves among us; and return once more to his household gods, maybe rejoice in our glorious destiny, as we have and do in that of his great and illustrious country.

The sculptor lives in the breathing stone, the painter in the glowing canvas, but he lives in the affections of the people, who in revealing the mysteries of the human heart, has shown that its virtues and its feelings are alike independent of station and of power.

D. P. Ogden, sixth vice-president, being next called

on, closed a forcible tribute to Mr. Dickens by pertinently reminding the company of the services and achievements of American authors, and of their claims to the gratitude and affectionate regard of their countrymen. He proposed—

The Republic of Letters—Having mankind for a constituency, it invites all the world to share the rich blessings it bestows.

Mr. C. A. Davis, after reading some letters from Governor Seward and other invited guests, closed with a humorous reply from his friend, Major Jack Downing—

To the Gentlemen of the Committee—for the dinner to Mr. Boz.

Washington, February 15, 1842.

There is nothing in nature would tickle me so desperately as to be able to go on to York and eat dinner along with Mr. Boz—but I can't nohow and noway in the world, and the Capting thinks it best that I wait here till Mr. Boz comes this way, as he wants me to take a share in shaking hands at the White House.

There are very few folks nowadays who desarve more civilities on the score of gratitude—for few folks now living or dead have done more to scrape the shins of the wicked—to plead the causes of the destitute and suffering, and to nail to the counter like a bad penny the hard-hearted and selfish.

As to larning and book-study, no matter how much a man has—if he keeps it all to himself and looks and feels wise, he is of no more use to his fellow-critters than a miser who stores away his gold in an old stocking, but if he tells what he knows and thinks, and puts it into sech shapes as let young and old, high and low understand and be instructed by it—then he is entitled to gratitude, and I hope he will get his full share of it, especially as he ain't likely to get anything else so long as some of our folks understand "copy-right" to mean "right to copy."

There is one class of writers that I and the Capting

have a shocking bad opinion of—it is them chaps that thinks there ain't sickness and sorrow and suffering and hard times enough in this world, and so they turn and rile up folks, and make muddy water betwixt them, and are never so happy as when they injure better people than themselves, and being ashamed to sign their own names to their dirty work, clap down "Brutus" and "Cato" and "Nebuchadnezzar" and "Judas Iscariot" and other old Roman and foreign Injuns. The Capting and I keep our eye on these chaps, and when we know who they are, they may as well look for a frost in June as an office, I tell you, Sonny. But when they use their pen in grubbing up tangled briars and making the path clear for a happy journey through life, the Capting is sure to remember them. You see how it was t'other day in that appointment to Spain; he asked no questions, just wrote doen the name of Geoffrey Crayon as nat'ral as putting on his mittens. So there is no telling yet how soon I may stand a chance to get a post office or land office as a reward for my long labours.

I did hope that Mr. Boz would come into the states down east, so as to take a look at Downingville, and begin the country at sunrise; but I suppose he thought it best to land first where he did on account of the compliment paid to his grandfather, who was a warm friend of the Pilgrims before they left home—and so they called it Bosting after him; and if it had not been for the ignorance or vanity of the early printers the spelling would be now as it was before the Revolution. The least, however, that can now be done is to correct that error, and bring it back to the good old Pilgrim spelling, "Boztown." It is due to old Mr. Boz, and to his great grandson who comes out in the middle of winter to see us. It will please infinitely, too, a good many honest old folks along up the northeastern boundary-line, who are unwilling to see izzards turned into esses and snaix crawling off under other spellings just to justify some new twistification instead of letting letters tell their own story.

I am sorry to hear that Mr. Pickwick and Samivel

Weller havint come out with Mr. Boz, specially Samivel, for I wanted to see him amazingly and have a chat with him. I think there is as much left of that critter as has yet been threshed out of him; but that is saying a good deal before such a man like Mr. Boz, who can put his rake on a stubble that others have cut before him and carry off more clear corn than the first reapers. I see that Mr. Boz let the old clock run down at hum. If he's willing I'll lend him one I bought of Samuel Slick. It's a wooden one, but can tick as loud as if it was all brass, and will run a plaguy long time if well wound up. If there is a spare hole to stick in another toast without alarming folks as Oliver Twist did when he asked for more, please scrooge in the following—

The Quill—May the ink it sheds in the cause of truth and justice (and in good old Anglo-Saxon lingo) wet in the priming of the war gun, while its feather-end tickles the nose of the base passions of all creation into good humour and happy smiles.

J. DOWNING, MAJOR, etc.

The president, Washington Irving, having proposed the following sentiment—

International Copyright—It is but fair that those who have laurels for their brows should be permitted to *browse* on their laurels.

Mr. Cornelius Matthews, one of the editors of *Arcturus*, having been called, rose and responded to the sentiment as follows—

I answer your summons, Mr. President, under some restraint. I am not quite sure that it becomes me, a humble lay-brother of the order of authors, to trouble a diplomatist and Spanish Minister, in any way, with the insignificant affairs of the fraternity. But when I recollect how the distinguished gentleman on your right, a monk at least if not a bishop, has been lately received in this great city of ours, I am re-assured : knowing how you, once an honoured member of the craft, are going forth from the country, its ambassador and representative, and how he, a man of letters, in full communion with the brethren, has just entered it—I think I may venture to say a word or two of rights which you hold in common. In speaking on the subject of an International Copyright, at this time, I would not be understood as being moved by any new impulse or sudden enthusiasm; but as uttering convictions carefully considered and long entertained.

That I am speaking in the presence of an eminent foreign writer—the universality of whose genius, appealing by its delineations to all classes and conditions of men, would seem to entitle him to an universal recognition of his rights—will, I believe, by no means diminish the force of what I may say.

It is argued, sometimes, I know, that authors have no rights; and a paper-dealing tradesman of this city, greedy of some sort of renown, has lately contended, if we could but get English Books at the cost of type and paper (the author being considered an impertinent third party), all the ends of good literature would be answered. I might ask this artful casuist, how it would suit his convenience—he being a man of some stamp and character among his neighbours—to come abroad in the open light of day—in a coat yet odorous of the fingers of the petit-larceny thief; a hat savouring of the burglar's fist; his pockets jingling with the transferred coin of a bank robber: but I look beyond this miserable economical subterfuge, and seek, somewhat farther down, the actual operation of an uncopyrighted Foreign Literature, reprinted without restraint. There is at this moment waging in our midst a great war between a Foreign and a Native Literature. The one claims pay—food, lodging, and raiment; the other battles free of all charges, takes the field, prepared for all weathers and all emergencies; has neither a mouth to cry for sustenance, a back to be clothed, nor a head to be sheltered.

The conflict between a paid literature and an unpaid is a fierce one while it lasts; it cannot last long. The one relies on the feeble and uncertain impulses of authorship; the other is driven on by all the restless interests of trade. What, sir, is the present condition of the

Field of Letters in America? It is in a state of desperate anarchy—without order, without system, without certainty. For several years past, it has been sown broad cast with foreign publications of every name and nature; what growth has ensued? No single work, so far as I can see, has sprung up as its legitimate result; no addition to the stock of native poetry or fiction; no tree has blossomed; no solitary blade struck through the hard and ungrateful turf. Whatever has been produced has been in spite of opposition from within and without; has been the bright exception, not the rule. Instead of being fostered and promoted, as it should be, our domestic literature is borne down by an immethodical and unrestrained republication of every foreign work that will bear the charges of the compositor and paper-maker.

Under the regulations of an International Copyright, the work of a British author would be published here in its order; would take its chance with other works, native and foreign; would be valued and circulated according to its worth; and would hold its rank in due subordination to the judgment passed upon it by the side of other compositions. What is the case now? A new work by the author of *Charles O'Malley* reaches this country— a pleasant, lively, vivacious picture of Irish life and dragoon service, well worthy of being printed by some prominent house, furnished to the libraries, and put in the hands of a liberal circle of readers, in due course of trade. This would be proper and natural. On the contrary, twenty, yea, fifty, or a hundred hands—for the giant of Republication is single-eyed and many-handed —are thrust forth, spasmodically to clutch the first landed copy; it is followed, watched to its destination; violent hands are perhaps laid on it to snatch it from its first possessor; it is reprinted; early copies are despatched into the country; new editions follow, in pamphlet, in book, by chapters in a thousand newspapers; the land is vocal with the unrestrained chuckle of the daily and weekly press over this new acquisition; while no other writer, whatever his merit, if his popularity be but a degree less, is listened to. What hope is there here for the native author?

The odds are tremendous; and I do not hesitate to
say, sir, that if he had thousands to lavish on the printing of a single work, a press in every village, a publisher of enterprise and spirit in every city, the purchased
control of fifty newspapers—he would be only beginning
to enter the field on anything like fair terms with Dr.
Lever. The one literature, the Foreign, is propelled
through the country by steam; the other, the Native,
halts after on foot or in such conveyances as a very
narrow purse may bargain for. Principles, it may be,
alien to our own, travel with the speed of lightning,
while national truths, in which we have the profoundest
interest, follow at a lacquey's pace behind. As an
American I feel this and I avow it. From the contemplation of that distinguished author, glorying in the
zenith of a reputation universal as the light of day, my
eyes turn away, and in the sequestered retreat, in the
cramped and narrow room, seek that other brother of
his, poor, neglected, borne down by the heavy hand of
his country, laid, like an oppressor's, upon him; and I
feel that the conditions of human life are hard indeed.
Far be it from me, sir, to indulge in idle repinings over
any of the inevitable sufferings of authors or of men;
still farther be it from me to cast any shadow upon the
general joy of this occasion; but I feel it my duty, as I
trust in God I always shall, to say something, wherever
I can, in behalf of the victims of false systems, the
children in this case—the orphans, rather, I might say
—who inherit the wide kingdom of Thought, and who
toil bitterly in secret, in labours not seen of the eye, that
the world may have enough of mirth and cheerful truth
to make the day wear through. Standing here to-night,
the representative, in some humble measure, of the
interests of American authors in this question, I say
they have been treated by this people and government
as no other of its citizens; that an enormous fraud practised upon their British brethren, has been allowed so to
operate upon them as to blight their hopes and darken
their fair fame. They have remonstrated, and will, until
the evil has grown too great to be encountered, or is
subdued. I might speak especially in behalf of the com-

pany of young native writers, who, seeing how well the
world was affected toward good literature, and moved by
some kindly impulses of nature, may have hoped in their
way to add something to the happiness, something to
the renown of their country. But we are advised how
others, who thought they had secured a constant and
enduring hold on the public good will by past character
and services, have also been affected by the present
injurious state of affairs.

You, sir, for example, in that retreat of yours, classical
in the world's affections, having matured a work of some
value and which you think ready for the metropolitan
market, take passage down the Hudson in company with
one of your farmer neighbours, who has, perhaps, just
fattened his fall stock to a grain : with your manuscript
in your pocket—recollecting, too, that in times past,
your handicraft has been held in some repute—you
flatter yourself you will find a prompt purchaser for
whatever you bring. You call, sir, on certain traders
in Cliff Street, you suggest the MSS. "For Heaven's
sake, Mr. Irving," is the response of the blandest member of the firm, the one that talks to the authors, "don't
plague us just now; we have a profound respect for your
talents, an ardent affection for American Literature : but
Mr. Bulwer's *Zanoni* has arrived, and we must have a
hundred hands on it before night. Call again, we shall
be happy to see you ! "

Then, sir, meditating on the patriotic courtesy of the
gentleman you have just left, you shape your course
toward a great Publishing House in Broadway : famous
heretofore for a certain solidity and selectness of publication, but having been lately bitten by the Number
viper—which, by the by, is encompassing the Earth,
like the Great Snake of the Hindoo Mythology—they
beg you, with some natural tears in their eyes, not to
interrupt them just then : "The Big Papers, the Mam-
moth Press, is on the alert : they must have *Handy
Andy* on the counter by Saturday or the tide will be
down with them : " and behold, sir, the author of the
Sketch Book, the illustrious historian of New York,
very much in the situation of the ostrich of the desert

having an egg to lay, but nowhere to lay it; and, like it, I might add, greatly disposed to hide his head for very shame. How has it fared, sir, in the meantime, with your sturdy neighbour and his charge? In robustious health, cheerful of spirit, with no misgivings whatever, he makes the voyage to New York; remembers many a hearty welcome, many a lucky market in times past; and has no sooner touched the wharf, than he is seized upon by a dozen or more red-cheeked hucksters, who well nigh embrace him from the joy they feel at his coming; he runs hastily over an inventory of what he has brought—so many turkies of a year old, so many spring chickens, so many cocks and hens, and before he has had a chance to unbutton his overcoat, his merchandise is off his hands, and he casts about in his mind at what comfortable chop-house he shall hold an interview of settlement, and reckon his gains over a snug meal and glass of choice cider.

Now, sir, I would ask, is not your brood of speckled fancies, as honestly begotten from the beginning, as his parti-coloured capons? Are not your historical truths as solid and substantial, as real to the mind as his gross-fed turkies to the body? Are not your racy courses of humour as much a solace and comfort to the soul as his web-footed waddlers to the palate? The property is as real, as actual in one case as the other; and why should it not command its price? That, sir, is a wretched country, or a wretched condition of things, where the best products of the best workman in any department are not in demand. And it is just so here at present.

The public taste is so deeply affected by the interested laudations of inferior authors by the republishers, that the value of literary reputation, as well as literary property, is greatly impaired. No distinction is made between good writers and bad; they all appear in the same dress, under the same introduction; and the judgment of the general reader is so perplexed that he cannot choose between Mr. Dickens and Mr. Harrison Ainsworth—between the classical drama of Talfourd and the vapid farce of Boucicault. As this system deepens and strengthens itself, as it does every day, an American celebrity will cease to have any semblance of the discriminating applause of a "contemporaneous posterity," and be regarded only as the confused shout of a distant crowd. I know that to many of our trans-Atlantic brethren their American reputation is dear and valued; and for their sakes I would not have a system endure by which its worth will be so surely diminished.

This brings me, gentlemen, to another aspect of the cause I am pleading with you. It has been a matter of surprise in some quarters that Mr. Dickens, a British writer, has addressed the American people on the subject of Copyright. Amid the happier visions which have crowded his English chamber for the last five or six years, are we quite sure that no Corsair face has ever looked in?—no eager visage of the ink-stained pirate, with a hand stretched stealthily towards the MS. on his desk, to snatch it away ere it was dry, and blazon it throughout the whole New World, as an acquisition honestly made? May not his brightest hours have been darkened, at times, by the fancy of a grim row of republishers rising before him—line upon line of readers, beginning at the Atlantic and stretching to the very verge of Oregon, with lines crossing them from Penobscot to the Mexican Gulf, all busy in the self-same task, turning page after page of what he has written—roaring with laughter, melting in tears—until the contemplation of it (with the thought that no honest penny was gained to him by all this pleasant show that was going forward) has become actually painful to his mind? And when, landing on our shores, these very readers, many of them, drew nigh and took him by the hand—in a very earnest, friendly grasp, too—and made solemn vows and protestations of friendship—was it less than natural that he should speak to them, in the confidence of frank discourse, of what had so often pressed painfully on his thoughts?

He was among brethren, in his own younger brother's house, and because he ventured to speak of a patrimony they held in common, with a like interest as himself, shall he be condemned?

But all this broadens into a general question, and one

L

to which we are bound to give heed. I will take it for granted, sir, that every gentleman within hearing of my voice is aware that fifty-six British Authors—and among them many that have given lustre to the age—applied to the American Congress for an international copyright, and were refused. I will also take it for granted that every gentleman here admits that there may be a good indefeasible right and property in a book as in any other estate. By what casuistry or jurisprudence does that which is property in one latitude in one civilized country cease to be property when transferred within the limits of another?

The most precious property of one country in another, as I regard it, is its books. To us, what is Germany, half so much as Goethe? Greece but Homer? And England is nearer and dearer to us by her long array of great writers, than by the constant intercourse of commerce, the closest compacts and treaties of amity. Her writers ask that this claim should be allowed; that all the relations of the two countries shall not be reduced to a gross, material standard; but that they shall have a property, as they have a right, in whatever of noble sentiment, or enduring thought they may impart to us; and that we shall have a like property with them. That we have heretofore enjoyed their labours free of charge, is nothing; that we have lived on their free bounty for a long time creates in us no claim—as it should no desire—to become perpetual almoners of theirs. A true spirit of national fair-dealing, not to say national dignity, would impel us to disclaim the charity, and persuade us to purchase what we read, as well as what we eat and wear.

I have said nothing, sir—and I might have said much —of the mutilation of books by our American republishers—that outrageous wrong by which a noble English writer, speaking truths in London dear to him as life, is made to say in New York that which his soul abhors. This, sir, silent and uncomplaining as it seems, is a despotism as gross as that of the rack and the thumb-screw, which wrings from men, under torture, falsehoods to flatter the tormentor. What right have I, sir, to stifle

the utterance of any manly spirit—to offer him oppor-
tunities of speech, and then, in bitterest mockery, abridge
the truth he would deliver? Soul speaks to soul through
all distances of time and space; and accursed should he
be that ventures to thrust his uncouth shadow as a
softening medium, between the two! We have friendly
treaties, Mr. President, by which property and person,
as commonly acknowledged, are sacred between the two
nations. Is it not worth the while of statesmen and
legislators to incorporate hereafter a provision by which
the great rights of Thought, of the soul speaking in its
highest moods, shall be cared for and guarded?

I desire to see the two sections of Anglo-Saxon Literature on either side of the great ocean, moving harmoni-
ously onward; they giving to us whatever they have of
maturity and art, and we returning, as we are bound, all
of freshness and vigour with which a new world may
have inspired us. I desire to see something of the great
debt, now accumulated for ages, which we owe to the
brotherhood of British writers, cancelled; first, in the
true honest currency of dollars and cents, known to the
Union as the representative value between man and
man; secondly, in works of genius, the growth of our
own soil, coloured by our own skies, and showing something of the influences of a new community, where
nature comes fresh and mighty to her task. A thousand
voices now slumber in our vales, amid our cities and
along our hill-sides, that only await the genial hour to
speak and be heard. Silence would no longer brood, as
it now does, over so many fair fields, nor, "moon-like,
hold the mighty waters fast." Alleghany would have a
voice, to which the Metropolis, with its hundred steeples
and turrets, would answer; gulf and river, and the broad
field would reply, each for itself, until the broad sky
above us should be shaken with the thunder tones of
master-spirits responding to each other; the whole wide
land echo from side to side with the accents of a Majestic
Literature—self-reared, self-sustained, self-vindicating!

I offer you, Mr. President—

An International Copyright—The only honest turnpike between the readers of two great nations.

L 2

Eloquent addresses were made by the Rev. Mr. Bellows and the Mayor, and among others these toasts were offered—

Mr. Kennedy proposed : *The Clergy of the City of New York*—who "allure to brighter worlds and lead the way."

Mr. Bellows answered : *Our Vernacular Tongue*—the English language—a recovery from the confusion of Babel destined yet to build a tower to reach to heaven.

By Mr. Bronson : *Master Humphrey's Clock*—Though it goes on tick, always in good credit.

By L. Gaylord Clark, editor of the *Knickerbocker: The Health of Sergeant Talfourd*—who stands among the tribe of our later dramatists like an ancient Grecian statue in a gallery of modern casts.

By R. H. H.—*The Works of our Guest*—Like Oliver Twist "we ask for more."

* * * * * * * *

The following account of the dinner is from Mr. Hone's diary—

"Feb. 19th.—The great dinner to Dickens was given yesterday at the City Hotel, and came off with flying colours. Two hundred and thirty persons sat down to dinner at seven o'clock. The larger room was ornamented with two illuminated scenes from the works of ' Boz,' busts of celebrated persons and classical devices, all in good taste; and the eating and drinking part of the affair was excellent. The president was Washington Irving (I beg pardon, ' His Excellency '). *Non nobis* was sung by Mr. Horn and a band of vocalists, who gave several glees during the evening. After the intellectual operation of eating and drinking was concluded, the president rose and began a prepared speech, in which he broke down flat (as he promised us beforehand he would), and concluded with the toast : ' *Charles Dickens, the literary guest of the nation.*' To this the guest made acknowledgment in an excellent speech, delivered with great animation and characterized by good taste and warm feeling.

An unusual feature in this festivity was the presence of a coterie of charming women, who were first stowed away in a small room adjoining the upper part of the hall, and who, with a laudable and irrepressible curlosity to hear me, and others equally instructive and agreeable, at the lower end, edged by degrees into the room, and finally got possession of the stage behind the president, to the discomfiture of certain pleasant old bachelors and ungallant dignitaries, but to the great delight of us who profess to have better taste in such matters. This flying squadron of infantry consisted of Mrs. Davis, Mrs. Colden, Miss Wilkes, Mrs. Dickens, Miss Sedgwick, Miss Wadsworth, the Misses Ward, Mrs. Burrows, Mrs. Parrish, Miss Anna Brigden and others, all of whom seemed to regret they could not take a more active part in the business of the evening. The dinner with the ball on Monday night is a tribute to literary talents greater than any I can remember; and if the English people do not repay it in some shape to our eminent men, they are no great things."

Professor Felton, in his address before the Massachusetts Historical Society on Washington Irving, gave the following interesting account of Irving's breakdown in his speech introducing Dickens at the dinner—

"Great and varied as was the genius of Mr. Irving, there was one thing he shrank with a comical terror from attempting, and that was a *dinner speech*. A great dinner, however, was to be given to Mr. Dickens in New York, as one had already been given in Boston; and it was evident to all that no man but Washington Irving could be thought of to preside. With all his dread of making a speech, he was obliged to obey the universal call and to accept the painful pre-eminence. I saw him daily during the interval of preparation, either at the lodgings of Dickens or at dinner or evening parties. I hope I showed no want of sympathy with his forebodings, but I could not help being amused with the tragi-comical distress which the thought of that approaching dinner caused him. His pleasant humour mingled with the real dread and played with the whimsical horrors of his own position with an irresistible drollery. Whenever it was alluded to, his invariable answer was, ' I shall certainly brcak down ! '—uttered in a half-melancholy tone, the ludicrous effect of which it is impossible to describe. He was haunted as if by a nightmare; and I could only compare his dismay to that of Mr. Pickwick, who was so alarmed at the prospect of leading about that ' dreadful horse ' all day. At length the long-expected evening arrived; a company of the most eminent persons, from all the professions and every walk of life, were assembled, and Mr. Irving took the chair. I had gladly accepted an invitation, making it, however, a condition that I should not be called upon to speak—a thing I then dreaded quite as much as Mr. Irving himself. The direful compulsions of life have since helped me to overcome, in some measure, the postprandial fright. Under the circumstances—an invited guest with no impending speech—I sat calmly and watched with interest the imposing scene. I had the honour to be placed next but one to Mr. Irving and the great pleasure of sharing in his conversation. He had brought the manuscript of his speech and laid it under his plate. ' I shall certainly break down,' he repeated over and over again. At last the moment arrived. Mr. Irving rose and was received with deafening and long-continued applause, which by no means lessened his apprehension. He began in his pleasant voice, got through two or three sentences pretty easily, but in the next hesitated, and after one or two attempts to go on, gave it up with a graceful allusion to the tournament, and the troops of knights all armed and eager for the fray, and ended with the toast: ' *Charles Dickens, the guest of the nation.*' ' There,' said he, as he resumed his seat under a repetition of the applause which had saluted his rising, ' there ! I told you I should break down, and I've done it.'

"There certainly never was made a shorter after-dinner speech; I doubt if there ever was a more successful one. The manuscript seemed to be a dozen or twenty pages long, but the printed speech was not as many lines. I suppose that manuscript may be still in existence; and if so, I wish it may be published. Mr. Irving often spoke with a good-humoured envy of the felicity with which Dickens always acquitted himself on such occasions."

CHAPTER VII

PHILADELPHIA

DICKENS left New York Sunday, March 6, in the afternoon and arrived in Philadelphia late that night. At the present time the traveller goes to the railroad station in the heart of the city, gets on a train which takes him through the tunnel under the Hudson River, and in two hours he is landed in Philadelphia. It was different in 1842, for, as Dickens wrote at that time, the journey was made by railroad and two ferries and occupied nearly six hours' time. On his arrival he went to the United States Hotel, which stood on Chestnut Street opposite the United States Bank. In *American Notes* he does not even mention the name of the hotel, and does not say whether it was good, bad or indifferent, while in almost every other city he visited he has something to say of the character of the hotel he stopped at. It is possible that the reason he said nothing of the United States Hotel was on account of the fact that, as he had complained in one of his letters to his friend, Thomas Mitton, the landlord had charged him for his rooms and board from the date he had engaged the rooms, instead of from the actual time of his arrival a week later.

At the time of Dickens's visit there were four daily papers in Philadelphia, and while there was neither a ball nor a dinner given in his honour, as in New York, and while there was no authorized reception given him, and while he spent his time in visiting the Penitentiary, water-works, and other public institutions, and was only in the city two days, all four of these papers informed the public very fully as to a reception which some of the papers said was authorized and others said was unauthorized.

That Dickens did not desire any public reception in the city was generally known is shown by the following notice which appeared in the *Philadelphia Gazette*, two weeks before his arrival in the city—

"Mr. Dickens will visit this city in a few days. He wisely declines all dinners, parades, shows, junketings and things of that sort, preferring to meet such private unostentatious hospitalities as a courteous people should extend to any gentleman, and a stranger."

Similar notices appeared in some of the other papers, but notwithstanding Dickens's wishes, there was at least one man who determined that if it could be accomplished, Dickens should hold a public reception, and being a politician of some influence, he had the following item inserted in the *Public Ledger* on Tuesday morning—

"*Mr. Dickens.*—This gentleman will, we understand, be gratified to shake hands with his friends between the hours of half-past ten and half-past eleven o'clock. He leaves for the South to-morrow."

That this announcement brought crowds to the hotel, and that it was a surprise to Mr. Dickens, can be seen by this short account of the affair which appeared in one of the morning papers the next day—

"*Boz.*—It was stated in one of the morning papers yesterday, that Mr. Dickens would be happy to see his friends between half-past ten and half-past twelve o'clock yesterday. And few men, we believe, have been more unexpectedly surprised at the number of unknown friends, than was Mr. D., especially as he was ignorant of the intention of any one to invent such an article. However, the public came, and Colonel Florence, who was present, introduced the numerous visitors until Mr. Dickens, who has been unwell for some time, was compelled to retire. We do not know, not having been present, how many called upon Mr. D., but probably a large number.

"Mr. Dickens was to visit the Eastern Penitentiary

at twelve o'clock, and after inspecting the place, was to dine with some friends. He expected to depart soon."

The *Philadelphia Gazette* did not believe the announcement of the reception was authorized, as shown by their account of the affair—

"*Mr. Dickens—Rudeness and Cruelty.*—Some of the morning papers contained a sort of semi-official announcement that Mr. Dickens would receive the calls of gentlemen between the hours of ten and twelve to-day. Consequently a crowd gathered there, and among others, curiosity led us to the United States Hotel. We found ' Boz ' in a large reception-room in the second storey, earnestly toiling away with all his might, shaking the hands of a dense crowd of people, as they promiscuously thrust out their digits, at the announcement by Colonel Florence, who appeared to be master of ceremonies. We understand that the invitation for gentlemen to call was wholly unauthorized, in consequence of Mr. Dickens's positive engagements and his rather delicate health, which must have suffered from the mistaken kindness and troublesome importunities of people before he reached this city. ' Boz ' has a very youthful look, with a profusion of hair and a winning smile, and a countenance decidedly affable. His voice, by which character is often indicated, we did not hear. We understand he will remain in town some days, and before he leaves, the citizens, doubtless, will have an opportunity of an introduction. But we beg of Philadelphians to respect this distinguished stranger, if they do not themselves. Do not obtrude upon his time and patience by needlessly taxing his physical energies, and thus rendering his visit one of *pain* rather than *pleasure*."

Colonel Florence, who seemed to have been the instigator of the notice advising the public of the reception, and who acted as a self-constituted major-domo of the affair, felt that these accounts of the reception did him an injustice, and protested to the editor of the *Gazette* against the wrong that had been done him, with this result—

"Colonel Florence has called upon us in behalf of himself and brethren of the 'Committee' and assured us that they acted yesterday in conformity with the wishes of Mr. Dickens. He doubtless expected a few gentlemen in company with the Committee, but under some sort of mistaken kindness, the notice was made public, and half the city besieged poor 'Boz' at his lodgings."

Colonel Florence was evidently not of the same political persuasion as the editor of the *Philadelphia Gazette*, who took an opportunity to give the Colonel and the Committee a lesson in politeness, and some instruction as to the manner in which distinguished strangers should be treated when visiting the city, without the guidance of "Tom, Dick and Harry."

"*Mr. Dickens and the Public.*—It will be a matter of deep regret if the presence of this distinguished private gentleman in this city should give rise to heart-burnings and criminations among any portion of the citizens of Philadelphia. We stated yesterday that the invitation to call upon Mr. Dickens was premature and unauthorized, yet he received those who did call with his characteristic ease and urbanity. It appears that a Committee, whether self-constituted or not the public have not been informed, addressed Mr. Dickens while in New York, begging him not to put himself into the hands of a 'clique' when he reached this city. That Committee remarked, among other very queer things—

"'It is needless to ask you whether you intend visiting Philadelphia. Doubtless you have determined this in your mind already; and, without doubt, many of the *soi disant* magnates of our city have conceived a multitude of plans for the *monopoly* of *Boz*, and it is of this that we complain; for we cannot conceive why you should be the *exclusive property* of a self-delegated clique, who may claim to be all in all, to the exclusion of all others.'

"Mr. Dickens replied, that when he reached Phila-

delphia, he should be ' exceeding glad to shake hands '
with these gentlemen, but doubtless he expected, as
they condemned ' exclusiveness ' and ' self-delegated
cliques,' that he should not be under their special control.   Neither could he have expected that his movements, even remotely, would be subject to their arrangements or dictation.   Yesterday, it appears, this self-same
Committee inserted in many of the morning papers, on
their own responsibility, a notice, that Mr. Dickens
would see his friends between 10 and 11.   We were
informed that Mr. D. *did* appoint this hour to receive
the Committee, but as his health was not good and he
had engagements elsewhere, which would prevent his
seeing the public promiscuously, he was expecting only
a few persons in his private apartment.   Doubtless the
Committee mistook the intentions of this gentleman in
their eagerness to be civil, but when Mr. Dickens found
a crowd below, with the complaisance of a gentleman,
he submitted to their calls, and the ceremony proceeded
for nearly two live-long hours !

"We protest against all this obtrusiveness and tres-
passing upon the time and patience of a private gentleman.   Especially do we reprobate all the official action
of men, who addressed him the absurd letter while in
New York.   They deprecate ' fawning ' or ' sycophancy.'
but yet huddle about this gentleman and obtrude themselves upon him in a manner which he has repeatedly
condemned, asked to be rid of, and which every gentleman despises.   To this committee and all other committees who are appointed, or who appoint themselves,
to superintend the movements of distinguished gentlemen who come among us, we would only say, leave Mr.
Dickens and all such people alone.   They visit us for
the purpose of seeing our institutions and to mingle
with society, and with such private hospitality as is
extended to them they will be well satisfied.   Beyond
this, they are capable of taking care of themselves and
of seeking out their own pleasures and amusements,
without the intervention of committees or the guidance
of ' Tom, Dick and Harry.'   Beyond this, it is positively rude, if not exceedingly impertinent, for people

promiscuously to trespass upon either the time or attention of private gentlemen, merely to gratify their vague, if not idle, curiosity."

The editor of the *Public Ledger* also took a whack at that Committee and pitched into them even stronger than his fellow-editor of the *Gazette*, in the following article—

"*Grand Reception of Boz—that Committee and the shaking of hands.*—The United States Hotel was thronged yesterday morning by a crowd of the admirers of Dickens, in consequence of the publication of a notice that he would be happy to meet *that* Committee and perform the agreeable task of shaking them and their friends by the hand, which he had promised to perform in coming to our city. The Committee and 'troops of friends' accordingly made their appearance, and agreeably to democratic usages voted him into the corner of his room, and commenced the delightful ceremony of introducing him to all the Smiths, Browns, Greens and Johnsons present. Boz looked considerably distressed at first, as he had other arrangements which he considered more important, but being assured that such was the custom here, he put the best face upon the matter possible, and suffered his arm to be almost shaken off without a groan. The whole ceremony was managed in a truly *simple*, and consequently republican, way and must have made a deep and lasting impression on Mr. Dickens. We cannot pretend to give a perfect report, nor would we attempt to make a full one, of the sayings and doings in the reception chamber. We shall merely say that the Committee did their utmost to render the affair interesting and imposing, and the friends exerted themselves to an equal extent to 'present' the intelligence of the city in a proper light to Boz.

"As a notice of one introduction will suffice to show what most of them were, we will simply give that. Imagine the illustrious Boz standing in one corner of the room, with a member of the Committee on each side, and a number of distinguished friends near him.

To accommodate all parties, the crowd in the room form an alley way to admit the 'friends' outside; the latter pass in at one door, Indian file, and after stopping to do the shaking, and express their opinion on the state of the weather, pass out in the same order through the other door. Everybody is excited, and some are so agitated as to be scarcely able to inform the introducing member what their names are. This was the case of an individual who bore the name of Brooks. On coming into the room, the introducing member asked the individual his name. 'Brooks,' replied he, in a tremulous whisper. 'Dukes, did you say?' rejoined the first. 'No, Brooks,' repeated the second in still greater agitation. 'Oh, Snooks, is it, very well—Mr. Snooks, Mr. Dickens, Mr. Dickens, Mr. Snooks.' Mr. Brooks gave Boz his hand and looked out of the window. Boz smiled fatiguedly, shook the proffered hand feebly and let it fall, when Mr. Brooks put it in his pocket and walked off as if he had been doing something he would not like to be caught at. The same form was gone through with for an hour or two, when Boz became restive and vowed he would sink under such hospitality unless relieved. One of the Committee then announced that the gentlemen 'with hearts in their hands' had to retire, as Mr. Dickens wanted their *room!* The 'friends' then went down, followed by 'that Committee!'"

Mr. Putnam, in the *Atlantic Monthly* article previously quoted, wrote regarding the unauthorized public reception referred to in the Philadelphia papers—

"A day or two after his arrival in Philadelphia, an individual somewhat prominent in city politics came with others and obtained an introduction. On taking his leave, he asked Mr. Dickens if he would grant him the favour to receive a few personal friends the next day, and Mr. Dickens assented. The next morning it was announced through the papers that Mr. Dickens would 'receive the *public*' at a certain time! At the

UNITED STATES HOTEL, PHILADELPHIA

PENITENTIARY, PHILADELPHIA

time specified the street in front was crowded with people and the offices and halls of the hotel filled. Mr. Dickens asked the cause of the assemblage and was astonished and indignant when he learned that all this came of his permission to the individual above mentioned ' to bring a few personal friends for an introduction,' and he positively refused to hold a ' levee.'   But the landlord of the house and others came and represented to him that his refusal would doubtless cause a riot, and that great injury would be done to the house by the enraged populace; and so at last Mr. Dickens consented, and taking his place in one of the large parlours upstairs, prepared himself for the ordeal.   Up the people came, and soon the humorous smiles played over his face, for, tedious and annoying as it was, the thing had its *comic* side, and while he shook hands incessantly, he as usual studied human character.   For two mortal hours or more the crowd poured in and he shook hands and exchanged words with all, while the dapper little author of the scene stood smiling by, giving hundreds and thousands of introductions, and making, no doubt, much social and political capital out of his supposed intimacy with the great English author.   This scene is substantially repeated in *Martin Chuzzlewit* when his new-made American friends insisted upon Martin's ' holding a levee,' having announced without his authority, as in the case of Mr. Dickens, that he would receive the public."

On Thursday, March 10, the day after Dickens left Philadelphia, the *Pennsylvanian* contained the following notice—

"Mr. Dickens left town yesterday morning for the south. On Tuesday, after having disengaged himself from the unexpected invasion of five or six hundred persons, he visited the Penitentiary; and having passed some time in a minute examination into the system practised there for reforming convicts, he dined with a small party of his Philadelphia friends, devoting the remainder of the evening to the enjoyment of other hospitalities which had been extended to him. It is to be regretted that his visit to Philadelphia has been so very brief, as this city prides herself upon her lions, which might perhaps have been seen quietly, affording an opportunity for pleasant recreation and comparative repose."

On Friday, March 11, the *Philadelphia Gazette* also had the following to say regarding the "lions" of the Capitol—

"Mr. Dickens, we rejoice to hear, has reached Washington in safety. There are too many ' lions ' there to have either one of them incommoded with attention. He left here Tuesday morning, slipped through the fingers of the ready-made Committee at Baltimore, and that evening was quietly and comfortably lodged in the Metropolis. Distinction is sometimes inconvenient, and greatness is often the source of much trouble."

While he was in Philadelphia, some of the "funny men" of the newspapers attempted either to exercise their wit with Dickens's hair as the subject, or else as a rebuke to those who were anxious to obtain one of his wavy locks as a memento. Here are a few of the attempts—

"Dickens is in danger of becoming bald, in consequence of the number of applications for a lock of his invaluable hair. We thought it would come to this."— *Public Ledger*.

"The Dickens he is ! The matter is not so serious, Mr. Ledger, as you seem to imagine, when it is known that there is a ' Balm in Gilead,' by which he can restore his hair to its pristine luxuriance and beauty. Go it, Boz, don't be selfish, give the ladies a lock of your hair, and when it is all gone, rub your bald pate with Balm of Columbia, to be had at 71 Maiden Lane, New York, corner of Third and Race, and Muth and Chestnut Streets, Philadelphia."—*Spirit of the Times*.

"Mr. Dickens narrowly escaped the fate of Samson

the other night at a social party in this city. Groups of the gay and beautiful crowded around him, eyeing his profuse flow of 'soap locks' with a most envious glance, and wishing all the while he could be thrown into a mesmeric sleep, that they could plunder his cranium of its drapery undiscovered. Not being able to furnish these bewitching ones with a lock of his hair, he gave the most of them a bit of sweet poetry, or a sentiment, coupled with his autograph."—*Philadelphia Gazette*.

"*A Shocking Bad Hat*.—It is said at the Boz ball the ladies bribed some of the waiters to bring them Charles Dickens's hat, and that the lovely dears plucked off all the nap, and put it in their bosoms as a memento of the great author. When asked why they did so, they said he would not part with his hair, and they wished something as near it as possible. When Boz saw his hat, he imagined it had the small-pox, by which calamity he accounted for the loss of the nap."—*Public Ledger*.

A certain Philadelphia confectioner, James Parkinson by name, utilized Dickens's visit to create a monumental tribute in sugar to the author, and incidentally to advertise the firm of Parkinson on Chestnut Street, and the *United States Gazette* published the following description of this work of art—

"*A Splendid Ornament*.—We see daily some evidence or other which brings the famous Boz to our mind —something contrived as a tribute to his worth, or as a vehicle to display a portion of those creations which have given to him so great a fame. The latest attraction of this kind is one which has just been completed by Mr. James Parkinson, of the firm of Parkinson, in Chestnut Street, where it is now to be seen. It represents a temple resting on a square rocky base, in each of the four sides of which there is a deep niche. In each of the niches is displayed with admirable truth and effect a tableau from Boz's works. On the top of this base lie imitations of the volumes of Dickens's works, and on them rests the famous clock

M

of Master Humphrey, having on one side of it ' Little Nell ' and on the other ' The Fat Boy.' Both on the front and back, standing on the vase, appear ' Mr. Pickwick ' and ' Samivel,' the figures modelled in sugar with great neatness and truth. Around the edges of the vase are placed twelve columns which support a flat ceiling appropriately ornamented, and from this spring a number of columns bearing aloft a dome of great beauty and lightness in its formation. The tracery of the upper part of the work is very rich, and altogether it wears a *bizarre* and most inviting appearance, showing much ingenuity and labour well applied. It is well worth seeing."

Here is another *bon mot* from the *United States Gazette*—

"*Charles Dickens.*—We are very happy to see him among our *living* authors, although his *Nell* has been heard of all over the country."

Even the poets of the Quaker City invoked their Muses, and the following is an example of the result—

WELCOME TO BOZ

By Mrs. C. H. W. Esling

Welcome, thrice welcome to our shores, thou champion of the poor,
Thou faithful chronicler of woes their weary hearts endure ;
Welcome we give thee with our hearts, our voices, and our hands.
And claim thee as in brotherhood, among our kindred bands.

Thy name is as a household word of most familiar tone,
It seems amid our good, or ill, a something of our own ;
A guide, a beacon from afar, a bright enduring ray
To lead the meagre child of want from vicious paths away.

How oft does pensive OLIVER at Mrs. Maylie's door,
Arise like a reality, our thinking minds before,
And little NELLY trudging on, unmurmuring all the while,
Leading her blind old grandfather for many a lengthy mile.

And poor heart-broken SMIKE, we hear his accents thin and weak,
We mark the tear of sorrow steal adown his hollow cheek ;
We note again his wistful gaze, with anxious watch grow dim,
When sweet home tokens came to all, but NOTHING came to him.

Their figures seem to haunt our walks where'er our footsteps tread,
Though NELLY and the blind old man are number'd with the dead,
And SMIKE, in his own chosen spot, is slumbering in his rest,
With the deep secret of his soul untold within his breast.

Unweariedly we think of them, but oh ! we wish again
To feel our bosom's pulses thrill unto another strain—
Unsatisfied with what we have, although a precious store,
We, like thy favourite OLIVER, still yearning, " ask for more."

U.S. Gazette,
  Tuesday, March 8, 1842.

CHAPTER VIII

WASHINGTON

DICKENS left Philadelphia Wednesday morning, March 9, for Washington. There was no railroad at that time running through from Philadelphia to the capital, and the first part of the journey was by steamboat down the Delaware River to Wilmington. Here the train was taken as far as the Susquehanna River to a point opposite Havre de Grace, Maryland, the river being crossed by a ferry boat, and the journey continued by rail. A stop for dinner was made at Baltimore, and Mr. Putnam relates the following incident which happened there—

"On reaching Baltimore the cars stopped while in the market-place. In a couple of minutes word had passed that 'Dickens was aboard the train.' Instantly the windows were darkened with faces, and all sorts of comments—but mostly kind and respectful—were made upon his looks and general appearance.

"A market woman near by, seeing the crowd, came up close to the windows, but she could not make out what all the excitement was about, and calling to a friend who was standing by, she loudly asked, 'What's the matter? What is it all about? Say, John, what is it?' 'Why,' answered the man, looking over his shoulder, 'they've got Boz here!' 'Got Boz,' said she. 'What's Boz? What do you mean?' 'Why,' said the man, 'it's Dickens. They've got him here!' 'Well, what has he been doing?' said she. 'He ain't been doing nothin',' answered the man; 'he writes books.' 'Oh!' said the woman indignantly. 'Is that all? What they should make such a row about that for, I should like to know?'"

After dinner the journey was continued by railroad, and Washington was reached in the evening. Mr. Putnam writes of the arrival at Washington as follows—

"On arriving at Washington Mr. Dickens went to his quarters at Willard's (Fuller's). But Willard's was not then the splendid hotel it now is. It was a low, two-storey building, with many odd additions which had been put up at intervals, and the rooms were small. But the house was well kept, and every attention was paid the visitors. There was a big triangle placed in the back-yard close to our rooms, and at all hours of the day and night it sent its summons to the servants. It was rather troublesome for a day or two, but we finally got used to it. Mr. Dickens had letters from distinguished English and American friends to all the leading members of Congress and other official dignitaries, and in due time Webster, Calhoun, Bell of Tennessee, and many others called to pay their respects. Among the rest was the Honourable R. C., then member of the Senate, from Massachusetts. I had often heard his splendid pleading at the bar; and after he left, I said to Mr. Dickens, ' That, sir, is one of the most remarkable men in our country.' ' Good God! Mr. P.,' answered he, ' they are all so! I have scarcely met a man since my arrival who wasn't one of the most remarkable men in the country! "

The Washington papers had less to say about Dickens than the Boston, New York and Philadelphia papers, and it will be seen that the further Dickens got away from those three eastern cities, the less attention the newspapers paid to him. On his arrival in Washington, the papers simply announced the fact, and the following from the *Daily National Intelligencer* of March 12 is given as a sample of these notices—

"Mr. Dickens, author of the admirable story of *Oliver Twist* and other of the most popular works of fiction known to the history of English literature, arrived in Washington on Wednesday last, accompanied by his lady, and took lodgings at Fuller's Hotel. These estimable strangers will remain in the city a few days, and then proceed south as far as Charleston."

On Thursday, the 10th, Mr. and Mrs. Dickens visited the Capitol, which event was chronicled in the Washington *Independent* the next day as follows—

"Charles Dickens, Esq., and lady visited the Capitol yesterday. Mrs. Dickens remained during the greater part of the time in the gallery, while the distinguished author was introduced upon the floor of the Chamber. In the House, he was presented to the venerable ex-president, but their brief conversation was interrupted by those who were eager to grasp the hand that has penned so many admirable stories. We have understood that the reporters have it in contemplation to do the honours of Washington, by a dinner to Mr. Dickens. He was formerly, we believe, of their profession. His works show the minuteness of many of his descriptions, that he has taken down human nature in shorthand."

If the intention of the reporters to give a dinner were carried out, there was no account of it in the newspapers. A search of the papers fails to disclose anything as to Dickens on Friday, but in the New York *Evening Post* of March 12 there is the following, telling of his doings on Saturday—

"Mr. Dickens has visited the President and the heads of the departments, and received the calls of a vast number of citizens and strangers at his lodgings. He has visited the Public Office to-day, the Patent Office, the National Institution, the new Post Office, and other public institutions. Monday, he is invited to a private dinner, with about twenty-five gentlemen, embracing some of the members of Congress, gentlemen of the press and several citizens, and from the character of the persons composing the party, there is no doubt it will be a ' feast of reason and a flow of soul.' Every person who becomes acquainted with him and his lady are pleased with them, and, we are happy to say, the people are not disposed to make fools of themselves, nor to inflict pain upon this intelligent and worthy stranger by any ostentatious parade."

On Sunday Dickens accepted two invitations to dinner, one at Mr. John Quincy Adams's and the other at Mr. Robert Greenhow's. No newspaper accounts of these two affairs have been discovered, but Mr. Philip Hone, who was at the Adams dinner, makes the following reference to it in his diary, and also of the levée at the President's house on Tuesday the 15th—

"*Washington, March* 15.—Dickens and his wife are here. There has not been much fuss made about him. They laugh at us in New York for doing too much, and have gone upon the other extreme. He has been invited to dine by several gentlemen to whom he brought letters. Amongst the rest, Mr. Adams invited him and his wife to dinner on Sunday at half-past two o'clock. (This early hour was fixed, I suppose, to keep up the primitive beauty of New England Republican habits.) Some clever people were invited to meet them. They came, he in a frock-coat, and she in her bonnet. They sat at table until four o'clock, when he said, ' Dear, it is time for us to go home and dress for dinner.' They were engaged to dine with Robert Greenhow, at the fashionable hour of half-past five! A most particularly funny idea, to leave the table of John Quincy Adams to dress for a dinner at Robert Greenhow's!

"This has been a day of great business. After our dinner party broke up, we went to the President's levée—the last of the season, and the crowd was great. The east room, which is one of the most splendid I ever saw, was a complete jam; but considering the facility of access, the sort of people who do the honours and those who receive them, the company was highly respectable! The first people in the land were there, and the women were well dressed. I noticed no gaucheries, no vulgarity, and I doubt if any society in any country, so organized, could have turned out so decorous and respectable an assemblage.

"Dickens was at the levée, and Washington Irving, and, so far as I could judge, Irving out-bozzed ' Boz,'

He collected a crowd around him; the men pressed on to take his hand, and the women to touch the hem of his garment. Somebody told me that he saw a woman put on his hat, in order, as she told her companions, that she might say she had worn Washington Irving's hat. All this was 'fun to them,' as the frogs said, but 'death' to poor Irving, who has no relish for that sort of glorification, and has less tact than any man living, to get along with it decently."

The Washington correspondent of the Baltimore *Patriot* wrote regarding the levée—

"The Dickens party left last night for the South. He was at the President's levée on Tuesday, and, while there, the greatest lion at the White House. The crowd oppressed him with kindness and thronged him wherever he moved. There was amusement and incident enough for a book, and if Boz does not make one of it, it will not be for want of a good opportunity to do so."

On Monday was given the private dinner referred to above, and no newspaper account of it can be found. Fortunately one of the guests who attended the dinner kept a diary in which he recorded an account of it, which appears in McKenzie's *Life of Charles Dickens*, published in 1870, and from which the following is taken—

"In Washington every attention was paid to Mr. Dickens. The Hon. B. B. French, who resided in that city at the time, kept a careful diary of events, a copy of which has been kindly lent me by H. M. Keim, Esq., of Reading. From this I learn that on March 10, 1842, Mr. Dickens visited the House of Representatives, with Mr. N. P. Tallmadge of the Senate. Two days later, he 'was in the house' nearly through its session. He was invited to a seat within the bar by some member, and occupied the selfsame chair in which Lord Morpeth sat nearly every day while he was in the city. In the following month (14th) he was entertained with dinner at Boulanger's; Hon. John Quincy Adams and General Van Ness were invited guests. Hon. George M. Keim was president, in the room of the Hon. John Taliaferro,

WASHINGTON FROM THE PRESIDENT'S HOUSE

THE PRESIDENT'S HOUSE FROM THE RIVER

who was expected to preside, but was unavoidably absent
from Washington, and Hon. M. St. Clair Clarke and
Hon. Aaron Ward were vice-presidents. The following
persons made the party : Mr. Dickens, Mr. Adams, and
General Van Ness as guests; General Keim, Mr. M.
St. Clair Clarke, General Ward, Messrs. Sumpter,
Roosevelt, Irwin, Cushing and Holmes of the House of
Representatives; and Messrs. Kingman, F. W. Thomas
(the author), Bache, Rice, John Tyler Jr., J. Howard
Payne, Frailey, Keller, Dimitry, Major Harrison,
Messrs. Samuel P. Walker, Robert N. Johnston, Sutton,
H. G. Wheeler, Riggs and B. B. French.

"Wit, sentiment, song-singing, story-telling and
speech-making occupied the time till eleven, when Mr.
Dickens arose and, in the most feelingly beautiful
manner possible, bade us good-night. The diarist
warmly eulogized the guest, saying, ' Dickens, by his
modesty, his social powers and his eloquence, has added
to the high esteem in which I was previously induced
to hold him. I believe every person present was delighted.' Mr. Keim proposed Mr. Dickens's health in
the following exalted terms : ' Philanthropy and Genius,
and a representative of both, now our guest in Washington, whom Washington himself would have rejoiced to
welcome.' Dickens, in reply, said, ' That if this were
a public dinner he supposed he would be expected to
make a speech; as it was but a social party, surely no
such effort would be expected of him; and when he
looked about the table and saw gentlemen whose positions in public life rendered it unavoidable that they
should either speak themselves or listen to the speeches
of others every day, his refraining upon this occasion
must be far more acceptable, and surely possess more
novelty than any remarks he might make—and he must
be allowed to presume that here, in the enjoyment of
the social hour, they will be happy to give their ears
some rest, and he should, therefore, consider himself
relieved from making a speech. He would, however,
say that, like the Prince in the Arabian Tales, he had
been doomed, since he arrived in this hospitable country,
to make new friendships every night, and cut their heads

off on the following morning. But the recollection of this night, wherever he might go, should accompany him, and, like the bright smiles of his better angel, be treasured in his mind as long as memory remains.'

"Among the subsequent toasts were ' The Health of John Quincy Adams,' ' The City of Boston ' and ' The Old Curiosity Shop '—among whose notions were the oldest wine, the newest wit, and the best cradle in the United States. After the evidence our guest had of the goodness of the former, we hope and trust they will give him the benefit of the latter.' After ' The Queen of Great Britain ' had been drunk standing, Mr. Dickens said : ' Allow me to assume the character of Mr. Pickwick, and in that character to give you ' The President of the United States,' which was also drunk standing. By this time the company had apparently reached a period of very pleasurable enjoyment, for after Mr. Caleb Cushing had responded to ' Our Country and our Guest —both in the first vigour of their youth, and both made great by the might of mind,' he proposed ' The Health of Mr. Pickwick.' At eleven o'clock Mr. Dickens arose and said, ' I rise to propose to you one more sentiment ; it must be my last ; it consists of two words—"Good Night." Since I have been seated at this table I have received the welcome intelligence that the news from the dear ones has come at last—that the long-expected letters have arrived. Among them are certain scrawls from little beings across the ocean, of great interest to me, and I thought of them for many days past in connection with drowned men and a noble ship, broken up and lying in fragments upon the bottom of the ocean. But they are here, and you will appreciate the anxiety I feel to read them. Permit me, in allusion to some remarks made by a gentleman near me, to say that every effort of my pen has been intended to elevate the masses of society, to give them the station they deserve among mankind. With that intention I commenced writing, and I assure you as long as I write at all, that shall be the principal motive of my efforts. Gentlemen, since I arrived on your hospitable shore, and in my flight over your land, you have given me everything I can ask

but time—that you cannot give me, and you are aware
that I must devote some of it to myself; therefore, with
the assurance that this has been the most pleasant evening I have passed in the United States, I must bid you
farewell, and once more repeat the words good night!'
"The guest was not to be let off without a parting
bumper, on Sheridan's plan—

'Let the toast pass,
Drink to the lass,
I'll warrant 'twill prove an excuse for a glass.'

For Mr. St. Clair Clarke proposed 'Mrs. Dickens: May
her stay amongst us be pleasant; may her return voyage
be comfortable, and, when she reaches home, may she
find her little ones as healthy as they surely will be
happy.'"

None of the Washington newspapers contained any
account of Dickens's reception at the President's levée
on Tuesday the 15th, but a correspondent of the New
York *Express* thus refers to some of the incidents
connected with it—

"'The last levée of the season, held by President
Tyler, was on the evening of Tuesday, the 15th instant.
"'The City and District seemed to have turned out
en masse at this last gathering of the People at the President's house. They came literally in clouds and in all
the various forms and shapes of the seven classes, now
dancing in like a lock of hair, or a feather, as a cirrus
cloud, worn like the cumulus in conical round heaps,
and now like the seventh class spreading out and running down. There were children in their nurses' arms,
and overgrown and over-aged children, a good many
years beyond second childhood. They run from the knee-
heigh to a grass-hopper of early infancy, to long Jim
Wilson of the Granite Hills that was, and the Surveyor-
General of Iowa that is. It was in the way of ascent and
descent of persons you might count somewhere from
seven inches to six feet seven inches, more or less.

"'And then for dressing! Goddess of fashion, what a figure do some of your votaries cut? An old woman just three steps from the grave, decked out in all the finery and gewgaw of her granddaughter. A grandmother with nineteen children (the grandchildren included) carrying as much sail as might interpret the feminine gender of a ship at sea—with quite *tourneau* enough to make ballast for a ship of almost any size, from a shallop to a seventy-four. Have you not heard of a man mad enough to curse his grandmother?

"'Such an unfilial act must have been where a very sensible grandmother, in some strange freak or other, metamorphosed herself from a sensible woman into a fool. Fools or not, there was much foolish dressing among the crowd, and not altogether confined to the old women. There was no lack of cast, colour or shape.

> "Black spirits and white,
>   Red spirits and gray,"

mingled in strange and odd confusion, everything in a word among the men, from muddy boots, holey coats and unshaven faces, to that pink of society, propriety, and sometimes foppishness seen in your kid gloves, oily hair and scented pocket-handkerchief. And then for the women, Heaven bless them all, they came sometimes like the graces, clothed in fleecy clouds and gauze veils, too spiritual, it seemed, to be touched, and sometimes, again, like so many patterns fresh from the quay of the street; some were bonneted, booted and spurred, it seemed, and some, again, like the witches of *Macbeth*—

> "Eye of newt, and toe of frog,
>   Wool of bat, and tongue of dog,
>   Adder's fork and blind-worm's sting,
>   Lizard's leg, and owlet's wing."

"'The greatest lion among the men was Boz, the never-ending Boz. He made his appearance between nine and ten, and the fifteen hundred or two thousand people present went in pursuit of him like hounds, horses and riders in pursuit of a fox in the chase. It

JOHN TYLER
President of the United States, 1842

was in this trying time that brawny arms, robustious waists and good understandings accomplished valorous feats. Alas for the weak, the modest and timid! Alas, too, for laces and silks, head-dresses, satin shoes, jewellery and alabaster necks. The pillory or the stocks would have been a heaven upon earth. "Where is Boz?" says one. "Where?" "There!" and a sea of heads appearing like the waves dancing in the river at the incoming of the tide are seen, staring poor Boz out of countenance. He is encompassed and as immovable as the men, and the crowd in sort of a funeral march revolve around him, reflecting some of the brightness in a smile or a word of their adored author. The Peruvians never worshipped the bright "god of day" with more fervour than the people did this bright emanation of that genius and truth which, after all, is from above, and for the possession of which so much more is due to the Creator than the creature; one could not but pity Boz with a full heart. There he stood like patience on a monument, and literally "smiling at grief."

"' Almost every countenance was a rueful one, because in the general press almost every one was kept in a most inconvenient and respectful distance. The people gazed, stared, opened their mouths, stretched their necks until the cords of their necks cracked and the limbs were extended to their utmost tension. This fever was kept up for some thirty or forty minutes, until Boz turned upon his heels to get rid of his two thousand good-natured American friends who had taken the President's house by storm. And there was no peace. Wherever he moved, it was like throwing corn among hungry chickens. They flocked around him here until he took leave of the President. He was then pursued to the dressing-room, and finally to his carriage, and probably to his house and chamber. In the general admiration, too, it is presumed that he found some dozen or two under his bed, in his bedroom closet, and perhaps, unconsciously, a bed-fellow with him. Well, "Hurrah for Boz," and "Hurrah for the Americans."

"' They who have seen him, of course, never will be smitten with blindness—and if any of the thousands who have run and jumped, screamed and halloed to see Boz should find themselves in print after the fashion and skill of Squeers and Squeers's accomplished school and family, for example, why, they must not complain.

"'"Madame Boz" was the next of the lions most gazed at in the general menagerie. An honourable M.C. played the agreeable, and the crowd spared the better half to gaze upon the great lion.

"' Washington Irving, the new Minister to Spain, who is here to receive his instructions, was turned upon next. The poor man placed himself somewhere in the East room, and the multitude came upon him like the billows of the ocean; first a crowd of women and then a crowd of men, some eager to take the author of The Broken Heart by the hand, and others content with a good stare, either with the naked eye or by the agency of a quizzing-glass. The squeeze around Mr. Irving for a half-hour was tremendous, and the people, having satisfied themselves here, turned their attention to new objects.

"' The President's Cabinet, Foreign Ministers, some of the tarrying judges of the Supreme Court, a sprinkling of Senators, two or three scores of representatives, fifteen hundred men, women and children, in every costume, and from every nook and corner of the country, made up the remainder of the medley. It was one to please everybody who could be pleased with a sight of the world at a focus. You might see it face to face, or at least through a glass darkly, and to add interest to the general variety, there was the Marine Band discoursing sweet music for the evening. The President, who keeps an open heart as well as an open house, found himself upon this occasion surrounded by troops of friends; but, after all, one could realize, in the labour and honour of office, the truth of the maxim—

"Untried, how sweet a court attendance :
When tried, how dreadful the dependence."'"

Dickens left Washington for Richmond on Wednesday, March 16, and on Friday, the 18th, the Daily National Intelligencer of Washington contained the following reference to his departure—

"Mr. and Mrs. Dickens left the city on Wednesday evening for Richmond, in continuation of their tour through a portion of the Union. They proceed from Richmond to Norfolk, thence up the Chesapeake Bay to Baltimore, whence they proceed by the Pennsylvania route to Pittsburgh and the Western States. During their short stay with us these interesting strangers have conciliated the warmest personal esteem by their frank and amiable deportment and the cordiality with which they received and appreciated the respectful attentions so extensively shown them by the inhabitants, resident and transient, of this city. We are requested by a friend to state that it was a source of much regret to them that their brief sojourn placed it out of their power to manifest their sense of these civilities, at least so far as returning the very numerous calls which they received during the few days they spent here. We are also requested to state that, as the arrangements of Mr. D. for his departure on Wednesday evening would have prevented his attending the theatre, the annunciation that he would do so was made without his authority."

The Editor of the *Intelligencer* was Mr. W. W. Seaton, and the latter part of this notice was written by reason of a request made by Mr. Dickens to Mr. Seaton in the following letter—

Washington, March 16, 1842.

MY DEAR SIR,

I am truly obliged to you for your kind note. I am so constantly engaged, however, that I think I *must* deny myself the pleasure of making an appointment with you, which I could scarcely keep without making a most uncomfortable scramble of it. I will report my knowledge of the lions to you, and you shall judge how I have been show-done.

In case I should forget it when we meet to-night, may I venture to ask two favours of you—or rather one favour with two heads?

It is that you will kindly (if you see no objection) let

my friends here know through the channel which is open to you, and over which you so ably preside, that whenever I make an appointment I keep it; and that it gives me great uneasiness to be placarded all over the town as intending to make a visit to the theatre, when I have given no authority to any person to publish such an announcement; and secondly, that, travelling as we do, we can never return the calls of our friends, in consequence of their immense number, and our very limited stay in any one place.

Let me take this opportunity of thanking you for the exceedingly kind attention I have received at your hands, and the pleasure I have enjoyed in your society and in that of your family. I need scarcely say that Mrs. Dickens desires me to say as much for her.

I am, my dear sir, with true regards,
Faithfully yours,
CHARLES DICKENS.

Mr. W. W. Seaton.

CHAPTER IX

RICHMOND, BALTIMORE AND HARRISBURG

DICKENS left Washington on Thursday, March 16, at four o'clock in the morning, having gone aboard the steamer the night before. He arrived at Richmond in the evening. He has given in *American Notes* a full account of the journey, but in the following, Mr. Putnam relates some instances that Dickens does not mention—

"Leaving Washington, Mr. Dickens took the steamer down the Potomac to Potomac Creek. He rose early in the morning to get a glimpse of Mount Vernon, for he cherished a profound respect for the great man who lies buried there. On arriving at Potomac Creek we found stages to take us to Fredericksburg, Virginia, and as usual Mr. Dickens secured his favourite seat on the box beside the driver. This ride and the negro drivers of the seven coaches is most graphically described in his *Notes*. The roads were bad past all description, and seemed to be impassable, but the negro drivers possessed great skill and drove through without accident.

"At Fredericksburg we took the cars for Richmond. After travelling a while we came to a very lonely and dismal-looking country. We passed plantations long ago deserted, the houses and barns rotting down, and the ground as barren of soil as a New England street. A gentleman told me that the vast pine barrens, stretching miles away, through which we were occasionally passing, were, years ago, the same as these barren fields, for only pines of the most meagre growth could grow on this slavery-cursed soil. I called the attention of Mr. Dickens to the sterility and ruin all around us, and he seemed astounded at the fact that the land was once fertile,

and the very 'garden of America'! Turning to his
wife, he exclaimed, 'Great God! Kate, just hear what
Mr. P. says! These lands were once cultivated, and
have been abandoned because worn out by slave labour!'
At sight of this widespread desolation his already deep
detestation of slavery became intensified.

"An incident upon the road added, if possible, to this
feeling. Stopping at a lonely station in the forest for
food and water, we noticed a coloured woman with
several small children standing by, who seemed to be
waiting for passage. After a little time we heard the
woman and children weeping, and some one in the car
asked the cause. A bluff, well-dressed man near us
answered: 'It's them d——d niggers; somebody has
bought them and is taking them down to Richmond, and
they are making a fuss about it.'

"Dickens heard the answer, and what impression this
separation of families made upon the mind of one who
loved so well the freedom and happiness of all human
beings may be imagined.

"At Richmond Mr. Dickens took rooms at the 'Exchange.' Here, as elsewhere, large numbers of the most
prominent people called upon him, and a dinner was
given in his honour. Here, too, he visited the tobacco
factories, and saw 'the happy slaves singing at their
work.' But it was a useless task to attempt to blind the
eyes or corrupt the heart of this friend of humanity. All
that was praiseworthy in our people and their institutions
he praised without stint; but he would not endorse any
wrong, especially that of slavery."

The morning after his arrival the Richmond *Enquirer*
contained the following mention of his arrival—

"*Mr. Dickens at Richmond.*—Mr. Charles Dickens
and lady reached Richmond Thursday evening on the
cars from Washington, and will remain with us till
Sunday morning, when he is compelled to return to
Baltimore. Thence he will go to Pittsburgh and the
north-western section of the United States. He has not
time to visit Charleston at the farther south. He will
return to England early in June after visiting the Cataract

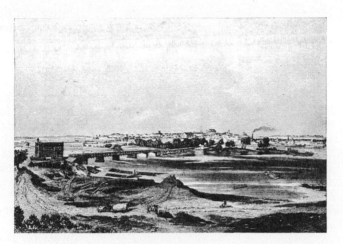

RICHMOND, VA.

EXCHANGE HOTEL, RICHMOND, VA.

178

of Niagara, Canada, etc. Some of his friends met him last night at a *petite* supper, got up by our friend Boyden of the ' Exchange.' "

The supper at the ' Exchange ' seemed to have caused some dissatisfaction amongst those who were not fortunate enough to be bidden to the feast, and the dissatisfaction was voiced through the Richmond *Star*, for on March 22 the *Enquirer* contained the following article explaining how the affair came to be arranged—

"The *Star* of yesterday morning, speaking of the Boz *Petite Souper*, says that ' a subscription was soon circulated among a select few, who, for some reason unknown to us, thus assumed the honour of representing the citizens of Richmond.' We hasten to correct this impression, as we do not wish the slightest trace of ill-feeling to be left from C. Dickens's visit to this city. The fact was that the gentleman who first waited upon him had been some time before selected by a meeting of their fellow-citizens to correspond with him and invite him to a public dinner. He had refused the dinner, and he now wished also to decline a supper, until he was told, as the *Star* states, that ' there were several gentlemen of Richmond who would be proud—happy was the word— to meet him at a social supper that evening.' When he had thus accepted, there was scarcely time to get up a supper (and no one but ' Mine Host of the Exchange ' could have done it in such quick time) and to bid in the guests.

"The subscription was not confined ' to a select few,' for it was intended and desired that all who pleased should participate in its pleasures. Scarcely any other magician than Boz (whose readers are found everywhere) could get together so many guests in so short a time."

The same issue of the *Enquirer* contained another article in which the writer expresses his opinion on Dickens's personality, and also a brief account of the supper, with a promise of a further account on Thursday—

"Mr. Charles Dickens left us on Sunday morning, with his lady, who received many visits from the ladies

N 2

of this city on Saturday. He had made an engagement
to be in Baltimore yesterday. Thence, he proceeds to
Pittsburgh, to Cincinnati, and down the Ohio to St.
Louis. He will return by the Lakes, and expects to
devote a week to the Cataract of Niagara. As the correspondent of the *New York Herald* says, ' he will then
visit the Canadas, and return to New York, whence he
will sail on June 7, to return to ' merrie England,'
and publish the first number of his new work on the 1st
of November. Wherever he travels, he multiplies by
masses the host of his personal friends, where before he
was cherished fondly for the pure fictions of his mind's
creation alone."

Mr. Dickens's visit to this city has produced precisely
that impression. He is very young for the great fame
which he has already won—only thirty years and six
weeks old—is a man of decided and varied talents—full
of wit and humour, with much good sense and much
practical knowledge of the world, with manners of the
most cordial sort; his heart in his hand. We have no
doubt his visit was as agreeable to himself as it was to
the citizens of Richmond. The supper Friday night was
unique. In eight hours' time, about one hundred gentlemen came together to pay their tribute to Dickens.
There was no labour of preparation in getting up the
Attic feast. The impulse of their feelings superseded
any such necessity. Many of the members of the Legislature co-operated with the citizens of the town, and contributed to the wit and joy of the evening. Boz was in
his happiest humour. But this fairy scene has vanished
like a dream, leaving behind it traces of light and ' pleasures of memory that can never fade away. The rose
has crumbled to pieces, but the perfume of the scattered
leaves still remains.' We have no room for further particulars to-day. We may be indebted to a friend who
took some notes of the first two speeches for a communication, embracing some short sketches of the brilliant scene. We may give this rapid delineation on
Thursday; but as all the toasts, speeches, etc., were
entirely improvisatore, we shall lose many good things,

unless the gentlemen who gave the toasts, etc., will be kind enough to put them on paper, and leave them with us for the use of our correspondent. We shall publish what we can save from the wreck of the evening. "

On Thursday the *Enquirer* published the further account of the supper which is given below in full. It contains a speech by Dickens which is not included in the published volume of his speeches. It will be seen that Mr. Ritchie, who presided at the supper, took much pride in the fact that their reception of the guest was on a more simple scale than those given in Boston and New York.

."CHARLES DICKENS

"The citizens of Richmond well recollect the sensation which was produced among them by the arrival of Charles Dickens on Thursday last. Every one seemed disposed to greet him with that cordiality which is so justly the pride of Virginians. It was well known, however, that he had declined receiving any more public manifestations of welcome during his sojourn in this country. On Friday, several of our citizens called on him to tender the hospitalities of the place to himself and lady. Among them were gentlemen who had been appointed by a prior meeting of the citizens to invite him to a public dinner, which he had declined in a correspondence already laid before the public. They now express to him the gratification which they would receive by meeting him at some festive entertainment, and he finally agreed to meet a few of his friends at a social supper that night at the Exchange Hotel, which was his headquarters during his sojourn in Richmond. Boyden was then placed in requisition and put his trumps to get up an entertainment which was worthy the man and the occasion. The appointed hour soon arrived (for it was past midday when the *petite souper* was first suggested), and about ninety gentlemen assembled to meet their guest.

"An hour or more was spent in conversation with each other and with Mr. Dickens, whose manners were open and frank, and whose kind-hearted simplicity won for him the favour of all with whom he conversed. The company proceeded from the drawing-room to the supper-room, and then partook of the elegant and *recherché* entertainment which had been prepared for them. Mr. Thomas Ritchie presided, assisted by Mr. James Lyons, General Pogram, Messrs. Faulkner and Carter and Preston (of the Senate of Virginia), as Vice-Presidents of the evening. The table was laid out with one broad stem, running across the room, from which diverged three parallel tables. The President occupied the middle of the cross-table, with Mr. Dickens to his right hand, and Acting-Governor Rutherford to his left, Vice-President Lyons facing him at the extreme end of the centre table, and the other Vice-Presidents at the heads of their respective departments.

"After the viands and substantials had been pretty well cleared off, the President of the night called upon the company to charge their glasses. He had a sentiment to offer them. He thanked the company for the honour they had done him by calling him to preside at such an entertainment, but never was a man put at the head of a firm with less corporate stock-in-trade than he was. No plan, no organization, not a regular toast prepared, not a set speech cut and dry. But he found some consolation in the capacities of the individual partners of the firm. When he looked around him, when he saw the hearts and heads of those who compose the association, he had no fear about all of the drafts he should draw upon them being duly honoured. He would, therefore, give his own sentiment, and put the ball in motion. Let it roll on, and let the good things go around the table. In this way we might crown our flowing cups with flowers, and the circling hours might glide on, gladdening and rejoicing, until after midnight.

"Never, indeed, had there been so little labour and so little preparation made in getting up an entertainment. It was scarcely six hours since the note was sounded in our streets that Dickens was to be at home to-night—scarcely six hours since the Fiery Cross was passed from hand to hand. But no labour was necessary to carry out the good work. The impulse of our feelings had superseded all such necessity, and the name of the magician who had brought us together had done the rest. And now behold the effect! Let this respectable company, brought together in so brief a space of time, speak the high compliment which could be paid to Mr. Dickens. Scarcely had that Fiery Cross been put in motion, when the clans of Roderick Dhu rush in such goodly numbers to the field, not to meet an enemy, but to meet a friend.

"We did not come here to welcome our guest after the fashion of our Northern brethren. We had no elaborate magnificence, no *éclat*, no elegant tableau to greet him, as those with which Boston and New York had received him. We bring around him no boast of literary circle. We have no Washington Irving to grace the chair; we have no Bryant present to celebrate his praises in rapturous strain. The literature of the Old Dominion was generally of another character, with some brilliant literary exceptions. Her forte was to be found in the masculine production of her statesmen, her Washington, her Jefferson, and her Madison, who had never indulged in works of imagination, in the charms of romance, and in the mere beauties of the *belles lettres*. ' But,' continued the President, ' we have something else to offer to our guest. We may vie even with Boston and New York in the warmth of our welcome. The sons of the sunny South have warm hearts and a cordial reception to give the man whom they admire, and who is there more entitled to our thanks for his literary labours than Charles Dickens? Has he not run up a debt with us all, and which we are all anxious to pay? Is there one among you whose saddest hours have not been soothed by the productions of his pencil? Is there one amongst you whose lightest hours have not still been more lightened by the emanations of his genius? Is there a man here to-night whose sensibilities have not been melted into tears by the pathos of the *Curiosity Shop*? or who has not been excited into laughter by the humours of the *Pickwick Club*? The works of Boz are our constant companions. We take him to our sick bed to cheer us; to our most private hours

to amuse and comfort us. But,' said the President,
' there is one charm in the writings of our guest to which
I delight to do justice. Mr. Dickens has passed over
the great, the glaring, the magnificent, in order to bring
out humble worth and unpretending merit. He has
sought the violet in its lowly bed, to give its perfume
to the light of day. He is no Troubadour, to sing
the warlike achievements of Knights; no Poet Laureate,
to celebrate the praises of Kings, Princes and the titled
great. His excursive imagination had wandered over
the whole surface of human nature, and instead of invest-
ing wealth or power with additional attractions, it had
seized upon the humble points in the human landscape,
had lighted them up with all the fire of his genius, and
given them that conspicuous position to which they were
entitled. He had caused us to feel for the humblest not
less than for the highest, and all to feel for all—for the
youthful tenant of the workhouse and for the poor and
pious Nell—that enchanting picture, or whose delicate
touches we are so indebted to the imagination of the
writer. This is one of the charms of his productions,
that it creates in us all a sympathy for each other—a
participation in the interests of our common humanity,
which constitutes the great bond of equality, and the
best basis for a free form of government. It is impossible for us not to feel respect for such a man, and not
to welcome him in the bosom of our society. Let us not
forget, too, how much we are deeply indebted to that
"miraculous organ" the Press for the communication of
these pleasures. No sooner is thought conceived and
transferred to Mr. Dickens's paper from his brain, in his
solitary chamber in distant England, than it is trans-
mitted by the Press, across the broad Atlantic, with the
rapidity of electricity.

   "' It was the Press which made us first acquainted with
Mr. Dickens. And now we have him in our midst
shall we not welcome him—tender him the hospitalities of the Old Dominion, and give him a cordial reception in this city? But will Mr. D. excuse me for
turning my address for a moment to a graver theme? I
am an older soldier,' said the President, ' than he is,

certainly not a better. And it is one of the maxims I have gathered from my own experience, one of the wisest, though paradoxical, lessons which should be learned both by men and by states, that it is infinitely harder to bear prosperity than adversity. I will not go into its philosophy, nor into the thousands of illustrations of which it is susceptible. It was the neglect of this principle which had prostrated the first genius of the age, Bonaparte, who had never found the word "impossibility" written in his dictionary, but who had his head so much turned by his successes that he braved the rigours of a Russian climate, and then perished, a victim of his folly, on the rock of St. Helena. The Romans were so sensible of this truth that, in the midst of their triumphant processions, they stationed in the car of the conqueror a monitor, whose business it was to remind him of the vanity of life and the mutability of all human fortunes. Nothing is better calculated to affect us than the early possession of the most brilliant fame. I beg my friend, therefore,' said the President, 'to excuse this digression, and to recollect that, though he has already done much, it is no reason why he should not do a great deal more for us. Young as you are, you have won a proud distinction in the Temple of Fame. I pray you not to let your success turn your head or paralyse your pen. But enough! It is my duty as well as my pleasure now to greet you as you deserve, and may I not (*addressing the company*) in your name and with all your hearts, extend to him the right hand of fellowship (*grasping his hand*)? (Cheers.) And now,' said the President, ' I propose the following sentiment—

"' *Charles Dickens, the Literary Guest of the Nation:* We welcome him to the hearths and hearts of the Old Dominion.'

"After the cheering which followed the annunciation of the President's toast had subsided, Mr. Dickens arose, and was greeted with renewed tokens of applause and welcome.

"He said: ' Mr. President and Gentlemen, I am most

truly grateful and obliged to you for the kind welcome which you have given me. I receive and acknowledge with gratitude this testimonial of your kindly feelings towards me. If it were possible to convey to you my sense and appreciation of your favours, I would indeed acknowledge as I receive your good wishes an hundred-fold. But, as I said at a social party a few nights since at Washington—a party somewhat similar to this—it is my misfortune to be passing through this country with almost as rapid a flight as that of any bird of the air—the American eagle excepted. (Cheers.) I find, in my career amongst you, no little resemblance to that far-famed Sultan of the thousand-and-one nights, who was in the habit of acquiring a new friend every night and cutting his head off in the morning. I find another resemblance to what we read in the history of that Sultan. He was diverted from his bad habit by listening to the tales of one who proved a favourite above all the rest, so I am stopped in my original intention by the hospitalities of the Americans. (Cheers.)

"' I say that the best flag of truce between two nations having the same common origin and speaking the same language is a fair sheet of white paper inscribed with the literature of each. (Cheers.) If, hereafter, I think of this night, if I remember the welcome which you have assured me, believe me, my small corner, my humble portion of that fair sheet shall be inscribed with the hos-pitalities I have received of the friends I have seen and made here. (Cheers.) It has been said, gentlemen, that an after-dinner speech may be too long. (Laughter.) If so, it may be said, with more truth, that an after-supper speech cannot be too short—(laughter)—and especially to those with whom to listen to a speech is no novelty—(laughter)—and among whom a man of few words is a rare and almost "literary phenomenon." (Great laughter and cheering.) I therefore deem it only necessary to say to you that I am almost deeply and sincerely obliged to you for your kindness. (Cries of "Go on.")

"' In reference to the admonition tendered to me by my worthy friend, your President, I will say that it has long been a thing near my heart. But I hope that I shall never need the monitor of which he reminds us. My situation forbids all paralysis of my pen—as I hope you will discover from November next, when I shall resume my literary labours. The hospitalities of America can never be forgotten among them. Your kindness, certainly, never.

"'Imagine me thinking of you to-morrow; imagine me on the railroad to Fredericksburg—on that *Virginia road* from Fredericksburg to the Potomac.' (Here the laughter and cheering was overpowering. The President exclaimed, 'No more of that, Hal, an you love me.') 'In fact, throughout all my travels in these parts I shall think of the pleasure I have enjoyed in the bosom of your society.' (Great cheering.)

"In answer to the call upon him, Mr. Lyons (First Vice-President) said that he rose with reluctance to utter a single word after the excellent addresses which had just been delivered by our distinguished guest and the venerable President of this meeting. But participating deeply, as Mr. L. did, in the general feeling of gratification experienced by all here at the presence among us of one who, distinguished as he was when he touched our shores, had added a new claim to our respect and admiration by the modesty with which he wore his honours, his gentlemanly demeanour and social temper, he could not refrain from expressing that feeling. He hoped to be pardoned for adding that he differed from the President in one sentiment uttered by him in his address, and he felt that he did not disparage that address when he said there was one sentiment in it from which he dissented. The President had said we could not vie with our Northern brethren in the offering which we could make to our guest—that we had not the large room, the splendid edifices and public shows, to exhibit, which they had, *nor* had we the means of gorgeous entertainment or literary treasures which they have. But we offer to our guest the highest tribute—it is no tribute to rank or title—to place or wealth—but the free homage which hearts that never bent to power pay to genius; and we offer him what we in Virginia, at least, regard as equal to any other offering to a friend—a hearty Virginian welcome. Having said thus much, Mr. Lyons would, in the spirit of the address (from Mr. Dickens) to which he listened with so much pleasure, conclude by offering—

"'*England and America, bound together by kindred ties:* May all their controversies be conducted in the true "Pickwickian" spirit.' (Laughter and cheers.)

"General Pogram (being called on by the Chair) gave a toast, with the usual happy vein of his remarks. But, unfortunately, the General is now absent, and neither the toast nor the speech can be given in detail. The President having called upon Mr. Faulkner, Third Vice-President, for a toast and a speech, Mr. Faulkner said he would discharge the duty which devolved upon his end of the table by complying with the call so far as to give an unpremeditated sentiment; a speech he must decline. He came there to give himself up to the full enjoyment of the evening—to see, to hear, to catch the accents of that youthful genius whose fame already fills the world. The bare idea of making a speech would drive back the genial current of his feelings to their fountain cells. It would make him think of the Senate Chamber or the bar and bring up reflections which it was his purpose to bury for a few brief hours. He could not, besides, so soon forget the admonition which our honoured guest had just given us upon the subject of 'after supper' speeches. The sentiment which had occurred to him was one suggested by the position which the worthy President himself held, and by the inimitable life and spirit with which he discharged the duties of the Chair to the honoured individual on his right—

"'*Our distinguished Guest:* His reception in this country shows that there is at least one kind of aristocracy to which the sternest Republicans are proud to pay the homage of their hearts—the aristocracy of genius and worth.'

"Mr. Vice-President Carter being called on by the Chair, gave the following toast—

"' *England and America—the parent and child—the home of* DICKENS *and* IRVING : May their future contests be in literature and not in arms.'

"Mr. Vice-President Preston, being called on by the Chair, gave the following toast—

"' *The knowledge of mankind—of the springs of human action, and the power to portray them, proclaims their possessor a nobleman everywhere.*'

"The ball was now fairly set in motion, and sentiment followed sentiment, or, as the President said, ' The good things went around.' Scarcely a character among those depicted by ' Boz ' was left unnoticed, from old Mr. Pickwick down to Little Nell. Presently one of the company arose and proposed the health of that part of Mr. D.'s family who were on the other side of the Atlantic. He proposed the *three* young ones who bore the name of our guest. In this he was corrected : ' *Four*,' said a near neighbour. An amusing dispute arose as to whether there were three or four. This was, however, decided by an official annunciation from the Chair that there were *four*. Accordingly, the company most cordially drank the health and prosperity of the four little Dickenses over the water.

"The passes of wit and sentiment between Boz and all who sat within conversational distance from him were frequent throughout the evening. The company were all previously assured of the power of pleasing possessed by their guest through the pen ; but they did not know, until this occasion, that he could be so happy in the use of the living faculty of speech. The sallies between himself and the President were constant and amusing. In one instance, when the latter complimented a character in the *Curiosity Shop*, Mr. D. retorted by denominating him a living ' curiosity.' In a few remarks addressed to the whole audience, he spoke with enthusiasm and delight, and with many humorous strokes, of his having met with a man who had gone through so many labours and yet preserved such a green heart, with all the freshness and sprightliness of a boy.

"But it is impossible for me to present the whole

tableaux to your readers. 'The fairy scene has vanished;' but we cannot say it has not 'left a wrack behind' it. It will not be easy for any one who was present to forget all that has passed. But one thing is indeed a subject of regret—that so many good things were said by the company at large which are lost to the public; that the toasts were improvisatore, and not written or taken down; that some very happy but short addresses are to be lost in oblivion for want of a historian. We lament that the modesty of gentlemen should have prevented their handing in their toasts, as was requested in this paper, and none are given except the toasts of the presiding officers. We shall have other and joyous feasts in this good city, but no literary guest can be more warmly received than has been perhaps the most popular author of the day.

"It was an Attic supper, which no one present will be apt to forget.

"One of the last sentiments drunk produced great enthusiasm. It was in these words—

"'*Charles Dickens, the Artful Dodger:* He has dodged Philadelphia and Baltimore, but he could not dodge the Old Dominion.'"

Mr. Gales Seaton, son of Mr. W. Seaton, editor of the *National Intelligencer* of Washington, happened to be in Richmond at the time of the Dickens visit. He wrote his father a very interesting letter relating to his own experiences with, and his personal opinions of, Dickens, and the letter is copied in full from *William Winston Seaton: a Biographical Sketch*—

". . . I wrote a hurried note last night, to advise you that Mr. and Mrs. Dickens proposed going to Washington this morning, a delay in the departure of the boat to Norfolk preventing their reaching Baltimore as soon as desired; so they go no farther south. I was amused at the earnestness with which he asked me if I was *sure* St. Louis is farther north than Charleston.

"C.'s letter reached me too late to allow me to comply with your wishes; and though I should, of course, have attended to your behests, it would have placed me more in the attitude of a lion-hunter than I like. Indeed, I have barely escaped as it is. I sent up my card to him, anticipating that I should find a crowd, and determined to pester him with very little of my chat, after offering my services. I thought I might approach him calmly, and, like Malvolio, ' quenching my familiar smile with an austere regard of control,' address him in the loftiest style of hospitable welcome. I had only time to frame an appropriate exordium, when his secretary informed me that Mr. Dickens had been expecting me, and would be glad to see me. Entering the room with somewhat of a tremor, for I knew not whether he would ' roar as gently as a sucking dove,' I was seized by the hand and almost slung across the room, and a dozen remarks and questions addressed me in a breath. For he was entirely alone and writing. In reply, I at first could only gasp, without much power of articulation; for I suppose few persons feel with more devotion the homage due to the majesty of genius than I. He proposed a walk, and we went to the French Gardens. I need not say that I was delighted with his affable, cordial, frank and conversible manner, a strong proof of which is that in ten minutes I nearly forgot his distinction as an author, and conversed with him on a variety of topics as they naturally arose. We discussed law, London, negro songs, Richmond, etc., and, in truth, if I were to sum up in one sentence the impression he left on my mind, it would be that he is a thorough good fellow. As you may suppose, from your own feelings, I sedulously avoided the crowded streets, having no idea of being pointed out as having seized Boz immediately and monopolized him. On our return, we found several gentlemen, and, with Mrs. Dickens, we walked to Church Hill. She spoke of the pleasure she enjoyed at our house, and their hope to see you again. Afterwards we went to the Capitol, but persons crowding in to see them, I made my bow, after a kind invitation from him to call whenever I felt disposed. I saw that he was likely enough to have people around him, and did not see him again that day; though I felt unquiet and restless, I must confess, and could hardly resist going again.

"On Saturday morning I sent up my card, and sat a short time; but he was at breakfast and expected a crowd of visitors, so did not go out. He had been up late at a supper the night before, and laughed at my reason for not attending it, that I should have been called on for a speech. He was, I hear, very happy, and every one else very insipid in their efforts, except Mr. Ritchie, with whom he was greatly pleased.

"At his levée, from twelve to two, I attended to present a lady and spoke a while with him. He and his wife offered to bear letters, etc., to you from me, which I declined and took leave. I knew last night that they were receiving friends, and I could with difficulty keep away from the ' Exchange.' Whether from gratified vanity or a purer feeling, admiration of genius or simply a liking for the man, I know not, but I do feel very sorry that he has gone. I have never seen a man in whom, in so brief a period, I was so greatly interested. His likenesses certainly flatter him, but they cannot give the charm of his face, his rich expression of humour and merriment when he laughs—his whole face lights up. And then if he is not a man of fine feeling, no confidence is to be placed in the face as an index of the heart. I do sincerely hope his life may be a happy and prosperous one. . . .

"Your affectionate son,
"GALES SEATON."

Dickens left Richmond Sunday morning, March 20, via Washington for Baltimore, where he arrived the next evening, going to Barnum's Hotel, which he said was the only hotel he stopped at in the United States where he was given enough water to wash himself.

The day after his arrival the daily papers all contained very brief notices announcing his arrival, of which the following from the Baltimore *Patriot and Commercial Gazette* is a sample—

"Mr. Charles Dickens and Lady arrived in this city last evening from Washington, and took lodgings at Barnum's Hotel. We understand it is their intention to remain for several days."

BALTIMORE

BARNUM'S HOTEL, BALTIMORE

Dickens wrote to Washington Irving in Washington on Monday afternoon on his way to Baltimore.

"We passed through—literally passed through—this place again to-day. I did not come to see you, for I really did not have the heart to say ' good-bye ' again, and felt more than I can tell you when we shook hands last Wednesday.

"You will not be at Baltimore, I fear? I thought at the time that you said you might be there to make our parting gayer."

Dickens had a pleasant surprise at Baltimore, for, as will be seen from this article from the *Patriot and In-quirer*, Irving did go to Baltimore.

"*Charles Dickens.*—This distinguished author has been in Baltimore for the last two days, and left this morning in the Susquehanna Railroad line for Columbia. Mr. and Mrs. Dickens received at their rooms at the City Hotel the ladies and gentlemen who extended to them the courtesies of social intercourse, and were entertained privately, as far as their limited sojourn with us would admit.

"Washington Irving was also in Baltimore, and left this morning for New York, whence he sails for Madrid early in April. It was very pleasant to meet in the social circles these distinguished representatives of American and English literature.

"Mr. Dickens made a visit yesterday to the Maryland Hospital and Penitentiary, as he takes a deep interest in studying human nature in such receptacles of misfortune and crime. The civilities extended to him in Baltimore were very quiet and unostentatious, and such as must have been gratifying to his feelings as a man.

"He takes the Pennsylvania works at Harrisburg to Pittsburgh; then to St. Louis; returns by the Lakes to New York, and sails for England in June. His distinguished reception in this country is a striking illustration of the influence of mind over mind, of the homage which all civilized nations pay to genius of the

o

pre-eminence of that best of all nobility—the nobility of nature.

"It is a fine feature in our Republican country, as indicating our attachment to Republican institutions, that this architect of his own fortune is received with ten thousandfold more distinction than titled nobility. Long may he live to delight and instruct the world with the beautiful creations of a genius which does honour to the age."

In a letter to Mr. Charles Lanman, written at Washington, February 5, 1868, Dickens thus refers to the intercourse between him and Irving in Baltimore, and the famous mint-julep which they enjoyed together in 1842—

"Your reference to my dear friend Washington Irving renews the vivid impressions reawakened in my mind at Baltimore the other day. I saw his fine face for the last time in that city. He came thence from New York to pass a day or two with me before I went westward, and they were amongst the most memorable of my life by his delightful fancy and general humours. Some unknown admirer of his books and mine sent to the hotel a most enormous mint-julep, wreathed with flowers. We sat, one on either side of it, with great solemnity (it filled a respectable-sized round table), but the solemnity was of very short duration. It was quite an enchanted julep and carried us among innumerable people and places that we both knew. The julep held out far into the night, and my memory never saw him afterwards otherwise than as bending over it with his straw, with an attempted air of gravity, after some anecdote involving some wonderfully droll and delicate observations of character, and then, as his eye caught mine, melting out into that captivating laugh of his, which was the brightest and best I ever heard."

It will be noticed that Dickens says that the julep was sent "by some unknown admirer." When he wrote the letter to Mr. Lanman, twenty-six years after he and Irving enjoyed the delectable drink, he had forgotten who the donor was; but it was a Mr. William Guy of Philadelphia, as shown by a letter he wrote to Mr. Guy, which is now in the possession of his grandson, Mr. E. Guy Miller, and which letter he had also forgotten having written. The letter is here given—

Barnum's Hotel, March 23, 1842.

MY DEAR SIR,

I am truly obliged to you for the beautiful and delicious mint-julep which you so kindly sent me. I have looked at it, but await further proceedings until the arrival of Washington Irving, whom I expect to dine with me *tête-à-tête*, and who will help me to drink to your health. With many thanks to you,

Dear Sir,
Faithfully yours,
CHARLES DICKENS.

— Guy, Esquire.

The *American and Commercial Daily Advertiser* on Friday, March 25, contained the following reference to Dickens's and Irving's doings on Wednesday—

"The Hon. Washington Irving was in this city Wednesday on his return from the National Metropolis, and left here for New York yesterday evening. To a private social circle Wednesday evening was afforded the high gratification of having within it two of the most popular literary men of the day—Charles Dickens and Washington Irving."

Dickens left Baltimore on the day following for Pittsburgh, by way of Harrisburg, and the incidents of this part of his journey by railroad to York, and thence by stage-coach to Harrisburg, are told by him in *American Notes.* He arrived in Harrisburg at 6.30 p.m., and, as he wrote, went to "a very snug hotel, which, though smaller and far less splendid than many we put up at, is raised above them all in my remembrance, by having for its landlord the most obliging, considerate and gentlemanly person I ever had to deal with."

The name of the snug hotel and the paragon of a landlord is revealed by George H. Morgan in his *Annals of Harrisburg*, in which he refers to Dickens's visit to that city as follows—

"In the spring of 1842, the English novelist, Charles Dickens, accompanied by his wife, being on a tour through the United States and Canada, visited Harrisburg on their way from Baltimore to Pittsburgh. They remained here overnight and the following forenoon at the Eagle Hotel, then kept by Henry Buehler, Esq. (Now Bolton House.) The distinguished author gives an amusing account of this visit in *American Notes for General Circulation*, published after his return to England, and celebrated for their severe reflection upon the institutions and manners of our countrymen."

No Harrisburg newspaper files for 1842 are obtainable, but the following, from an account written by Chief Justice Ellis Lewis of Philadelphia, shortly after Dickens's second visit to the United States in 1868, to Dr. R. S. McKensie, literary editor of the *Philadelphia Press*, describing a meeting with Dickens at Harrisburg in 1842, is interesting—

"In the year 1842 I resided at Williamsport, Lycoming County. I had been in Philadelphia, and on arriving from that city at Buehler's hotel, in Harrisburg, I found quite a crowd of people in the house and surrounding it. The news was circulated that the celebrated Charles Dickens was at the hotel. Some alleged that he had gone to the Capitol to witness the proceedings of the Legislature, then in session. There was a great desire to get a sight of this distinguished man. I confess that my own desire was to get away from the crowd, and to avoid participating in the eager anxiety which our citizens generally display to pay court to distinguished strangers from abroad. Accordingly, I went immediately to the packet boat, then lying at the wharf in the canal, although its time for starting for Williamsport had not arrived by several hours. I found in the cabin of the boat my old friend Samuel R. Wood, a

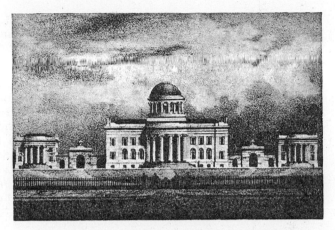

OLD CAPITOL OF PENNSYLVANIA, HARRISBURG

THE BOLTON HOTEL (FORMERLY EXCHANGE),
HARRISBURG, PA.

Where Dickens stayed in 1842

Quaker gentleman of Philadelphia, in company with a lady and gentleman. To these latter my friend Wood honoured me by an introduction. They were Mr. and Mrs Charles Dickens, who had come on board the packet boat with the same object which had brought me there—to avoid the crowd and the display of attention. I need not say that I was much gratified with my new acquaintance.

"One circumstance made a deep impression on my mind. It happened during our intercourse on the canal packet boat. I was much pleased with the social and genial disposition of Mr. Dickens, and was impressed with the great difference which appeared to exist, at that early time in their lives, between the husband and wife. She was good-looking, plain and courteous in her manners, but taciturn, leaving the burthen of the conversation to fall upon her gifted husband. In the course of the conversation I told him that I had a little daughter at home who would be delighted if I could present her with his autograph, written expressly for her. He consented to give it. Our mutual friend, the good Quaker Warden of the Eastern Penitentiary, Samuel R. Wood, bustled about and prepared a sheet of foolscap, with pen and ink. Mr. Dickens took up the pen, and commencing at the top of the sheet, wrote—

"'Yours faithfully, CHARLES DICKENS.'

"Mr. Wood remarked: 'Thee begins very close to the top of the sheet.' 'Yes,' said Mr. Dickens; 'if I left a large blank over my name somebody might write a note or a bond over it.'

"'Does thee suppose that a judge of the court would do such a thing?' said Mr. Wood; and Mr. Dickens replied, 'I did not intimate anything of that kind. The paper might soon pass out of the judge's possession and be made use of by others. But I do not suppose that judges of courts in America are any better than the judges in England.'

"The autograph was written for my daughter Juliet and was delivered to her. She is the wife of Hon. James N. Campbell, formerly Member of Congress, recently American Minister to Sweden and now residing in Philadelphia."

The canal boat on which Dickens embarked left on Friday, June 25, at 3 p.m., and his own account of the trip is familiar to all who have read *American Notes*.

Mr. Philip Hone made the same journey five years after Dickens, and the following extracts from Mr. Hone's diary, written as it was by an American, will show the reader how little Dickens exaggerated the discomforts of the trip—

"*June* 11.—At three o'clock we embarked on the canal boat *Delaware* on a canal voyage of more than two hundred miles. The weather is pleasant and we have an agreeable set of passengers, not too many. The day does very well, but the sleeping is tolerably uncomfortable (there is not much of *that*, however). The delay on this, the first day of the voyage, is rather discouraging; there has been a breach in the canal which has caused an accumulation of loaded boats, but the scenery is splendid. Just at the sunsetting (a more glorious one I never saw) we came to the junction of the Susquehanna and Juniata rivers, fifteen miles from Harrisburg, where the boat crosses the dam, the towpath being conveyed across a long bridge of light and delicate construction, on piers of massive and solid masonry. At the mouth of the Juniata is a handsome mansion and a fine estate of four hundred acres called Duncan's Island, belonging to a lady of that name, whose character seems to be worthy of such a position. Here we leave the Susquehanna and follow the course of the Juniata—beautiful stream, standing in romantic and picturesque scenery.

"*Canal: June* 13.—This canal travelling is pleasant enough in the daytime, but the sleeping is awful. There are two cabins, in which the men-folk and women-folk are separated by a red curtain. In the former apartment the sleepers are packed away on narrow shelves, fastened to the sides of the boat, like dead pigs in a Cincinnati pork warehouse. We go to bed at nine o'clock and rise when we are told in the morning; for the bedsteads are formed of the seats of the tables. ' A couch by night, a chest of drawers by day ! ' If I should ever be so happy as to sleep in my own bed again, my comfort will be enhanced by the remembrance of my present limited, hard, sheetless dormitory.

"*June* 14.—An extra car brought in from Holidaysburg, at six o'clock this morning, to take the Portage Railway across the Allegheny mountains to Johnstown —thirty-six miles—which is effected by ten inclined planes, five ascending and five descending. It is somewhat exciting, but nothing when you get used to it. The scenery of these mountains is astonishingly grand, wild beyond description.

"*June* 15.—Our canal voyage has been pleasant on the whole, though tedious. We arrived at the ' Birmingham of America ' at 11 o'clock this evening. I regretted the necessity of entering the city at night, but its appearance was quite a novelty; bright flames issuing from the foundries, glass works, rolling mills, and heavy clouds of smoke making the night's darkness darker, gave us a grand entry into Pittsburgh."

CHAPTER X

PITTSBURGH, CINCINNATI, LOUISVILLE AND CAIRO

MR. AND MRS. DICKENS arrived in Pittsburgh at 9.30 p.m. Tuesday, March 29, and only one newspaper, the *Morning Chronicle*, made any mention of their arrival, and that was the following brief notice in the issue of March 30—

"*Boz in Pittsburgh.*—Charles Dickens and lady arrived in the city last night about 9.30 on his way to St. Louis, and took lodgings at the Exchange Hotel. We understand the managers have given him an invitation to visit the Theatre to-night."

And under the "List of Arrivals" at the principal hotels, in the same paper is given—

"Charles Dickens and Lady—England."

It will be seen that in the papers of the Western cities which Dickens visited the references to his visit are much more brief than in the Eastern papers. This is explained by the fact that at that time very little attention to local news was given by the papers of the West, as the towns were small and the inhabitants were all familiar with local affairs, and desired the news from the East and from Europe.

Dickens and his party, as noted above, took up their lodgings at the "Exchange," which Dickens wrote was "a most excellent hotel." Dickens's opinion as to the character of the "Exchange" was not undeserved, as it was ranked by travellers of the day as above the average of Western hotels. In a book published in Baltimore in 1836, the author wrote that the hotel had "genteel plate-ware and cutlery and good attendance," and that

PITTSBURGH, PA., 1843

the "servants do not wear wooden or iron-bound shoes,"
from which fact the author observes that "guests may
sleep undisturbed when late arrivals and their luggage
make their appearance." He also stated that their charge
was $1·50 per day, while other hotels charged only $1·25.

Another writer also speaks of this hotel having fine
cutlery with the name of the hotel stamped upon it,
which seems to have been an unusual thing in those
days.

While the Pittsburgh newspapers gave very little
information about Dickens's goings while here, Dickens
himself has given a pretty full account in *American
Notes* as to how he passed his time.

Dickens left Pittsburgh for Cincinnati on the morning of April 1, on the steamer *Messenger*, and the
following day the editor of the *Morning Chronicle* rather
boasts of the fact that the author was not treated and
flattered as he had been in the East—

"Mr. Dickens and lady left our city yesterday, on
board the steamboat *Messenger*, on his westward trip.
As Birney Marshall said he would be treated in the
West, so he was treated in Pittsburgh. He was not
bespattered with that fulsome praise with which he was
bedaubed in the East, and which, we have not the least
doubt, was as disagreeable to himself as it was sickening to all sensible men. In the words of the editor of
the *Louisville Gazette*, we admired his genius, and were
prepared to greet him with warm and friendly hearts,
to grasp him by the hand, and give it a good Republican
shake; we let him see us as we were, and if he chooses
to 'write us in his book,' it will be no fault of ours if
we are classed among the Dogberries who beset his first
arrival. Many of our citizens called upon him, and
were delighted with the man whose writings had contributed so greatly to their enjoyment. We doubt not
he was better pleased with the quiet hospitality of his
reception in Pittsburgh, than he would have been if
we had got up a 'Boz Ball' or any other 'Gnome Fly'
to welcome him."

The following are extracts from the private diary of

Mr. Charles B. Scully, who was a prominent attorney of Pittsburgh at the time of Dickens's visit—

"*Monday, March* 28—Mr. Charles Dickens arrived to-night at the Exchange Hotel.

"*Tuesday, March* 29—At 12 noon a remarkable event, a thing I never expected, happened to-day. Went to the Exchange Hotel and was shown up to room No. 12, and, on announcing our name to Mr. Putnam and Mr. D'Almaine, was introduced to Mr. Charles Dickens, the greatest author of the age. He gave us a cordial hand-shake. I wished him welcome and he thanked me most politely. I was then introduced to Mrs. Dickens, who very easily and in a friendly manner reached out her hand. I took a seat beside her and spoke of her fortune in having such good weather. She said this was a remarkable country of ours and she was delighted with it. I told her she would admire its vastness more when on the broad waters of the Ohio and Mississippi. She said she hoped she would not be too nervous, as she was alarmed at the dreadful accidents on our rivers from boiler explosions. I recommended her to take a boat with Evans's safety valves, and she said she would. She told me Mr. D'Almaine was an old friend of her husband. I told her that Mr. Dickens had as many admirers of his literary productions here in proportion as in the East, although we showed it in a more plain and less extravagant way than our Eastern brethren, and were more democratic. She smiled very graciously.

"Mr. Dickens is much like his portrait, or likeness, as published in his works, a full, thoughtful face, a round dark eye, large mouth, wavy hair, and sparse whiskers. I never saw an English woman (Mrs. D.) like her, a modest and diffident demeanour, fair hair, blue eye and round features. Both are very pleasant, in their appearance. Mr. Dickens stood while I was in the room and is very fidgety, as it struck me, and quick. He appears to see everything that is going on : for instance, when I was speaking to Mrs. D., in a low tone, of boats with safety valves, he ran over to the window where I was sitting and said, 'What is that you say of safety valves?' We then talked a few minutes about boats, and I bowed and shook hands and left. Afterwards went to the 'Exchange' and serenaded Mr. Dickens.

"*Friday, April* 1—Mr. Dickens left our city on the steamboat *Messenger* for the great West. Saw him alight from his carriage and go aboard. There was a considerable crowd waiting to see him."

The Mr. D'Almaine whom Mr. Scully met in Dickens's room at the "Exchange," was the English portrait-painter mentioned in one of Dickens's letters to Forster describing his stay in Pittsburgh. In this letter he wrote : "We were there received by a little man (a very little man) whom I knew years ago in London. He rejoiceth in the name of 'D.G.,' and when I knew him was in partnership with his father in the Stock Exchange and lived handsomely in Dalton. . . . I lost sight of him nearly ten years ago, and he turned up t'other day, as a portrait-painter in Pittsburgh. . . . He dined with us every day of our stay in Pittsburgh (there were only three), and was truly gratified and delighted to find me unchanged—more so than I can tell you."

The only other item to be found in the *Pittsburgh Chronicle* relating to Dickens is the following from the issue of April 4—

"M. G. Searle, Esq., had the distinguished honour of attending the last distinguished visitors to our city— Mr. Charles Dickens and lady—on board the steamer *Messenger*, Captain Baird. Mr. Searle is the regular agent for all respectable steamboats coming to and departing from Pittsburgh."

It will be noticed that this item does not state whether the *Messenger* was equipped with Evans's safety valves or not. Dickens, in *American Notes*, has described the trip down the Ohio river to Cincinnati as "miles and miles and miles " of solitude "unbroken by any sign of human life or trace of human footsteps." It is not uninteresting to compare Dickens's account of the Ohio river with another account by a fellow-countryman, Mr. Archibald Prentice, editor of the *Manchester Times*, who made the trip six years later on the *Messenger*, the same boat on which Dickens made the journey. Mr. Prentice had read Dickens's account, and referred to it in his own as follows—

"What might be expected after this description, but an unbroken solitude and an eternal monotony relieved by an occasional deformity? The map of the country through which the river flows might show that a considerable population and immense tracts of cultivated land are close upon its banks; a look at a ' river grade ' might show that between Pittsburgh and Cincinnati there are no fewer than forty-seven landing-places, most of them at rising towns and villages; and it might thence be concluded that the solitude is not exactly such as Daniel Boone and Charles Dickens found it. But still there might be expected the absence of all beauty; still it might be expected from Dickens's description that the eye would be more strongly arrested by the mere dry *grisly skeletons* of trees than by luxuriant foliage; still it might be expected that, so far as the beautiful and picturesque were concerned, there was nothing to be found between the ' Dan of Pittsburgh ' and the ' Beersheba ' of Cincinnati—nothing to tempt the passenger to leave the ladies' cabin for the roof of the deck. The passengers do not sit sociably after dinner in the cabin —don't they? Why, no man with any eye in his head would sit still to pass unseeing a single turn in this *belle rivière*, as the French truly named it. Constantly winding, every quarter of a mile presents a new form of beauty. At one place we have steep hills on each side clothed with trees growing as if they never could grow old; at another the ends of ridges, with magnificent monarchs of the forest filling the hollows between them; at another the high banks receding half a mile or a mile on each side, presenting a combination of lawns and trees as might be expected around an English nobleman's seat; at another, islands of surpassing beauty; clearings which indicate the cultivation that is

STEAMER " MESSENGER "

On which Dickens travelled from Pittsburgh to Cincinnati

going on behind. I grudged every moment spent at the breakfast, dinner or tea tables. I spent hours alone at the highest elevation where the steersman, perched aloft for a good look-out, steered the long light steamer through its tortuous course; and after a brief twilight, I felt as one might feel after listening a whole day to the grandest and most beautiful strains of music—sorry that it was over, yet fatigued with the very intensity of the pleasure enjoyed. The next day was Sunday, and we enjoyed the same succession of splendid pictures. . . . Early next morning we found the vessel lying in shore in a fog, so dense that we could not see ten yards on either side—strange contrast to the preceding night. Perhaps in such a mist Charles Dickens might have come down the river, only he does not say so. The sun soon dispelled the fog, and then the river was before us again in all its glory, winding, and its high banks receding—the white houses and villages and small cities increasing in number as we went onwards."

While the six years that had elapsed between the time of Dickens's trip and Mr. Prentice's may have been long enough for the change in scenery, so far as to allow the white houses, villages and small cities to have been built, it would hardly account for the "trees growing as if they never could grow old," so that possibly the difference in the two accounts may be explained by the mist, as suggested by Mr. Prentice.

Dickens, in describing his arrival at Cincinnati, writes of "the broad wharf where the boat was moored; with other boats and flags and moving wheels, and hum of men around it, as though there were not a solitary rood of ground within the compass of a thousand miles."

The broad paved wharf is still there, but the number of steamboats has diminished. In fact, the glory of the Ohio and Mississippi rivers has departed so far as passenger boats are concerned owing to both these rivers being now paralleled with railroads.

Dickens arrived at Cincinnati on the morning of Monday, April 4, and took up his quarters at the Broadway Hotel, only a short distance from the steamboat landing. Dickens's opinions of the American newspapers was fully expressed in one of his letters to Forster, in which he wrote : "Of course I can do nothing but in some shape or other it gets into the newspapers. All manner of lies get there, and occasionally a truth so twisted and distorted that it has as much resemblance to the real fact as Quilp's leg to Taglioni's."

This was hardly true with regard to the newspapers of Cincinnati, as they published nothing of his doings except the bare fact of his arrival, as shown by the following—

"Mr. Dickens and his lady have, we are informed, arrived in the city."—*Daily Chronicle*, April 4, 1842.

"Mr. Dickens and Lady arrived in our city yesterday morning and have taken rooms at the Broadway Hotel. We understand that they will be at home to-day from 11 o'clock until 3 o'clock."—*Daily Republican*, April 5, 1842.

"*Charles Dickens*.—This gentleman reached our city yesterday and took lodgings at the Broadway Hotel."—*Cincinnati Gazette*, April 5, 1842.

There were certainly no lies in these three items, and a careful search of succeeding issues of these newspapers fails to show that they even made any mention of his doings in the city, or of his leaving the city on the following Wednesday morning. That the Cincinnati newspapers made absolutely no mention of him, or his attire, or any personalities whatever, may partly explain his very favourable opinion of that city, for he wrote : "Cincinnati is a beautiful city, cheerful, thriving and animated. . . . The society in which I mingled was intelligent and agreeable," etc. Surely the people of the city, when they read *American Notes*, might have said : "This is indeed ' praise from Sir Hubert,' and so far as we are concerned, we have no fault to find with the book."

Dickens, writing to Forster from Cincinnati on the morning of his arrival, said : "About half after eight we came ashore and drove to the hotel, to which we

CINCINNATI LANDING

BROADWAY HOTEL, CINCINNATI

had written on from Pittsburgh, ordering rooms, and which is within a stone's throw from the wharf. Before I had issued an official notification that we were 'not at home,' two judges called . . . and we fixed for an evening party to-morrow night at the home of one of them."

The judge at whose house the party was held was Judge Timothy Walker, and the following is an extract from his manuscript diary—

"*April* 5, 1842.—Had a visit from Charles Dickens and Lady. Rode with them around the city and gave them a party in the evening. Liked them much. Have read all his works and with great interest. Felt intimate with him before I saw him. Like him still better now."

That the feeling was mutual is shown by an extract from one of Dickens's letters to C. C. Felton, from Montreal, May 21—

"I saw a good deal of Walker at Cincinnati. I like him very much. We took to him mightily at first, because he resembled you in face and figure, we think."

While Dickens liked Judge Walker, he did not seem to like the judge's friends, for he wrote Forster concerning the party: "In the evening we went to a party at Judge Walker's and were introduced to at least one hundred and fifty first-rate bores, separately and singly." That one of the bores was disappointed in Dickens is shown by a description of the party by a young lady, which is copied from Mackenzie's *Life of Charles Dickens*.

"I went last evening to a party at Judge Walker's, given in honour of the hero of the day, Mr. Charles Dickens, and with others had the honour of an introduction to him. M—— had gone to a concert and we awaited her return, which made us late. When we reached the house, Mr. Dickens had left the crowded rooms and was in the hall, with his wife, about taking his departure when we entered the door. We were introduced to him, and in the flurry and embarrassment of the meeting one of the party dropped a parcel containing shoes, gloves, etc. Mr. Dickens, stooping, gathered them up and restored them with a laughing remark, and we bounded upstairs to get our things off. Hastening down again, we found him with Mrs. Dickens, seated upon a sofa, surrounded by a group of ladies, Judge Walker having requested him to delay his departure for a few moments, for the gratification of some tardy friends who had just arrived, ourselves among the number. Declining to re-enter the room where he had already taken leave of the guests, he seated himself in the hall. He is young and handsome, has a mellow, beautiful eye, fine brow, and abundant hair. His mouth is large, and his smile is so bright it seems to shed light and happiness all about him. His manner is easy and negligent,—but not elegant. His dress was foppish; in fact he was overdressed, yet his garments were worn so easily they appeared to be a necessary part of him. He had a dark coat, with lighter pantaloons; a black waistcoat embroidered with coloured flowers; and about his neck, covering his white shirt front, was a black neckcloth, also embroidered in colours, on which were two large diamond pins connected by a chain; a gold watch-chain, and a large red rose in his button-hole completed his toilet.

"Mrs. Dickens is a large woman, having a good deal of colour and is rather coarse, but she has a good face and looks amiable. She seemed to think that Mr. Dickens was the attraction and was perfectly satisfied to play second, happy in the knowledge that she was his wife. She wore a pink silk dress trimmed with a white blond flounce, and a pink cord and tassel wound round her head.

"He appeared a little weary, but answered the remarks made to him—for he originated none—in an agreeable manner. Mr. Beard's portrait of Fagin was so placed in the room that we could see it from where we stood surrounding him. One of the ladies asked him if it was his idea of the Jew. He replied, 'Very nearly.' Another laughingly requested that he would give her the rose he wore as a memento. He shook his head, and

said, 'That would not do; he could give it to no one—
the others would be jealous.' A half-dozen then insisted on having it, whereupon he proceeded to divide
the leaves among them. In taking the rose from his
coat, either by design or accident, the leaves loosened
and fell upon the floor, and amid considerable laughter
the ladies stooped and gathered them. He remained
some twenty minutes, perhaps, in the hall, then took his
leave. I must confess to considerable disappointment
in the person of my idol. I felt that his throne was
shaken, although it could never be destroyed."

Dickens left Cincinnati on Wednesday morning,
April 6, on the steamer *Pike*, as the *Messenger*, on
which he had arrived, had gone on to St. Louis. He
arrived at Louisville about midnight and put up at the
Galt House, which he says in *American Notes* is "a
splendid hotel, and we were as handsomely lodged as
though we were in Paris, rather than hundreds of miles
beyond the Alleghanies."

The Louisville Courier Journal said in 1870 that when
Mr. Dickens came to that city in 1842, he stopped at the
Galt House, whose landlord, Throckmorton, was a high-
strung Southerner of much character and influence, the
intimate of Clay, Crittenden and all the worthies. Mr.
Dickens had not been there long when Mr. Throckmorton visited him and offered his services in introducing him to the first families of Kentucky. "Sir, are
you the publican who keeps this inn?" inquired Mr.
Dickens. "Yes, sir," he replied. "Then," said Mr.
Dickens, "when I have need for your services, I will
ring for you."

This story is given for what it is worth, and it is
probably not worth much, for while it might not have
been customary in England for the landlord of an hotel
to offer to introduce his guests to the best people of the
town, still, Dickens was always considerate of others,
and knowing as he did that the manners and customs
of the United States at that time were different from
those of England, it is certain that he would have recognized that the landlord's offer was made in all serious-

P

ness and kindness to the stranger, and that he would have taken the offer in the spirit in which it was meant, and would not have met the offer with such a supercilious reply.

Dickens left Louisville the next day by the steamer *Fulton* for St. Louis, boarding the boat at Portland, a suburb of the city. In *American Notes* Dickens mentions a visitor to the boat in the person of a man named Porter, who was seven feet eight inches in his stockings. Mr. Philip Hone in his diary also mentions Porter, whom he saw on a trip from Pittsburgh to St. Louis in 1847—

"At the last dock, the new passengers all went ashore to see Porter, the Kentucky giant. He keeps an hotel and makes a good living out of the curiosity of travellers who stop to drink with him. The Captain introduced me to him. This mighty piece of humanity is seven feet eight inches in height, thirty-five years of age. I stood by his side, he stretched out his arm at right angles to his body, and it was six inches over my head. I fear that this last one of the *race* of giants will have run his earthly *race* ere long."

Mr. Prentice, whose description of the Ohio river is previously quoted, also saw the Kentucky giant, and wrote concerning him—

"He is much respected and has been one of the councilmen of the city. He told me that Lord Morpeth called upon him at his coffee-house, and that he was much pleased with his lordship's plain, unpretending manner. He did not like Dickens, who had sent for him. ' He had a double gold chain outside his waistcoat,' said Porter, ' and such breastpins, that I thought he looked like one of our river gamblers,' a class of persons who, it seems, particularly affect a show of jewelry."

The *Fulton*, on its journey down the Ohio, passed Cairo on the morning of Saturday, April 9, and it is pretty certain that Dickens was up early to get a view of the Eldorado on which he and so many of

VIEW ON THE OHIO RIVER BETWEEN CINCINNATI AND
LOUISVILLE

LOUISVILLE

his countrymen had invested their funds.   Here is what he wrote in *American Notes* describing his first view of Cairo—

"At length, upon the morning of the third day, we arrived at a spot so much more desolate than any we had yet beheld, that the forlornest places we had passed were, in comparison with it, full of interest.   At the junction of the two rivers, in ground so flat and low and marshy that at certain seasons of the year it is inundated to the housetops, lies a breeding-place of fever, ague, and death, vaunted in England as a mine of Golden Hope, and speculated in, on the faith of monstrous representations, to many people ruin.   A dismal swamp, on which the half-built houses rot away; cleared here and there for the space of a few yards, and then teeming with rank unwholesome vegetation, on whose baneful shade the wretched wanderers who are tempted hither, droop and die and lay their bones; the hateful Mississippi circling and eddying before it, and turning off upon its southern course a slimy monster, hideous to behold; a hotbed of disease, an ugly sepulchre, a grave uncheered by any gleam of promise; a place without one single quality, in earth or air or water, to commend it—such is the dismal Cairo."

On the return trip from St. Louis to Cincinnati he passed Cairo the second time, and he again wrote—

"In good time next morning, however, we came again in sight of the detestable morass called Cairo, and stopping there, to take on wood, lay alongside a barge, whose starting timbers scarcely held together.   It was moored to the bank, and on its side was painted ' Coffee House,' that being, I suppose, the floating paradise to which people fly for shelter when they lose their houses for a month or two beneath the hideous waters of the Mississippi.   But looking southward from this point, we had the satisfaction of seeing that intolerable river dragging its slimy length and ugly freight abruptly off towards New Orleans, and passing a yellow line which stretched across the current, were again upon the clear

P 2

Ohio, never, I trust, to see the Mississippi again save in troubled dreams and nightmares."

If any good American thinks to-day that this description of Cairo was overdrawn or exaggerated, let him look at the picture "High Water at Cairo" (1844), and read the following description of that flood which occurred just two years after Dickens saw the place—

"In 1844 the houses at Cairo, at the confluence of the Ohio and Mississippi, were nearly submerged. The swollen rivers were fourteen miles wide between the opposite shores of Kentucky and Missouri. Movable property of every kind, fences, cattle, lumber, furniture and entire houses (wooden ones of course) were floated down the Mississippi and other rivers. A building was seen driving down the Mississippi while several persons from the windows were calling for assistance, which on account of the torrent-like velocity of the stream could not be afforded them. Many lives were lost, and the amount of property destroyed by the flood is beyond all estimate. Many people and dead bodies floated down the Mississippi. A house, with a whole family inside it, went over the falls of the Ohio. Boats passed over fields and plantations, far beyond the limits of the river, and took the frightened from the upper stories and roofs of their houses, to which they had been driven for refuge from the waters. The levels or embankments made at different places, as defences against the river, were broken through."

Can any one say after reading this description of the 1844 flood that Dickens, in writing *Martin Chuzzlewit*, had drawn on his imagination in describing Eden? It would almost seem that his picture might with truth have been made darker. Can any reader of the present day be surprised that Dickens never wanted to see Cairo again?

The following is a description of Cairo written in 1856, and reprinted from *Lloyd's Steamboat Directory*, published in Cincinnati in that year. It will be seen that even fourteen years after Dickens saw the place it had only one thousand inhabitants, and that although it was the terminus of the Illinois Central Railroad at that time, the largest in the United States, it might still have been, without exaggeration, the prototype of Eden—

"Cairo is advantageously situated in Alexandria County, Illinois, at the southern extremity of the State, on a point of land formed by the confluence of the Ohio and Mississippi rivers, one hundred and eighty-four miles below St. Louis, and one thousand miles above New Orleans. The situation at the junction of these two great rivers affords one of the finest positions for a commercial city that can be found in the Western States; but owing to some natural defects in the locality, the growth has been less rapid than it would have been in more favourable circumstances. The banks of the Ohio at this point are low, and the surrounding country is still lower. These occasional overflows and the marshy nature of the soil are supposed to affect the health of the neighbourhood; but by the industry and ingenuity of man these natural disadvantages have already been removed, to some extent, and there is no reason to doubt that all such obstacles to the improvement of the place will, in the course of time, be entirely removed. A level or embankment, twenty-six feet high, has been erected at a cost of $1,000,000 to protect the town and adjacent country from overflows. Since this great work was completed, Cairo has improved very rapidly. It is the southern terminus of the Illinois Central Railroad (the longest railroad in the United States), which extends to Chicago and Rock Island. A line of first-class steamers will soon be in operation between Cairo and New Orleans, leaving each place daily and conveying the United States mail. When we consider what New Orleans has effected in order to overcome the natural disadvantages of soil and situation, we cannot question the ability of Cairo to obviate those minor inconveniences which at one time threatened to interfere with her prosperity. Judging from what has been done already, we may safely predict that this place will soon become a flourishing emporium, and command the immense trade of the West, North-west, and South.   The tardy growth of Cairo, in earlier times, has been ascribed in a great measure to the illiberal policy of the English Company which purchased the land some years ago, and attempted to establish a monopoly of the whole ground, of which they retained the ownership, and making mere tenancy of all the settlers.   A better system now prevails; another company, of far more progressive character than the preceding one, has obtained possession of the land, men of energy and pecuniary means have been induced to settle on the place; improvements of various kinds have been carried into effect, and still greater ones are in contemplation.   Two excellent papers have been established.   The population at present is 1000, and is rapidly increasing."

The "View of Cairo," facing this page, is also produced from the same book as the description of the town.

VIEW OF CAIRO, 1856

HIGH WATER, CAIRO, 1844

214

CHAPTER XI

ST. LOUIS AND THE PRAIRIE

Dickens wrote Forster from Richmond on the 17th of March, referring to his contemplated visit to St. Louis—

"I am going to break my resolution of accepting no more public entertainments in favour of the originators of the printed document overleaf. They live upon the confines of the Indian territory, some two thousand miles or more west of New York? Think of my dining there! And yet, please God, the festival will come off—I should say about the 12th or 15th of next month. . . ."

The printed document, Forster wrote, was a series of resolutions moved at a public meeting attended by the principal citizens, judges, professors and doctors, urgently inviting to that city of the Far West the distinguished writer, then the guest of America, and tendering to him their warmest hospitalities.

A search of the existing files of the St. Louis newspapers fails to discover any account of the meeting at which the invitation to Dickens was extended or any copy of the printed documents to which he referred; but on April 6 the St. Louis *Republican* contained the following brief notice of further action by the Committee—

"The Committee formed some time since to invite Mr. Dickens to this city have agreed to tender him, upon his arrival, a public ball and such other hospitalities as may be in accordance with his wishes and present mode of travelling."

Dickens arrived in St. Louis after a journey by water from Pittsburgh of 1,230 miles, having travelled the entire length of the Ohio River and up the Mississippi River from Cairo.   The day after his arrival the *Republican*, noting his arrival, said—

"*Boz*—The veritable Charles Dickens and Lady arrived last evening on board the *Fulton* from Louisville.   They took us a little by surprise, for we did not expect them before Tuesday; but no matter, he will find a cordial welcome in this far land of the West.   Though our fare may be homely, it will not be given with stint or grudging, but from honest hearts, though uncourtly. Rooms have been taken for them at the Planter's House."

The Planter's House was one of the hotels which Dickens was surprised to find 2000 miles west of the Atlantic Ocean, and in one of his letters to Forster had this to say about it—

"The inns in these outlandish corners of the world would astonish you with their goodness.   The Planter's House is as large as the Middlesex Hospital, and built very much on our hospital plan, with long wards abundantly ventilated and plain whitewashed walls.   They had a famous notion of sending up at breakfast-time large glasses of new milk with blocks of ice in them as clear as crystal.   Our table was abundantly supplied at every meal.   One day when Kate and I were dining together in our room, we counted sixteen dishes on our table at the same time."

Monday, the day after their arrival, was spent looking around the city and receiving the calls of some of the citizens.

On Tuesday the *Republican* contained the following with regard to the programme for the entertainment on that and the next day—

"*Boz*—Yesterday a number of our citizens, we understand, paid their respects to Mr. Dickens and his lady. Those who called speak in the highest terms of the gratification afforded them by the visit.   To-day the Committee which had in charge his entertainment treat him to a view of the prairie, a sight which he seems very desirous of enjoying. To-morrow evening he is to be treated to a soiree. This mode has been adopted in preference to a ball, as it furnishes to all an opportunity of gratifying their feelings, which call them together, and will not interfere with the scruples of propriety of any."

There must have been at that time some of the good people of the city who looked upon dancing as the amusement of the wicked, so, as the *Republican* said, a soiree was given, in order not to interfere with the "scruples of propriety of any."

Dickens has given his own version of the trip to the prairie, but Dr. J. F. Snyder, who was a boy residing in Belleville, Illinois, at the time, and saw the arrival of the party in that town, has written a very interesting account of his recollection of the event for the *Journal of the Illinois Historical Society*, from which the following extracts are taken—

"Beside Mr. Dickens and the drivers of the four teams, there were nine men and no ladies in the party, only two of whom I could identify and can now remember. These were John J. Anderson, a banker, and George Knapp of the Missouri *Republican*. They were all young men connected with the newspapers and business interests of St. Louis, bent upon affording their famous guest a glimpse of the grandeur of Illinois, the 'two large baskets and two large demi-johns,' with ice and other extras, taken along, indicating the picnic aspect of the 'jaunt,' and intent to make it as pleasant for him as possible. Seated in the several conveyances with one of their number on horseback as guide, they crossed the Mississippi in the early morning on one of the Wiggins Company ferry-boats. At that season of the year the miry road across the seven miles of soft loamy soil of the American bottom, and the succeeding seven miles of sticky clay uplands to Belleville, usually rendered travelling over it slow and difficult, and was, in fact, at times almost impassable.

"Returning home at about eleven o'clock in the forenoon of that 15th day of April from an errand upon which I had been sent to the eastern part of the village, I had reached the public square when the line of carriages came pulling through the mud up Main Street from the West. In doubt as to whether they formed a funeral procession or transported some kind of show, I stopped to see them pass by. Just then Philip B. Foulke, editor of the Belleville *Advocate*, and in later years our Congressman, came down the street to the court-house, and I asked him who those travelling strangers were. He had, a few minutes before, interviewed the horseman who had arrived in advance of them to have luncheon prepared for the party, and was hurrying into the court-house—circuit court being in session —to inform the bench and bar the object and purpose of the novel expedition that had excited my curiosity. Startled by hearing that Boz, the author of the *Pickwick Papers*, was actually there, I turned about and, keeping abreast of the first carriage, followed it up the street until it stopped at the door of the Mansion House. On the way I was joined by several other boys, my daily associates, not one of whom perhaps had ever heard of Charles Dickens, but attracted by the unusual appearance of so many strange vehicles, went along gazing at them with open-mouthed wonder.

"When the barouche conveying Mr. Dickens halted at the curbstone, he was the first of its four inmates to step from it to the sidewalk, and did so with a look of evident relief. It was a perfect day 'overhead,' warm for the middle of April, with clear sky and the refreshing air of early spring. The landlord, Mr. McBride, came bustling out, bareheaded, to receive the company, and was introduced to the famous writer by one of his travelling companions. The man introduced as ' Mr. Dickens ' was (to me) a disappointing surprise. In fact, my youthful ideal of the genius who created Mr. Pickwick, Sam Weller and the Widow Bardell was badly shattered. It is natural for the average man, woman or boy, when hearing about any noted individual, to form a definite idea of that person's appearance; or, upon reading an interesting book, to draw an imaginary portrait of its

ST. LOUIS

PLANTER'S HOUSE, ST. LOUIS

218

author. Mr. Dickens was, on that day, a very ordinary-looking man indeed, with no external indication of true greatness. In the estimation of ' us boys ' he compared very unfavourably with Col. Richard M. Johnson of Kentucky, the slayer of Tecumseh, and late vice-president, who had, a short time before, visited Belleville, and had been given a grand reception with brass band accompaniment.

"The ' Mansion House,' on the north-east corner of Main and High Streets, is still there. Solid and substantial, though a dingy-looking relic of a past age in the midst of modern progress, it is yet (1910) serviceable as a business house, and, with pride, is pointed out to strangers by the older residents as the hostelry where Mr. Dickens was entertained in 1842. Of it he says : ' There was an hotel in this place . . . an odd, shambling, low-roofed outhouse, half cowshed and half kitchen, with a coarse brown canvas tablecloth, and tin sconces stuck against the walls to hold candles at supper-time.' The Mansion House was really a large, roomy brick building, fully up to date in all respects, two storeys high, with long two-storey frame addition, erected only three years before by the Rev. Thomas Harrison, and was well arranged, well furnished and conducted in first-class style by his daughter and her husband, Mr. and Mrs. Wm. J. McBride.

"Mr. Dickens and companions on arrival were escorted by the landlord up-stairs and to rooms provided with water, towels, etc., where they might perform their ablutions and ' dress for dinner '; and the carriages, from which the horses were unhitched and taken to the stable, were left standing in front of the hotel.

"Court having adjourned for the noon recess, Colonel Niles, Governor Koerner, Phil Foulke and two or three other members of the bar, with several citizens, came up to the Mansion House to pay their respects to the famous guest. Judge Breese and Jo. Gillespie declined to accompany them.

"With boyish curiosity and eagerness to see all that was going on, I followed Mr. Dickens unasked, and no doubt unwanted, to the foot of the stairs, and waited there until he came down and was introduced to the lawyers and some of the other visitors. I was in close proximity to his coat-tail when he was presented to ' Dr. Crocus,' and was an interested witness to that interview which, as narrated in Chapter XIII of the *American Notes*, is substantially correct, with the exception that the landlord, Mr. McBride, was not addressed as ' Colonel.' He was a quiet, unobtrusive, upright man, an exemplary citizen and rigid Methodist, but not a colonel. The man portrayed as ' Dr. Crocus ' was an adventurer calling himself Dr. Angus Melrose—perhaps an assumed name —who had a few months before alighted in Belleville as a lecturer on phrenology, then a very popular fad, and incidentally offering his professional services for the healing of all known diseases.

"To Mr. Dickens's question, ' Do you think soon of returning to the old country? ' Mr. Melrose answered, ' Not yet awhile, sir, not yet. You won't catch me at that just yet, sir. I am a little too fond of freedom for that, sir. Ha, ha! It's not so easy for a man to tear himself from a free country such as this is, sir. Ha, ha! No, no! Ha, ha! None of that till one's obliged to do it, sir. No, no! ' In this grandiloquent declaration the doctor was very evidently, as Mr. Dickens intimated, ' playing to the galleries,' but he also intended Mr. Dickens to understand that he was speaking ironically and, by innuendo, expressing his contempt for American institutions. With proverbial English obtuseness of perception, however, Mr. Dickens failed to catch the doctor's covert meaning.

"Dr. Melrose was over six feet in height, and robust in proportion, with florid face and long nose. Of friendly, social disposition, he was a fluent talker, speaking correct English with broad Scotch accent. To Mr. McBride he stated that he had recently graduated in medicine at the Edinburgh University, and having but limited means, to gratify his desire to see America he had recourse to the lecture platform, phrenology and the practice of medicine to defray expenses of touring the country. He remained in Belleville several months, but though immortalized as ' Dr. Crocus ' by the *American Notes*, very few persons now living retain the slightest recollection of him.

"For half-an-hour or more Mr. Dickens was surrounded by a throng of citizens, to several of whom he was formally introduced, but to none of whom he addressed anything more than curt, commonplace remarks. It was plain that he was both bored and amused by the curiosity and evident disappointment of the crowd inspecting him, and seemed glad when the dinner-bell ended the impromptu reception. The glimpse obtained of him from the open dining-room door, when all were seated at the long table, left no doubt as to the ample justice he was doing to the ' chicken fixings ' specially prepared for him. Dinner over, he strolled out on the sidewalk in front of the hotel, viewing part of the town in the range of his vision, while conversing with his St. Louis friends until the horses were brought from the stable and all was ready to move on again.

"' From Belleville,' says Mr. Dickens, ' we went through the same desolate kind of waste, and constantly attended, without the interval of a moment, by the same music ' (the croaking of bullfrogs). Here again, with the American bottom vaguely in mind, he drew upon his memory and it failed him. The road from Belleville to Lebanon—then almost the entire twelve miles through dense woods, broken here and there by the farms of Governor Kinney and other old settlers—is over high, undulating and beautiful country, remote from sloughs or swamps or other habitats of the festive mosquito or musical frog.

"The hotel at Lebanon was more fortunate than the one in our town in catching the fancy of the novelist, and he accorded it this dubious praise : ' In point of cleanliness and comfort, it would have suffered by no comparison with any English ale-house, of a homely kind, in England.' It was a large barn-like frame building, called the Mermaid Hotel, with a large square sign on a tall post in front, on which was painted a full-sized mermaid standing on her tail on the waves, holding a looking-glass before her with one hand and combing her golden tresses with the other. The house was owned and conducted as an inn and stage by Captain Lyman Adams, a retired New England sea captain of kind and genial disposition who ended his days there, highly respected and esteemed by all who knew him.

"After dining on the prairie, Mr. Dickens and party returned to Lebanon and passed the night at the Mermaid Hotel. The next morning he arose at five o'clock, and after a short walk about the village, returned to the tavern and amused himself for some time in the inspection of its public rooms and backyard, which seems to have afforded him more genuine enjoyment than his view of the prairie."

The party arrived in St. Louis on their return on Wednesday afternoon, and the following from the Belleville *Advocate* of April 21 is a fair sample of American journalism, as practised in the average country newspaper at that time—

"Mr. Charles Dickens (the renowned English novelist) passed through this town on Monday the 12th inst. to take at least a bird's-eye view of the Looking-Glass Prairie, or the Reflecting Mirror, as it may be truly termed, of our whole prairie region. After which when he returned to St. Louis, and while on the evening of the 12th was participating with the literati of St. Louis in a splendid entertainment given him at the Planter's House, Governor Kinney, being then in the city, sent a respectful letter of welcome to him as a visitor to the Far West; enclosing therein, as a specimen of his own writing, his answer to ' an old friend,' a farmer, on the subject of taking and reading the newspapers, etc. In answer to which letter, the next day previous to his departure, Mr. Dickens left the following note to the Governor, at the Planter's House, which I have obtained permission to publish. We understand that Boz, alias the old Dickens, was much enraptured with the scenery which this short romantic tour opened to his view, and does not regret, in the least, the time occupied to gratify the curiosity which led him to perform it.

"'*Planter's House, St. Louis, April* 14, 1842.

"'MY DEAR SIR,

"'I am truly obliged to you for your letter of welcome and congratulation, which has given me real pleasure. Accept my cordial thanks, and believe me,

"'Faithfully yours,

"'(*Signed*) CHARLES DICKENS.'"

The same issue of the *Advocate* contained the following communication—

"MR. EDITOR,

"It is understood that Mr. Dickens, after visiting the Looking-Glass Prairie and taking a view of the scenery thereof (which may be considered an index to the whole prairie volume of Illinois), intimated an intention on his return to his native country, to give a picturesque view of the novelty, real beauty and sublimity of our whole prairie system; which, we have no doubt, will be both instructive and entertaining to his readers at home and to his admirers in the Far West.

"Should he be able, with his pen, to give the public, and particularly the old bachelors who are fond of novels, a more lucid and enchanting description than Governor Kinner did at the celebration on the last 8th of January in this place, we must acknowledge that he can beat the extemporaneous effusion of a Sucker."

On the evening of the return from the prairie the soiree at the Planter's House occurred, and Dickens, on writing to Forster, refers to it—

"We had a crowded levee at St. Louis. Of course the paper had an account of it. If I were to drop a letter on the street it would be in the newspaper the next day, and nobody would think its publication an outrage. The editor objected to my hair as not curling sufficiently. He admitted an eye, but objected again to my dress as being somewhat foppish and indeed rather flash."

Here is evidently the article to which Dickens referred, and the reader can judge whether it was so objectional as to warrant such strong condemnation as he gave it—

"We knocked at the door, gave our name to a gentleman usher, and were introduced to Charles Dickens and his Lady. Dickens stands very straight, is of medium length, and has a good figure. His manner of introduction is free and easy, frank. His head shows large perceptive faculties, a large volume of brain in front of the ears, but not a large causality. His eye is to our perception blue, dark blue and full. It stands out slightly and is handsome—very beautiful. It is the striking feature of his physiognomy.

"His hair has been described as very fine. We did not find it remarkably so. It is slightly wavy, and has a glossy soft texture. We had thought from his portraits that it was thick, but did not find it so. He wore a black dress coat, with collar and facings of velvet, a satin vest with very gay and variegated colours, light coloured pantaloons, and boots polished to a fault. His neck was covered by a low rich satin stock, with a small bow and large appendages, which were arranged rather carelessly, and fastened with a double pin united by a chain, and so disposed as to hide his shirt bosom entirely.

"No shirt collar appeared, but the wristbands were turned back over the cuffs of his coat. Small thin whiskers run along in front of his ears. One or more rings ornamented his fingers. Dickens is thirty years and one or two months old. He does not look older. No one would suspect from inspection that he is the genius his works prove him to be. The world has scarcely furnished an example of a man who has written his way to so widespread a fame as his in so short a time."—*St. Louis Organ.*

The *Republican* on Friday, April 15, contained only the following very brief note on the soiree—

"*Boz.*—A large number of ladies and gentlemen paid

MANSION HOUSE, BELLEVILLE, ILLINOIS

Where Dickens stayed in 1842

NEIL HOUSE, COLUMBUS, OHIO, 1844

their respects to Mr. Dickens and lady at a soiree given at the Planter's House on Wednesday night. Yesterday they left St. Louis on the *Messenger* for Louisville and Cincinnati. From the latter place they will proceed to Portsmouth, and from there by the Ohio Canal to the lakes, visiting Niagara Falls, and return to the east."

CHAPTER XII

THE RETURN TRIP—ST. LOUIS TO NEW YORK

As stated in the previous chapter, Dickens left St. Louis Thursday, April 14, on the return journey east, on the steamer *Messenger*, on which he had travelled from Pittsburgh to Cincinnati, and in *American Notes* he has told of his trip down the Mississippi and his opinion of that "filthy river," and how he took his last look at "the detestable morass called 'Cairo.'" The boat arrived at Louisville on Sunday the 17th, and he remained over night at the Galt House, leaving there the next day on the *Ben Franklin*, which he said was "a beautiful mail steamboat," and arrived at Cincinnati at 1 a.m. on Tuesday. The following are the only notices that can be found in the Cincinnati newspapers referring to his return to that city—

"Mr. Dickens arrived in town yesterday and took lodgings at the Broadway Hotel. He leaves to-day for New York, via Columbus."—*Cincinnati Gazette*.

"Charles Dickens, Esq., and Lady arrived yesterday by the mail boat *Ben Franklin* and took rooms at the Broadway Hotel. He leaves this morning via Columbus and the Lakes, for the Falls of Niagara, on his route to New York."

Dickens has given a very full account in *American Notes* of the trip to Niagara Falls, but his secretary, Mr. Putnam, in his account has told of some incidents of the journey which are not related by Dickens. It is interesting to compare Dickens's story with Putnam's, and the latter is therefore copied in full.

"The coach was crowded with passengers, and, as usual, Mr. Dickens secured his favourite seat on the

box with the driver. We travelled all night, and a weary
journey it was. Mrs. Dickens sat on the back seat, and
my place was on the middle seat by the window in front
of her. Opposite me, through the night, sat a well-
dressed man; but all night long he poured out a rain
of tobacco spittle which, from the motion of the coach,
fell on us in showers. I tried to screen Mrs. Dickens,
but notwithstanding my efforts, and the aid of a thick
veil, she could not escape the disgusting results.

"Arriving at Columbus, we stopped at the Neil House,
an excellent hotel; a few hours were given to rest and
sleep, and afterwards Mr. Dickens received for an hour
or two the ladies and gentlemen who called upon him.
The plan of travel was to get to Sandusky City on Lake
Erie, take a steamer to Buffalo, thence go to Niagara,
and thence to Canada.

"At Columbus we hired a stage-coach exclusively for
our party, and the stage company sent an agent with
the driver to go through with us. The upper portion
of Ohio was largely at that time an unbroken forest, and
the accommodations for travellers were very poor.
Nothing but corn-bread and bacon could be obtained at
the log cabins on the road, and so our good landlord of
the Neil House had a basket of provisions put up for us
to dine upon. The road was pretty good at first, but
did not improve as we went on. We had, however, a
good stage-coach to ourselves and a good team and
driver. So for many miles we went on quite well. The
driver, at intervals of a dozen miles or so, would commence blowing his horn, to give notice at the station a
mile or more ahead, that a relay of horses was to be
ready. It was evidently unusual for an 'extra' to go
through on that road, and while we changed horses all
the people in the log tavern and its neighbourhood
would assemble to look at us, and they generally found
out by questioning the driver that it was 'Boz' who
was travelling with an 'extra' toward the lake. Soon
after noon we came to a pleasant nook in the woods, not
far from a log-cabin, and our basket of provisions was
opened and the cloth spread upon the grass. I obtained
a pitcher of cool water at the cabin near by, and dinner

was ready. I trust I shall be excused if I mention here a little instance of the kindne s of heart always shown by Charles Dickens. The driver and his friend, who were now waiting with the coach a little distance, had dined at the log tavern which we passed a half-hour before. But before *we* dined, Mr. Dickens, heaping up a large quantity of oranges, apples, nuts and raisins, which we had brought for dessert, and a quantity of wine added, requested me to take them to the driver and his companion, which I did. It was a little incident; but it was characteristic of that man throughout life to *remember others*.

"After dinner I returned the pitcher, taking the basket and dishes with me to the log cabin, and the people were greatly pleased and surprised when I made them a present of the whole. We hurried off again, as the road was constantly growing worse and night not far distant.

"At the next place for changing horses—a log cabin and stable standing all alone in the forest—we alighted for a few moments and went in. An elderly woman received us and gave us seats. In an adjoining room there were two tall, good-looking young girls, her daughters, spinning. They seemed quite desirous to know, and were too bashful to ask, who the strangers were. Being curious to see if, in the midst of the almost unbroken forests of Northern Ohio, the inmates of that lone cabin had ever heard of Charles Dickens, I incidentally mentioned his name. ' Is it indeed ! ' said the girls, and with brightened eyes and looks of pleasure on their handsome faces they came and sat down where they could see Mr. and Mrs. Dickens. The coach was soon ready, and with a few words and a kind ' good-bye ' to the woman and her daughters from Mr. and Mrs. Dickens, we went on our way. I told Mr. Dickens that the girls had read his books and were happy to have seen him; and the incident seemed to gratify him, as weil it might.

"We soon began to know something of the exquisite softness of ' corduroy roads.' Some dozen miles of this kind of road now lay before us, and as they talked of 'building a good road there some time or other' no repairs had for a long interval been made in the 'Corduroy'; consequently holes nearly large enough to bury coach, horses and all were constantly occurring, which, however, the driver managed with great skill to avoid. It was a wondrous talent that put the wood and iron of that coach together, for it did not seem possible that it could long remain unbroken.

"Mrs. Dickens had the back seat to herself; as the terrible jolting increased, Mr. Dickens, taking two handkerchiefs, tied the ends of them to the door-posts on each side, and the other ends Mrs. Dickens wound around her wrists and hands. This contrivance, to which was added the utmost bracing of the feet, enabled the kind and patient lady to endure the torture of the 'Corduroy.' Mr. Dickens and myself occupied the middle seat, with our arms wound tightly around the other door-posts, and Mrs. Dickens's maid Ann occupied the front seat facing us. Mr. Dickens on his side, and I on mine, kept a sharp look-out ahead as well as we could, and when we saw—as we did almost every minute —an uncommonly large hole into which the wheels must go, we shouted 'Corduroy!' and prepared ourselves for the shock. But preparation was of little avail, for with all our strength we found it impossible to keep our places, but were constantly tumbling upon each other and picking ourselves up from the bottom of the coach. At last we got through the swamp, and thankfully left the 'Corduroy' behind us. As night came on a smart thunder-shower passed over us, and by the gleams of lightning we followed the winding forest road. The driver told us we should reach Upper Sandusky a little before midnight and stop there till morning. This was good news, for perhaps there never yet was a set of travellers more utterly worn out than ourselves. We looked forward with pleasure to supper, good clean beds and a few hours' sleep. The time seemed very long, but at last, about eleven o'clock, when yet a mile or more from the place, our driver began to blow his horn to rouse the people at the tavern. In due time we arrived. The log tavern was a long, low structure, a storey and a half high. We got out of the coach, sore and lame, and soon sat down to a supper of bacon, bread and butter and hot tea. Mr. and Mrs. Dickens had a room on the ground floor, and into it all the trunks and baggage—including overcoats and shawls—were carried. Mr. Dickens called my attention to the fact that there were no fastenings to either of the doors of his room, but said, ' I can pile all the trunks up against the doors, and no one can possibly get in without waking us.' Mrs. Dickens was naturally rather nervous, for the place certainly looked new and strange. We heard that an ' Indian Council ' had just been held at the lodge near by and there were hundreds of Indians at that time in the vicinity, and everything looked like being in a wild and uncivilized country.

"So ' Boz ' and his wife went thankfully to rest, and the landlord, lighting a tallow candle, showed me up a flight of outer stairs into the chamber or loft of the cabin. There were two beds in the room, and one was already occupied by a man who snored in splendid style. I was too tired to mind that, and got into bed as soon as possible. But it was useless to try to sleep. The bed literally swarmed with bugs, and I found it impossible to close my eyes. After trying in vain for some time to endure the torment, I dressed and went down the stairs again out doors. It was in April, and the night air was piercing cold. I could not obtain an overcoat or shawl, for they were all in Mr. Dickens's room and I would not alarm Mrs. Dickens by trying to get in. So I took to the coach. It was better than standing out doors, but as it was lined with leather, it was not very warm. I spent the night in useless attempts to catch a nap.

"As daylight began to glimmer ' I crowed ' very loudly several times, hoping that the old darkey who did the chores would think it was morning and get up and light the fires. But the ruse didn't succeed, though the ' crowing ' was very well done, indeed.

"As soon as it was light, I got out and crept to the cabin. While I was standing there, Mrs. Dickens, with a face full of trouble, and rubbing her wrists and hands,

came from her room to the tin wash-basin provided for
the public, which stood upon a stump near the door. I
bade her good morning and asked how she had rested
' Oh, Mr. P.,' said she, ' I have been almost devoured
by the bugs ! ' I then related my ' experience,' which
excited both her mirth and sympathy, and calling to
her husband, said, ' Charles, Charles, just come here
and listen to what Mr. P. suffered last night ! ' I then
told my experience again without any embellishments—
none were needed—and with laughter and kind words
Mr. Dickens heard it and has duly chronicled it in his
' notes.'

"We had breakfast, and, the coach being ready, we
all got in and were on the point of starting, when the
landlord mentioned that the ' Bill wasn't paid ! ' ' The
bill not paid ? Good heavens ! Mr. P., the bill not
paid, sir ! Why, how is this ? I hope you have not
neglected it before, have you ? '

" I apologized to the landlord and explained that I had
never before forgotten to pay all bills ; but having spent
the night in the coach, I had no consciousness of having
stopped anywhere or owing anything ; with which explanation Mr. Dickens nodded and smiled his satisfaction. The landlord, however, seemed not well
pleased, but received his money sullenly, and we went
on our way.

"Our stage-coach ride across Ohio ended at Tiffin, a
small town which we reached about noon, from whence
was a railroad to Sandusky City on Lake Erie. The
good landlord at Tiffin, finding who were his guests, did
his best to please, and also to let the entire town know
that ' Dickens was at his hotel.' And when we left the
house for the depot, he had a large kind of wagon on
springs, with seats very high, on which Mr. and Mrs.
Dickens were placed. I think the driver was instructed
to pass through all the principal streets of the place
before he reached the railroad station, for we went at
a slow pace and were a long time going ; and the people
awaited us in groups, as if by appointment, at the street
corners and at the windows and doors of the houses ;
and if the inhabitants of Tiffin, Ohio, did not on that

occasion see ' Boz ' and his wife, it certainly was not the fault of that good landlord or of his carriage driver.

"The change from coach and corduroy to the rail was most grateful, and in the evening we reached Sandusky City. A lake steamer made her appearance in the harbour the next day, and we embarked for Buffalo.

"At Buffalo our travellers gladly welcomed their letters from home which were awaiting them there, and it was here that Mr. Dickens received from Carlyle and other eminent English writers the letters endorsing his views upon the subject of ' International Copyright Law.'

"It was but a short ride from Buffalo to Niagara. Mr. Dickens had been repeatedly warned not to expect too much of Niagara and told that people were often disappointed in their anticipation of the grandeur of the scene.

"As we crossed on the ferry-boat, Dickens gazed at the falls in astonishment! When midway over, he looked around for a few moments and said solemnly, as if to himself, ' Great God! How can any man be disappointed at this ! '

"Rooms had been engaged at the Clifton House, and now the tired travellers looked forward to a season of perfect rest and quiet. In this they were not disappointed. It was much too early in the season for visitors, and with the exception of a few English officers and gentlemen residing in the neighbourhood, there was no company to call upon them. The time allotted to be spent at Niagara was full of pure enjoyment, and when it was over they started for Toronto, thence to Kingston, Montreal and Quebec. At all these places Mr. Dickens and his wife were most cordially received by the government officials, officers of the army, and the resident English population. The time was pleasantly passed in rides and visits, and also in some private theatricals, in which Mr. Dickens and several English officers took part."

Dickens left for Niagara Falls on the afternoon of Tuesday, April 26, and remained in Canada until

Monday, May 30, when he left Montreal for New York, and as everything in Canada was entirely to his satisfaction no effort has been made to collect the newspaper accounts of his stay in British America.

He arrived in New York on the afternoon of Wednesday, June 1, where he remained that night, and the next morning went back up the Hudson River to visit the Shaker village, Lebanon and West Point, returning to New York on Monday. The stay in Canada and return trip to New York are all fully described in *American Notes* and in his letters to Forster.

Dickens left New York for home on Tuesday, June 7, on the sailing vessel *George Washington*. The New York newspapers made no mention other than the simple fact that he had sailed. Mr. Philip Hone, who was one of a number of American friends who went aboard the boat to bid the Dickens party farewell, writes in his diary under date of June 8 as follows—

"Yesterday was quite a day of jubilee with me. On coming down to breakfast I found a kind note from Mr. James G. King, to attend, with one of my lady folk, a parting breakfast given at Highwood, to Mr. and Mrs. Charles Dickens. Margaret and I went over at ten o'clock, where we found the Boz and Bozzess, Mr. and Mrs. Archibald Gracie, Miss Wilkes and the Doctor, Mr. and Mrs. Colden, Miss Ward and the charming family of our host and hostess. We had a breakfast worthy of the entertainers and the entertained; and such strawberries and cream! The house and the grounds and the view, and the library and the conservatory were all more beautiful than I have ever seen them. Having been favoured with an invitation from Grinnell, Minturn & Co., the owners of the ship *George Washington*, to accompany Mr. and Mrs. Dickens to Sandy Hook, I left Margaret to take Mrs. Colden and Miss Wilkes in the barouche to town and was driven down to Jersey City, where by previous arrangements a steamboat was sent to take us aboard, and we embarked with a 'hurrah' from the people assembled on the dock. We found on board the steamboat a large party of gentlemen, among whom were the owners, Rev. Dr. Wainwright, Drs. Francis Cornell and Wilkes; Mr. Chapman of Boston; Judge Warren of New Bedford, Mr. Crittendon, the distinguished Kentucky Senator; Charles King, D. C. Colden, Simeon Draper, James Bowen, Harry Carey, J. Prescott Hall, R. M. Blatchford and his son, and other gentlemen—a right pleasant merry company. We went delightfully down to Sandy Hook, where the ship lay at anchor. Soon after we came aboard a cold collation was spread, to which, and to an infinite number of bottles of champagne wine, the utmost justice was done. Speeches and toasts and bright sayings went round, of all which Dickens was the most fruitful theme. I gave his health in the following toast : ' *Charles Dickens*—the welcome acquired by literary reputation has been confirmed and justified by personal intercourse.' At the conclusion of this jolly repast, we took leave of the passengers with many hearty shakings of the hands and good wishes, returned to the steamer, towed the ship to the point off Sandy Hook, and, having cast her off and given three cheers, returned in proper style. She went ' on her journeying ' and was soon out of sight, and our party returned to the city about six o'clock."

About the middle of August there appeared in some of the New York newspapers a letter dated "July 15—Devonshire Terrace, Parkgate," addressed "To the Editor of the *Morning Chronicle*," and signed "Charles Dickens." A search of the obtainable files of the New York newspapers fails to discover this letter, but Mr. Hone in his diary gives the following extract from it—

"Though in my travels from city to city I, of course, found much to be pleased with and astonished at, yet the total difference between our good old English customs and the awkwardness, the uncouth manners and the unmitigated selfishness which you meet everywhere in America, made my journey one of a good deal of annoyance. I do not think Americans, as a people, have much good taste. To a person brought up among them, and in their own way, of course, the glaring faults that strike a stranger do not appear; but to any well-bred man from abroad, the effect of the prevalent features of the American character is by no means agreeable.

"It may be said that I, of all persons, ought to be blind to the dark spots of American character, treated as I have been by the American people. I do not agree with this view of the case. I did not seek their attention, their dinners and their balls. On the contrary, these things were forced upon me; many times to the serious inconvenience of myself and my party. The kindness of a friend, if it is troublesome and officious, often annoys as much as the injuries of an enemy. The Americans have most of the faults of both the English and the French, with very few of their virtues. I never thought that I was petted merely for *myself*; but as a kind of a *monster*, to look at, and imbue my keepers with somewhat of the notoriety that enveloped myself. I can freely and confidently say that this was the case, almost without exception."

Mr. Hone could not believe that a guest who had been so recently honoured to such an extent as Dickens could be guilty of such "wilful unappreciation" and "gross ingratitude," and wrote a letter to him calling for his "avowal or denial of this unworthy piece of splendid impudence," and on October 6 he received the following reply—

Broadstairs, Kent, England,
September 16, 1842.

My DEAR SIR,
    I am very much obliged to you for your friendly letter, which I have received with real pleasure. It reached me last night, being forwarded from London to this seaside fishing town, where we are enjoying ourselves quietly until the end of the month. I answer it without an hour's delay, though I fear my reply may lie at the post office some days before it finds a steam packet to carry it across the ocean.

The letter to which you refer is, from beginning to

end, in every word and syllable, the cross of every *t* and the dot of every *i*, a most wicked and nefarious forgery. I have never published one word or line in reference to America in any quarter, except the copyright circular, and the unhung scoundrel who invented that astounding lie knew this as well as I do. It has caused me more pain, and more of a vague desire to take somebody by the throat, than such an event should perhaps have awakened in an honourable man. But I have not contradicted it publicly, deeming that it would not become my character or elevate me in my own self-respect to do so. I shall hope to send for your acceptance, next month, my *American Notes*. Meanwhile, and always, and with cordial remembrance to all friends,

I am, my dear sir,

Faithfully yours,

CHARLES DICKENS.

CHAPTER XIII

It may seem to the reader that, as the question of an International Copyright between the United States and Great Britain having been settled in 1891, any extended reference to it at the present time might be considered something in the nature of a post-mortem held long after the corpse had been interred. That the subject, however, was one to which Dickens referred in no uncertain words whenever the opportunity presented, not only while in the United States, but also after his return to England, and as it was a subject on which the American papers in 1842 had much to say both for and against,—these seem to the writer sufficient reasons for including a chapter on the subject in this book.

Dickens himself, in a letter to one of his sons, has said that whatever he put his hands to he did with all his powers, and it will be seen later that while in the United States in 1842, so far as the subject of International Copyright was concerned, he was instant in season; and also, as some of his critics believed, out of season.

There can be no doubt as to the abstract justice of an International Copyright Law, and that at the time of his first visit to America, Dickens himself believed he had suffered personally by reason of the piracy of his books by publishers in the United States, as he himself said, "Of all men living, I am the greatest loser by it." He wrote to Mrs. Pardoe referring to the "American robbers," as he called the publishers: "The existing law allows them to reprint any English book without any communication whatever with the author or anybody else. My books have all been reprinted on these agreeable terms." This statement was literally true, as all of Dickens's works were reprinted in the United States, most of them in monthly parts, just as soon after the arrival of the original numbers from England as possible, and some of these reprints sold at as low a price as six cents a copy. The writer believes that while this resulted in a temporary loss to the author, the final result, although he did not reap the benefit till 1868, was that his books were more widely read in the United States than in England, where the price of the monthly parts was one shilling, almost twenty-five cents, or five dollars for the bound volume. It is doubtful whether Dickens would have had so many readers in the United States if it had not been for those cheap reprints.

Horace Greeley said in the *New York Tribune*, during Dickens's visit in 1868 : "The fame as a novelist which Mr. Dickens had already created in America, and which, at the best, has never yielded him anything particularly munificent or substantial, is become his capital stock in the present enterprise," a statement which his biographer Mr. Forster said was faithfully and truly put. This capital stock, as Greeley called it, earned Dickens such dividends that he was able to return to England after his second visit with about £20,000 pounds ($100,000) in his pockets as the result of his readings. This amount was considered at the time so enormous for a lecturer or reader to receive that some of the comic papers published cartoons showing Dickens carrying home his profits in a carpet bag.

Many American authors were also strongly in favour of an International Copyright for the reason that they believed it increased the number of pirated editions and, of course, the number of readers of the works of foreign authors, for as long as publishers would reprint the novels of such authors as Dickens, Charles Lever, Lytton Bulwer and others without paying any royalty, there was little show for the American authors' works being printed when the authors required a royalty. Mr. Cornelius Mathews, in his speech at the Dickens dinner in New York, said on this phase of the subject—

"What is the present condition of the Field of Letters in America? It is in a state of desperate anarchy—without order, without system, without certainty. For several years past, it has been sown broadcast with foreign publications of every name and nature; what growth has ensued? No single work, so far as I can see, has sprung up as its legitimate result; no addition to the stock of native poetry or fiction; no tree has blossomed; no solitary blade struck through the hard and ungrateful turf. Whatever has been produced has been in spite of opposition from within and without; has been the bright exception, not the rule. Instead of being fostered and promoted, as it should be, our domestic literature is borne down by an immethodical and unrestrained republication of every foreign work that will bear the charges of the compositor and paper-maker."

Several of Dickens's biographies written since his death have stated that the prime object of his visit in 1842 was to agitate the passage of an International Copyright Law. Some of the English critics, in reviewing the *American Notes*, made the same statement, and when the writer of a review of the book in the *Edinburgh Review* gave the same reason for the trip, Dickens not only asked the editor of that periodical to correct it, but he also wrote the following letter, published in *The Times*, January 16, 1843, emphatically denying the statement—

"*Devonshire Terrace, Sunday, January* 15.

"*To the Editor of* THE TIMES.

"SIR,
"In your paper of Saturday you thought it worth while to refer to an article on my *American Notes*, published in the recent number of the *Edinburgh Review*, for the purpose of commenting on a statement of the reviewer's in reference to the English and American Press, with which I have no further concern than that I know it to be a very monstrous likening of unlike things.
"I am anxious to give to another misrepresentation

made by the same writer, whoever he may be—which *is* personal to myself—the most public and positive contradiction in my power, and shall be really obliged to you if you will allow me to do this through the medium of your columns.

"He asserts ' That if he be rightly informed, I went to America as a kind of missionary in the cause of International Copyright.' He is wrongly informed, and reports without inquiry a piece of information which I could only characterize by using one of the shortest and strongest words in the language. Upon my honour, the assertion is destitute of any futile aspect or colouring of truth.

"It occurred to me to speak (as other English travellers connected with literature have done before me) of the existing laws—or want of laws—on the subject of international copyright, when I found myself in America, simply because, unexperienced at the time in the American public, I believed they would listen to the truth, even from one presumed to have an interest in stating it, and would not long refuse to recognize a principle of common honesty, even though it happened to clash with a miserably short-sighted view of their own profit and advantage.

"I am, Sir, your obliged servant,
"CHARLES DICKENS."

When Dickens, after his first speech at the Boston dinner, found that his remarks on the subject had been met with so much opposition by some of the editors and publishers, he came to the conclusion that he would keep up the agitation and strike while the iron was hot, with the result that in nearly every speech he made thereafter he referred to the subject, and with added argument and fire.

Dickens, in his speech at the Hartford dinner, again spoke in very strong terms, voicing his indignation on the subject; and, referring to the speech, he wrote Forster from New York on February 24, saying: "I had no sooner made my second speech than such an outcry began, for the purpose of deterring me from doing the like in this city, as an Englishman can form no notion of." The following is an extract from the *Hartford Times*, which is an example of the "outcry" Dickens refers to—

"Mr. Dickens alluded in his remarks to an International Copyright Law. In Boston he also alluded to the same subject, intimating that England had done her duty and it now remained for the United States to follow suit. It happens that we want no advice on the subject, and it will be better for Mr. Dickens if he refrains from introducing the subject hereafter, but it is not pleasant to pursue the subject further at this time."

In the letter to Forster above quoted, Dickens wrote referring to the New York dinner : "The dinner committee here (composed of the first gentlemen in America, remember that) were so dismayed that they besought me not to pursue the subject, *although they every one* agreed with me. I answered that I would. That nothing would deter me; that the shame was theirs, not mine; and that I would not spare them when I got home, I would not be silenced here. Accordingly, when the night came, I asserted my right, with all the means I could command to give it dignity, in face, matter or words," etc.

It will be noted from the date of this letter (February 24) that it was written after the dinner, which occurred February 19, and from the absence of any reference to any remarks by any of the other speakers, the inference would be that the subject was ignored by them, and that Dickens himself was the only one who said anything at all on the subject which he had so much at heart. Just why Dickens did not tell Forster that the President, Washington Irving, proposed the sentiment "International Copyright," which was responded to by Mr. Cornelius Mathews, is difficult to understand, for in other letters he had written that the best people amongst the authors and editors were in accord with him. The facts are, however, that Mr. Mathews made a very strong plea for the copyright, as shown by the following brief quotation from his address—

R

"Standing here to-night, the representative, in some humble measure, of the interests of American authors on the question, I say they have been treated by this people and government as no other of its citizens; that an enormous fraud practised upon their British brethren has been allowed so to operate upon them as to blight their hopes and darken their fair fame. . . .

"By what casuistry or jurisprudence does that which is property in one latitude in one civilized country cease to be property when transferred within the limits of another?"

Mr. Mathews spoke for nearly twenty minutes on the subject, and concluded: "I offer you, Mr. President, *An International Copyright*—the only honest turnpike between the readers of two great nations."

It is difficult, at this late day, to understand how the dinner committee should beg Dickens not to speak on the subject, although they every one agreed with him, and then have the very subject he says they wished him to keep silence upon put on the programme as one of the set subjects to be spoken upon by one of the guests who was himself an American author. The only reasonable explanation that can be given for Dickens ignoring this in his letter to Forster is that his treatment by some of the newspapers, not only on account of his advocacy of the copyright, but also on account of their remarks about his personality, manners and attire, had so angered him that it was impossible for him at that time to speak or write on the subject in a fair or impartial manner.

As an indication of how the better class of newspapers treated the subject, the following editorial from the *New York Tribune*, February 14, probably written by Horace Greeley himself, is given—

"We have heard rumours that Mr. Dickens has ventured to allude, in his replies to complimentary addresses, to the gross injustice and spoliation to which he and foreign authors are exposed in this country, from the absence of an International Copyright or some other law protecting the rights of literary property. We trust he will not be deterred from speaking the frank, round truth by any mistaken courtesy, diffidence or misapprehension of public sentiment. He ought to speak out on this matter, for who shall protest against robbery if those who are robbed may not? Here is a man who writes for a living, and writes nobly; and we of this country greedily devour his writings, are entertained and instructed by them, yet refuse to protect his rights as an author that he may realize a single dollar from all their vast American sale and popularity. Is this right? Do we look well offering him toasts, compliments and other syllabub while we refuse him naked justice—while we say that every man may take from him the fruits of his labours without recompense or redress?

"It does very well in a dinner speech to say that fame and popularity and all that are more than sordid gold; but he has a wife and four children, whom his death may very possibly leave destitute—perhaps dependent for their bread—while publishers who have grown rich on his writings roll by in their carriages; and millions who have been instructed by them contribute not one farthing to their comfort. But suppose him rich, if you please, the justice of the case is unaltered. He is the just owner of his own productions as much as though he had made axes or horseshoes; and the people who refuse to protect his right ought not to insult him with the mockery of thriftless praise. Let us be just, and then generous. Good reader! if you think our guest ought to be enabled to live by and enjoy the fruits of his talents and toil, just put your names to a petition for an International Copyright Law, and then you can take his hand heartily if he comes your way and say, if need be, ' I have done what is in my power to protect you from robbery!' The passage of this act of long-deferred justice will be a greater tribute to his worth and achievements than acres of inflated compliments soaked in champagne."

This editorial speaks entirely in favour of the copyright solely on the grounds of the personal injustice to Dickens, but a week later (February 21) the *Tribune*

R 2

contained another editorial, presumably written by Horace
Greeley, the editor, arguing in favour of the law for a
very different reason : that of the injustice to American
authors.

"*Justice to Authors.*—We publish on our last page
the speech of Mr. Mathews in regard to International
Copyright, for which we especially ask the consideration
of our readers. The question is one of universal, and
by no means trifling, interest, and is destined to attract
attention more largely than hitherto. We must be
permitted to add a few words in support of its positions.

"How shall it be contended by any unwarped, in-
genuous mind that the author has not a clear, absolute,
indefeasible right of property in his own productions in
every part of the world? What possible act of human
wit or effort shall give a clear title if his does not? How
shall it be maintained that the man, whether citizen or
alien, who slays the deer in the common forest, who lures
the fish from the wild mountain stream or tracks the bee
to his secret hive, shall have exclusive property in the
spoils which he has appropriated from the common
stores of the race, while the author who builds out into
infinite space—who peoples dreary chaos with the bright
and beautiful creations of his genius, shall have none,
but be left the prey of all who covet, and whose covet-
ousness will, of course, be just in proportion to the
value and productiveness of the fruit of his labours.
The denial of protection to the rights of authors is
not even impolitic and unjust, but a positive and flagrant
robbery.

"More absurd is the cavil which affirms the intangi-
bility of literary property, the impossibility of defining
and securing it.

"Society submits to Law and Government mainly to
ensure the protection of those rights which stretch out
beyond reach of the individual's sword-arm—beyond the
range of his rifle. It is emphatically because the rights
of the author are easily subverted that we invoke for him
the protection of that shield which should be as broad
as the domain of civilized existence.

"We loathe to speak of this matter in the light of
policy when the demand of justice is so clear and urgent.
All who are in literary vocations well know that our
robbery of the foreign author dooms the American to
neglect and want; for what bookseller will buy his
manuscript when he can reprint the last popular London
novel from fair type and shining paper without even
the ceremony of saying 'By your leave'? Thus ten
British books to one American are read by our people,
and the intellect and taste of the country kept intermin-
ably in colonial vassalage.

"The author should hold his book by the same tenure
as his wheat, if he were a farmer, or his axes if a black-
smith. The copyright is at best a grudging restoration
of part of what society has unjustly taken. *Barnaby
Rudge* belongs to Boz, and *Bracebridge Hall* to Irving,
just as clearly and perpetually as the Astor House to
Mr. Astor or the ox to the grazier. If justice were done
by our laws, Genius would no longer be forced by
hunger to pander to the depravity of the age, to the
narrow prejudice of a nation. We should no longer
pamper Ainsworths and Marryats while famishing
Coleridges and Wordsworths—— But we have not
space to pursue this theme. People of the United
States: We ask you to petition Congress for Justice
to Authors. We appeal to you to urge upon our Government that true and lofty National Policy which aims to
nerve the heart that beats, the arm that strikes for the
Elevation of Man!"

Having started the agitation and begun the fight in
his Boston speech, and seeing the manner in which the
discussion was carried on in the American Press,
Dickens was not the man to let the matter drop. One of
the means which he adopted to add fuel to the flame is
shown by the following extract from a letter to Forster—

"I will tell you what *I* should like, my dear friend,
always supposing that your judgment concurs with mine,
and that you would take the trouble to get such a document. I should like to have a letter addressed to me by

the principal English authors who signed the International Copyright Petition, expressing their sense that I have done my duty in the cause. I am sure I deserve it, but I don't want it on that ground. It is because its publication in the best journals here would unquestionably do great good. As the gauntlet is down, let us go on."

Forster's judgment did agree with Dickens, and he procured the joint letter which Dickens desired addressed to him personally, and also a second, with the same signatures, addressed "To the American People."

The principal agitation against the Copyright Law came from the publishers who had been reprinting Dickens's works, and on April 26 a convention was held in Boston for the purpose of taking action on a memorial to Congress asking that a duty be placed on foreign books, and also protesting against the passage of an International Copyright Law. The following extract from the *Boston Mercantile Journal* gives briefly an account of the action taken at this meeting, and a synopsis of the memorial—

"*Convention of the Book Trade.*—The Convention of persons engaged in the manufacture of books was held, last evening, at the hall beneath the Boston Museum. There were printers, publishers, type-founders, paper-makers, book-binders, engravers, etc., present. The meeting was called to order by Charles A. Wells, and was subsequently organized by the choice of Samuel G. Goodrich, President, John Prentiss of Keene (N. H.), and Harrison Gray of Boston, Vice-Presidents, and Samuel D. Warren, Secretary.

"Mr. Goodrich, on taking the chair, said that the committee had taken pains to collect facts and obtain specific information on the subject referred to them, which they had incorporated in a general form into the Memorial, which he then accordingly read.

"The Memorial sets forth that in fixing duties on foreign books, regard should be had, firstly, to the revenue; secondly, to the various arts and trades dependent on their production; thirdly, the effort which may follow, considering books as instruments for the diffusion of knowledge.

"The Memorial then takes up the subject of our International Copyright Law—and undertakes to show by various arguments and reasons that the enactment of such a law would be impolitic, would be injurious to the interests of the country, is not required by justice, and ought not at this time to be carried into effect. Some interesting statistics are embodied in the Memorial, from which it appears that the number of persons employed in the various arts connected with printing and publishing is not less than 41,000—and those who are dependent upon them for their support amount to four times that number. The capital invested is almost $15,000,000, and the total productions not short of $27,000,000.

"After the Memorial was read, Mr. Bowen of Cambridge rose and objected to the Memorial as embracing two subjects not necessarily connected with each other, viz. Protection to American Industry and International Copyright. He believed that many persons who would cheerfully agree to the sentiments expressed in the first part of the Memorial would disapprove of the views contained in the latter part—and he therefore would move that the document be recommitted, with instructions to report one Memorial relating exclusively to the subject of the protection of books, printing materials, etc., and another, if it should be thought necessary, relating to an International Copyright.

"On this question a protracted debate ensued, in which several gentlemen took part—among them were Mr. Brown, Mr. Goodrich, Harrison Gray, Colonel Parker, J. H. Jenks and G. W. F. Mellen. The motion was rejected. A motion was then made by another gentleman to strike out that part of the Memorial relating to the International Copyright Law. This was also rejected by an overwhelming vote. The Memorial was finally adopted with only a trifling modification."

Dickens, on February 24, wrote Forster a letter in which he said regarding the proposed law: "Washington Irving, Prescott, Hoffman, Bryant, Halleck, Dana, Washington Allison, every man who writes in this country, is devoted to the question, yet not one of them dares to raise his voice and complain of the law."

Dickens's agitation of the subject, however, must have given these authors courage and overcome their timidity, for later they all signed a memorial to Congress in favour of the proposed law, and Dickens himself carried this memorial to Washington to Henry Clay, who was to present it to the Senate. Dickens wrote Forster regarding this memorial, that he was going to assist Mr. Kennedy, the Chairman of the Committee of the House of Representatives, in writing the report favouring its passage.

On April 29 Dickens wrote from Niagara Falls to his Boston friend, Mr. C. C. Felton, a letter enclosing four copies of some document relating to International Copyright, in which he said: "My first idea was, publicity being the object, to send one to you for a Boston newspaper, another to Bryant for his paper, a third to the *New York Herald* (because of its larger circulation), and a fourth to a highly respectable journal at Washington (the property of a gentleman and a fine fellow named Seaton, whom I know there), which I think is called the *Intelligencer.* . . .

"Whether to limit its publication to one journal, or to extend it to several, is a question so very difficult of decision to a stranger that I have finally resolved to send these papers to you and ask you (mindful of the conversation we had on this head one day in that renowned oyster cellar) to resolve the point for me. . . . If you see Sommer, take him into our council. The only two things to be borne in mind are, first, that if they are to be published in several quarters, they must be published in all simultaneously; secondly, that I hold them in trust, to put them before the people."

Dickens also wrote the next day (April 30) to the "fine fellow" at Washington, who was Mr. W. W. Seaton, the editor of the *National Intelligencer* of that city, advising him of the important documents, of which the following is an extract—

"I have received some documents from the greatest writers of England, relative to the International Copyright, which they call upon me to make public immediately. They have taken fire at my being misrepresented in such a matter, and have acted as such men should.

"They consist of two letters, and a memorial to the American people signed by Bulwer, Rogers, Hallam, Talfourd, Sydney Smith, and so forth. Not very well knowing, as a stranger, whether it would be best to publish them in newspapers or in a literary journal, I have sent them to some gentlemen in Boston and have begged them to decide. In the event of their recommending the first-mentioned course, I have begged them to send a manuscript copy to you immediately."

It will be noticed that Dickens did not tell either Mr. Felton or Mr. Seaton that he himself had, through his friend Forster, procured the writing of these letters and memorials. The manner in which Dickens obtained these manuscripts, and procured their publication in the newspapers, shows that he was equally as adept in the means by which public sentiment is created through the public press as any press agent or "publicity man" of the great corporations of the present day.

Felton and Seaton evidently decided to publish the documents in the newspapers, as they appeared in Bryant's paper, the *New York Evening Post* on May 9, 1842, and probably in the other papers which Dickens mentioned, and they are here reprinted as they appeared in the *Evening Post*.

"*Niagara Falls, April* 30, 1842.

"*To the Editor of* THE EVENING POST.

"SIR—I found awaiting me in the post office in Buffalo certain letters from England, of which the following are copies. I ask the favour of you that you will publish them in your columns; and I do so in order that the people of America will understand that the sentiments that I have expressed on all public occasions since I have been in these United States, in reference to a law of International Copyright, are not merely my individual sentiments, but are, without any qualification, statement or reserve, the opinions of the great body of British authors represented by the distinguished men whose signatures are attached to these documents.

"That they are also the opinions of the native writers of America they have sufficiently shown in their earnest petitions in the legislatures upon this subject.

"I would beg to lay particular stress upon the letter from Mr. Carlyle; not only because the plain and manly truth it speaks is calculated, I should conceive, to arrest attention and respect in my country, and most of all in this, but because his creed in this respect is, without the abatement of one jot or atom, mine. And because I have never considered, and never will consider, this question in any other light than as plain right or wrong—justice or injustice.

"I am, sir, your faithful servant,
"CHARLES DICKENS."

"*London, March* 28, 1842.

"DEAR DICKENS,

"The deep interest we take in the efforts you have been making for the cause of International Copyright impels us to express to you our earnest sympathies with your cause and cordial wishes for its success. Our feeling, like your own, is not prompted by a desire that authors on this side of the Atlantic should obtain some palpable reward of their industry from the mighty public who enjoy its fruits—but is established by the conviction that on the issue depends the question whether the intellect of America shall speedily be embodied in a literature worthy of its new-born powers—or shall be permitted to languish under disadvantages which may long deprive the world of the full development of its greatness. Assured that in promoting this object you will make the best return for that generous appreciation which your genius has received from our Transatlantic brethren, and which we have learned with grateful and unmingled delight,

"We are your obliged and grateful servants—

"Edward Lytton Bulwer.	Henry Hallam.
Thomas Campbell.	Sydney Smith.
Alfred Tennyson.	H. H. Milman.
T. N. Talfourd.	Samuel Rogers.
Thomas Hood.	John Forster.
Leigh Hunt.	Barry Cornwall.

"To CHARLES DICKENS, Esquire,
"*United States.*"

"TO THE AMERICAN PEOPLE.

"We, the undersigned, in transmitting to one of our most eminent English authors the following memorial for an International Copyright between the United States and Great Britain, are willing that our claims should be considered part of our interests in urging them.

"Addressing a great nation—chiefly united to us by a common ancestry; speaking the same language and indebted to the same hereditary sources for models in literature and authorities in science, we venture to hope that a prayer which asks for labours not less useful to America than Great Britain, those rewards which can only be proportionate to the estimation in which, by Americans, the labours may be held, will need little argument to advance it with the legislature and people of the United States, provided that no counterbalancing disadvantage can be proved to arise from its concession.

"Independently of grace or generosity to ourselves, we conclude that the question of International Copyright can only be viewed by enlightened Americans—first, as affecting the interests of American authors; secondly, as influencing those of the American reading public.

"With regard to the first, we respectfully submit that a greater curse cannot be inflicted on American authors nor a more serious injury on American literature than a state of law which admits gratuitously the works of foreign authors in the same language. It is impossible that an American writer can hope for adequate remuneration in any branch of literature so long as he can be met by the publishers with a declaration that they can publish the best English works without paying a farthing for the copyrights. The necessary consequence must be that the energy of American industry and genius, so remarkable in every other department of human intellect, will be greatly chilled and oppressed in the general departments of literature. Against all possible exertion of native authors is arrayed a wholesale system of competition existing only by means of piracy and smuggling. And we are convinced that the ultimate consequences of inundating the American market with English works, for which no remuneration is paid to the author, must be the extinction of American literature as an adequate, honourable and independent profession.

"With regard to the second—the only interest the American public have is in the supply of English works in as cheap a form as at present, and there can be no doubt that this would continue to be the case were a copyright established. Works are sold at a low or high price, not in proportion as there is a copyright or not, but in proportion as they can obtain a larger or smaller community of readers. The noble cultivation of the American people, which forms a reading public almost commensurate with the entire population, renders it the obvious interest of every author (and every publisher) to adapt his price to the means of all his readers, and we venture to predict that were an International Copyright established not one popular English work would be sold in the United States at a higher price than at present. So far, if this be true, the American public will be no losers. But will they be no gainers if they have removed from their own writers and men of genius the great impediment to a purely national literature?

"We do not pause to inquire if there be any separate or oligarchical interests against us in this great question; because we venture to trust that in a country, the institutions of which are based on foundations so broad, the minor and selfish interests which cannot be supported by simple justice are not suffered to prevail. And also, because we cannot conceive that concession to our prayer would disturb or invade one solitary vested right.

"On the other hand, in our sanguine anticipations from a legislature willing to be just to others, and honourably jealous of the fame of the people it represents—in arts and letters, no less than in arms and commerce—we look forward with pleasure to the new and firm bond that the law we pray for must establish between our American brotherhood and ourselves. Such a law must naturally and obviously bind the large body of our writers to peace and amity with the public they may then justly consider as their own, and whatever tends to connect the intelligence of one country with that of another must exert a deeper and more permanent influence than they who superficially regard this question as one of mere pecuniary profit to English authors can foresee upon the tranquillity and civilization of the world.

"Edward Lytton Bulwer.   Henry Hallam.
Thomas Campbell.   Sydney Smith.
Alfred Tennyson.   H. H. Milman.
T. N. Talfourd.   Samuel Rogers.
Thomas Hood.   John Forster.
Leigh Hunt.   Barry Cornwall."

" *Templeland* (*for Lonaon*),
"*March* 26, 1842.

"MY DEAR SIR,
    "We learn by the newspapers that you everywhere, in America, stir up the question of International Copyright, and thereby awaken huge dissonance where all else were triumphant unison for you. I am asked my opinion of the matter—and requested to write it down in words.

    "Several years ago, if memory err not, I was one of the many English writers who, under the auspices of Miss Martineau, did sign a petition to Congress praying for an International Copyright between the two nations, which properly are not two nations—but one—*indivisible* by Parliament, Congress or any kind of human law or diplomacy, being already united by Heaven's act of Parliament and the everlasting law of Nature and fact. To that opinion I still adhere and am like to continue it.

"In discussion of the matter before any Congress or Parliament, manifold considerations and argumentations will arise which are to me not interesting nor essential for helping me to a decision. They respect the time and manner in which the thing should be, not at all whether the thing should be or not. In an ancient Book, reverenced, I should hope, on both sides of the ocean, it was thousands of years ago written down in the most decided and explicit manner, ' Thou shalt not steal.' That thou belongest to a different ' nation ' and can steal without being certainly hanged for it gives thee no permission to steal. Thou shalt not in any wise steal at all ! So it is written down for Nations and for Men in the Law Book of the Maker of this universe. Nay, poor Jeremy Bentham and others step in here and would demonstrate that it is actually our true convenience and expediency not to steal. Which I, for my share on the great scale, and on the small, and in all conceivable scales and shapes, do also firmly believe it to be. For example, if nations abstained from stealing, what need were there of fighting—with its butcherings and burnings, decidedly the most expensive thing in this world ? How much more two nations which, as I said, are but one nation, knit in a thousand ways by Nature and Practical Intercourse, individual brother elements of the same great Saxondom to which in all honourable ways be long life !

"When Mr. Robert Roy Macgregor lived in the district of Menteith on a Highland border two centuries ago, he, for his part, found it more convenient to supply himself with beef by stealing it alive from the adjacent glens than by buying it killed in the Stirling Butcher's Market. It was Mr. Roy's plan of supplying himself with beef in those days, this of stealing it. In many a little 'Congress' in the district of Menteith there was debating, doubt it not, and much specious argumentation this way and that before they could ascertain that, really and truly, buying was the best way to get your boof, which, however, in the long run, they did with one assent find it indisputably to be, and accordingly they hold by it to this day.

"Wishing you a pleasant voyage and a swift and safe return, I remain always,
          "My dear Sir,
               "Yours very sincerely,
                    "THOMAS CARLYLE.
"To CHARLES DICKENS, Esquire,
     "*In the United States*."

The same issue of the *Evening Post* also contained the following editorial, which is a plea not only for justice to English authors and publishers, but also for the authors and publishers of the United States—

"We publish in this sheet several papers received this morning from Mr. Dickens relating to the subject of an International Copyright. The 'Address to the American People,' with so many illustrious names among its signatures—Campbell and Hallam and Rogers, Bulwer and others worthy to be placed by their side—will be read with a strong and respectful interest. The letter of Mr. Carlyle to Mr. Dickens is highly characteristic of the writer.

"It is a mistake to suppose that if we refuse to make an arrangement for securing to the authors of America and Britain a copyright in both countries, the advantage of the injustice would be on our side; that if wrong be committed for want of such an arrangement, the profits of the wrong will go into the pockets of American publishers. American authors are every year producing more and more works for the republication of which there is a demand in England. Within the last year the number of books written by American authors which have been successful in Britain is greater than that of foreign works which have been successful in this country. Robertson's work on *Palestine,* Stephens' *Travels in Central America,* Caltin's book on the *North American History,* Cooper's *Deerslayer,* the last volume of Bancroft's *American History,* several works prepared by Anthon for the schools—here is a list of American works republished in England within the year which we might easily enlarge, and for which we should be puzzled to find an equivalent in works written in England within the same time and republished here. Our eminent authors are still engaged in their literary labours.

"Cooper, within a fortnight past, has published a work stamped with all the vigour of his faculties, Prescott is occupied in writing the *History of Peru,* Bancroft is engaged in continuing the annals of his native country, Sparks is still employed in his valuable historical labours, and Stephens is pushing his researches in Central America with a view of giving their results to the world. We were told the other day of a work prepared for the press by Washington Irving, which would have appeared ere this but for the difficulties in the way of securing a copyright for it in England as well as here. He has done this, however, we presume, on his way to Spain.

"The success of so many of our authors will have the effect of raising up a host of literary adventurers among us. In no part of the world are hope and emulation so easily awakened as here. There is no part of the world where a few brilliant examples have so powerful an influence in calling up rivals and competitors in the same path to fortune or to fame as in this republic. We shall have men preparing themselves by intense study, and exercising their faculties to the utmost to reach the same eminence which has been attained by other authors, their countrymen, and, if possible, to go beyond it. In a conversation which we had the other day with an eminent American author, now abroad, he remarked that if American literature continued to make the same progress as it had done for twenty years past, the day was not very far distant when the greater number of books designed for readers of the English language would be produced in America.

"If we look back to the year 1820 and compare the state of authorship in our country at that time to what it is now; if we consider how barren our literature was then and how prolific it has now become; if we look at the quality of the works produced at the two different periods, and the reward received by their authors, we shall find ourselves obliged to admit that the prediction is a very probable one.

"The plea against an international copyright, that it gives our publishers an advantage over those of Great Britain, is not true, or if true, is true for the present moment only. If our publishers enrich themselves at the expense of British authors, British publishers enrich themselves at the expense of ours, and will continue to do so from year to year until the advantage will be shifted from our side to theirs. The policy of our country is to secure for its authors the benefit of an International Copyright before that time arrives."

Notwithstanding all this agitation for the copyright law by both English and American authors in 1842, it was not till 1891, nearly fifty years later, that an International Copyright between Great Britain and America was put into effect.

S

CHAPTER XIV

THE PRESS DINNER AT DELMONICO'S

[The account which follows is copied from the *New York Tribune*, Monday, April 20, 1868.]

OVER two hundred members of the Press of the United States, on Saturday evening at Delmonico's, united in a testimonial dinner to Mr. Dickens, previous to his departure for England. The following is the preliminary correspondence on the subject—

New York, Jan. 22, 1868.

MR. CHARLES DICKENS—Dear Sir: On behalf of the members of the Press of New York, we beg to solicit the pleasure of your company to dinner at such time as may suit your convenience, upon your return to this city in the coming spring. Inasmuch as Saturday evening is the one of all the week that the largest number of our busy journalists are free from business, we venture to suggest the appointment of that evening for the proposed meeting, but trust that you will not allow this suggestion to prevent you from designating another.

We beg to add that it has been a rule of our meetings thus far that no mention be made of them in the public prints; but remembering that previous to your departure from England to the United States you accepted an invitation to a dinner of which the London Press made notice, we shall be happy to waive our rule in case you should so desire, since our sole wish is to arrange the entertainment as may best accord with your convenience and preference.

Permit us to ask the favour of an early reply to this note, and at the same time to tender you the sincerely good wishes of those in behalf of whom we write, and of ourselves individually.

Believe us, dear sir, very cordially your friends,

DAVID G. CROLY AND OTHERS, COMMITTEE.

The reply of Mr. Dickens was as follows—

Philadelphia, February 1, 1868.

DEAR SIRS—I beg to acknowledge the receipt of your letter of the 22nd of last month, and to explain to you that I should have done this sooner but that I could not until now be sure of my engagements.

It will give me very great pleasure to accept your invitation, provided that Saturday, the 18th of April (the only day at my disposal before my departure), should suit your convenience.

In reference to your kind suggestion of your readiness to depart from your usual rule of privacy, if I should desire it, I assure you that I have no such wish, and that I leave the matter wholly in your hands.

Very cordially reciprocating your good wishes, I am always, dear sirs, faithfully your friend,

CHARLES DICKENS.

The hour appointed was 5 o'clock p.m., at which time the company assembled in the parlours adjoining the large dining-room, appropriated to the event. At 6 o'clock Mr. Dickens appeared, though suffering from a temporary illness; and, escorted by the Hon. Horace Greeley, who had been selected to preside, proceeded to the dining-hall. This room was decorated with the arms and flags of England and the United States. The guest of the evening sat at the right hand of the president at a table which was placed on an elevated dais at one side of the room; while several other tables were stationed at right angles with this. A fine band of music was in attendance in an adjoining room, and favoured the company with choice selections, and the national airs of the two countries represented by the distinguished guest and his entertainers. The decoration of the tables and the room was in exceedingly good taste, and the rare flowers that graced the board filled the room with the genial breath of spring. The bill of fare was excellent, and by an ingenious nomenclature the different dishes were made to compliment some well-known personages in the walks of literature.

Among the names of gentlemen present were the following : Horace Greeley, Henry J. Raymond, Samuel Bowles of the *Springfield Republican;* W. H. Hurlbut, George William Curtis, James Parton, M. Halstead of Cincinnati, Charles Eliot Norton, George H. Boker, J. T. Fields, Charles F. Briggs, *Putnam's Magazine;* D. G. Croly, *New York World;* Richard D. Kimball, Oliver Johnson, *The Independent;* Charles Nordhoff, *The Evening Post;* John Russell Young, *New York Tribune;* John R. G. Hassard, *New York Tribune;* Professor E. L. Youmans, C. P. Dewey, *Commercial Advertiser;* General Joseph R. Hawley, *Hartford Courant;* G. W. Demars, *Albany Evening Journal;* the Reverend H. N. Fields, E. C. Stedman, Samuel Sinclair, *New York Tribune;* A. J. Schen, *New York Tribune;* F. J. Ottarson, *New York Tribune;* Colonel T. B. Thorpe, D. W. Judd, *Commercial Advertiser;* Dr. William A. Hammond, J. W. Simonson, Augustus Maverick, *Evening Post;* S. S. Conant, *New York Times;* George Sheppard, *New York Times;* W. W. Hardy, *Philadelphia Inquirer;* A. D. Richardson, R. S. Chilton, C. B. Seymour, *New York Times;* F. E. Carpenter, Henry E. Sweetser, *New York World;* Charles H. Sweetser, *Evening Mail;* Thomas MacElrath, J. F. Cleveland, the Hon. William Orton, Thomas Nast, *Harper's Weekly;* E. H. Clement, *New York Tribune;* Edwin De Leon, *New York Citizen;* J. Smith Homans, *Banker's Magazine;* Whitelaw Reid, *Cincinnati Gazette;* B. C. Howard, *Evening Mail;* W. W. Warden, *Philadelphia Inquirer;* William Stuart, Lester Wallack, J. H. Hackett, Leonard W. Jerome, John Bonner, J. H. Osgood, John R. Thompson, William Young, Howard M. Ticknor, J. D. Lippincott, Philadelphia; and S. S. McClure.

At about 9 o'clock the president arose amid loud applause, and upon the restoration of silence, said—

SPEECH OF MR. GREELEY

Gentlemen of the American Press:—It is now a little more than twenty-four years since I, a young printer, recently located in the City of New York, had the audacity to undertake the editing and publishing a weekly newspaper for the first time. Looking around at that day for materials with which to make an engaging appearance before the public, among the London magazines which I purchased for the occasion was *The Old Monthly*, containing a story by a then unknown writer—known to us only by the quaint designation of "Boz." (Great applause.) That story, entitled, I think, at that time "Delicate Attentions," but in its present form entitled "Mr. Watkins Tottle," I selected and published in the first number of the first journal with which my name was connected. (Applause.) Pickwick was then an uncomical, if not uncreated character. (Laughter.) Sam Weller had not yet arisen to increase the mirth of the Anglo-Saxon race. (Cheers.) We had not heard as we have since heard of the writer of those sketches, whose career then I may claim to have in some sort commenced with my own—(great laughter); and the relation of admirer and admired has continued from that day to the present. (Applause.) I am one of not more than twenty of the present company who welcomed him in this country on an occasion like this a quarter of a century ago. When I came to visit Europe, now seventeen years ago, one of my most pleasant experiences there, and one of my pleasantest recollections of Europe, is that of buying in one of the furthest cities I visited—the city of Venice on the Adriatic—an Italian newspaper, and amusing myself with what I could not read—(laughter)—a translation of *David Copperfield*, wherein the dialogue between Ham and Peggotty, with which I was familiar in English, was rendered into very amusing Italian. (Laughter and applause.) And so, friends, I claim a sort of humble connection with the prophet and priest of humanity

who is our guest this evening—(applause)—the man
who, best in this generation when many have worthily
attempted to preach from that magnificent text of the
ploughman-poet of the world, "A man's a man for a'
that," has preached the best sermon from that text, and
perhaps, I may say the most also—whose works from
first to last have been instinct with not only the still,
sad music of humanity such as one—only one strain of
the great epoch of the time; but with the cheering,
hopeful, triumphant music of humanity also; the
humanity of the future, the elevated, enlightened and
glorified humanity which must and shall yet be.
(Applause.) Friends and fellow-labourers, we honour
ourselves to-night in honouring the most successful,
the most thoroughly successful, literary man of our
time. (Applause.) A man who, we may say, is not
ashamed of having come up, as most of us have come
up, from the lower rounds of the ladder of the Press,
and though none of us have reached such a height as
he has, still, I say his success is a sign of hope and
encouragement to every one of us. We are successful
in his triumph. We have each in seeing what he has
done, how nobly, how worthily he has done it, with
what thorough success he has preached the gospel of
humanity, until even nobles and kings have listened in
admiration—I say we have in this success of his an
encouragement to every one of us, saying, "Go up
higher"; do not fear to say your best, for there has
been created a public (if there was not a public thirty
years ago) ready and eager to listen to the noblest and
most humanizing thoughts which the best of us is now
prepared to put before the public. Friends and fellow-
labourers, as I am to set you an example to-night of a
short speech, I will, without further prelude, ask you
to join me in this sentiment: "Health and happiness,
honour and generous, because just, recompense to our
friend and guest, Charles Dickens." (Tremendous
applause and three hearty cheers for Charles Dickens.)

RESPONSE OF MR. DICKENS

Gentlemen, I cannot do better than take my cue
from your distinguished president, and refer in my first
remarks to his remarks in connection with the old
natural association between you and me. When I
received an invitation from a private association of
working members of the Press of New York to dine
with them to-day, I accepted that compliment in grateful remembrance of a calling that was once my own,
and in loyal sympathy for the brotherhood which, in
the spirit, I have never quitted. ("Good, good!" and
applause.) To the wholesome training of severe newspaper work when I was a very young man I constantly
refer my first successes; and my sons will hereafter
testify of their father that he was always steadily proud
of that ladder by which he rose. (Great applause.) If
it were otherwise, I should have but a very poor opinion
of their father, which, perhaps, upon the whole, I have
not. (Laughter and cheers.) Hence, gentlemen, under
any circumstances, this company would have been
exceptionally interesting and gratifying to me. But,
whereas I supposed that, like the fairies' pavilion in
the *Arabian Nights*, it would be but a mere handful,
and I find it turns out, like the same elastic pavilion,
capable of comprehending a multitude, so much the
more proud am I of the honour of being your guest;
for you will readily believe that the more widely representative of the Press in America my entertainers are,
the more I must feel the goodwill and the kindly
sentiments toward me of that vast institution.
(Applause.) Gentlemen, so much of my voice has
lately been heard in the land, and I have, for upwards
of four hard winter months, so contended against what
I have been sometimes quite admiringly assured was
a "true American catarrh"—(laughter)—a possession
which I have throughout highly appreciated—(renewed
laughter)—though I might have preferred to be naturalized by any other outward and visible signs—(shouts

of laughter)—I say, gentlemen, so much of my voice has lately been heard that I might have been contented with troubling you no further from my present standing-point, were it not a duty with which I henceforth charge myself, not only here, but on every suitable occasion, whatsoever and wheresoever, to express my high and grateful sense of my second reception in America, and to bear my honest testimony to the national generosity and magnanimity. (Great applause.) Also, to declare how astounded I have been by the amazing changes that I have seen around me on every side, changes moral, changes physical, changes in the amount of land subdued and peopled, changes in the rise of vast new cities, changes in the growth of older cities, almost out of recognition, changes in the graces and amenities of life, changes in the Press, without whose advancement no advancement can take place anywhere. (Applause.) Nor am I, believe me, so arrogant as to suppose that in the five-and-twenty years there have been no changes in me, and that I have nothing to learn and no extreme impressions to correct when I was here first. (A voice, "Noble!" and applause.)

And, gentlemen, this brings me to a point on which I have, ever since I landed here last November, observed a strict silence, though tempted sometimes to break it, but in reference to which I will, with your good leave, take you into my confidence now. (Laughter and applause and cries of "Silence.") Even the Press, being human—(laughter)—may be sometimes mistaken or mis-informed, and I rather think that I have in one or two rare instances known its information to be not perfectly accurate with reference to myself. (Laughter and applause.) Indeed, I have now and again been more surprised by printed news that I have read of myself, than by any printed news that I have ever read in my present state of existence. (Laughter.) Thus, the vigour and perseverance with which I have for some months past been collecting materials for, and hammering away on a new book on America, has much astounded me—(renewed laughter)—seeing that all that time it has been perfectly well known to my publishers on both sides of the Atlantic that I positively declared that no consideration on earth should induce me to write one. But what I have intended, what I have resolved upon (and this is the confidence I seek to place in you) is, on my return to England, in my own person, to bear, for the behoof of my countrymen, such testimony to the gigantic changes in this country as I have hinted at to-night. (Immense applause.) Also, to record that wherever I have been, in the smallest places equally with the largest, I have been received with unsurpassable politeness, delicacy, sweet temper, hospitality, consideration, and with unsurpassable respect for the privacy daily enforced upon me by the nature of my avocation here and the state of my health. (Applause.) This testimony, so long as I live, and so long as my descendants have any legal right in my books, I shall cause to be republished as an appendix to every copy of those two books of mine in which I have referred to America. (Tremendous applause.) And this I will do and cause to be done, not in mere love and thankfulness, but because I regard it as an act of plain justice and honour. ("Bravo!" and cheers.)

Gentlemen, the transition from my own feelings toward and interest in America to those of the mass of my countrymen seems to be a natural one; but whether or no I make it with an express object. I was asked in this very city, about last Christmas-time, whether an American was not at some disadvantage in England as a foreigner. The notion of an American being regarded in England as a foreigner at all, of his ever being thought of or spoken of in that character, was so uncommonly incongruous and absurd to me that my gravity was, for the moment, quite overpowered. (Laughter.) As soon as it was restored, I said that for years and years past I hoped I had had as many American friends, and had received as many American visitors, as almost any Englishman living—(applause)—and that my unvarying experience, fortified by theirs, was that it was enough in England to be an American to be received with the readiest respect and recognition anywhere. Hereupon, out of half-a-dozen people suddenly spoke out two, one an American gentleman with a cultivated taste for art who, finding himself on a certain Sunday outside the walls of a certain historical English castle famous for its pictures, was refused admission there, according to the strict rules of the establishment on that day; but who, on merely representing that he was an American gentleman on his travels, had not to say the picture gallery—but the whole castle was placed at his immediate disposal. (Laughter.) The other was a lady who, being in London, and having a great desire to see the famous Reading Room of the British Museum, was assured by the English family with whom she stayed that it was unfortunately impossible, because the place was closed for a week and she had only three days there. Upon that lady's going to the Museum, as she assured me, alone to the gate, self-introduced as an American lady, the gate flew open, as it were magically. (Laughter and applause.) I am unwillingly bound to add that she certainly was young and extremely pretty. Still, the porter of that institution is of an obese habit—(laughter)—and according to the best of my observation of him not very impressible. (Great laughter and cheering.) Now, gentlemen, I refer to these trifles as a collateral assurance to you that the Englishman who shall humbly strive, as I hope to do, to be in England as faithful to America as to England herself, has no previous conception to contend against. ("Good, good!") Points of difference there have been, points of difference there are. Points of difference there probably will be between the two great peoples. But broadcast in England is sown the sentiment that these two peoples are essentially one—(great applause)—and that it rests with them jointly to uphold the great Anglo-Saxon race, to which our president has referred, and all its great achievements before the world. ("Bravo!" and applause.) If I know anything of my countrymen—and they give me credit of knowing something—if I know anything of my countrymen, gentlemen, the English heart is stirred by the fluttering of those stars and stripes as it is stirred by no other flag that flies except its own.   (Tremendous applause and three cheers.)

If I know my countrymen, in any and every relation toward America, they begin, not as Sir Anthony Absolute recommended that lovers should begin with a little aversion, but with a great liking and a profound respect—(great applause); and whatever little sensitiveness of the moment, or the little official passion, or the little official policy now or then here or there may be, take my word for it that the first enduring great popular consideration in England is a generous construction of justice. ("Bravo!" and cheers.) Finally, gentlemen, and I say this subject to your correction, I do believe from the great majority of honest minds on both sides there cannot be absent the conviction that it would be better for this globe to be ridden by an earthquake, fired by a comet, overrun by an iceberg, and abandoned to the Arctic fox and bear, than that it should present the spectacle of those two great nations, each of whom has, in its own way and hour, striven so hard and successfully for freedom, ever again being arrayed the one against the other. (Tumultuous applause, the company rising to its feet and greeting the sentiment with enthusiasm.) Gentlemen, I cannot thank your president enough, or you enough, for your kind reception of my health and of my poor remarks; but believe me, I do thank you with the utmost fervour of which my soul is capable. (Great applause.)

The band then played "God Save the Queen," the company joining with enthusiastic voices.

The President then said: Gentlemen, our great New York poet—whereby I do not designate Bryant nor Halleck, they are Yankee poets—(laughter); I speak, of course, of our New York poet, Walt Whitman—(laughter)—commences his great epic with this striking line—

> "I celebrate myself"

(laughter)—in that spirit which I may designate the spirit of the age (laughter). This being a dinner of the Press, I perceive that the Press proposes to celebrate itself—(laughter); and first and foremost, as the New York Press was the instigator of this dinner, and is largely represented therein, the New York Press proposes to speak for itself. (Applause.) I ask you then, gentlemen, to join in the sentiment: "The New York Press," and I ask the Hon. Henry J. Raymond to respond to it. (Three cheers for Henry J. Raymond.)

Speech of Mr. Raymond

Mr. President and Gentlemen, it seems to me, as I have no doubt it seems to every one of you, that the Press of America ought to respond, at this moment, through some appropriate organ, to the noble and generous sentiments expressed by our guest to-night. I have no commission and claim no right to speak for the Press of the United States. (A voice: "Yes, you have.") I am here officially, and only officially, to speak for a section, a segment of that great Press. ("No, no.") But on behalf of that section, and I think with the assent of the whole Press with which that section is so closely, so constantly, so intimately, and so proudly connected, I may say that we deem it an honour to us, the Press of New York and the Press of America, that we have had an opportunity to greet on this occasion the guest who sits at my left hand. ("Bravo, bravo!") The Press of New York, from its geographical position, to say nothing else, maintains a quasi prominence among the Press of the country. That Press has maintained an independent existence, not only in itself, but through its organization. For many years (if I may say many in speaking of the few years during which I have been connected with it) it has had an organization in form as a "Press Club"; and it is among the most pleasant of my recollections in connection with the Press of New York that in that form of organization it has been our good fortune at various times to greet as guests, and to entertain, with whatever hospitality we were able to extend to them,

gentlemen ot distinction and position who did us the
honour to visit us from the countries of Europe. I
remember almost the first of those occasions when that
truly great man, then recently expelled from the office
of Governor of Hungary, Kossuth, the exile—(applause)
—came to this country, and charmed so many of our
people by the seashore and in the depths of the densest
wilderness of the West, and in great cities, and everywhere he went, by the silver voice in which he uttered
such sweet words in behalf of liberty and freedom, and
by that sad, solemn eye with which, as our eloquent
orator Rufus Choate has said, "he seemed constantly
to be beholding the sad procession of unnamed demi-
gods who had died for their native land." He was one
of the most honoured guests of the New York Press.
Then came to us and honoured us by his presence, as
he had honoured England and the world by his services,
that great statesman whom your people serve [*turning
to Mr. Dickens*], now honour as they honour few among
their dead or their living, Richard Cobden. (Great
applause.) Then, too, came to us, and greeted us with
the right hand of brotherhood, your great brother in
literature, William M. Thackeray. (Renewed applause.)
And, I may say, of the many things that touched the
hearts of our people, none touched them more nearly,
or struck home more closely, than the feeling and
eloquent words of the heart in which he spoke to us
of his brother in letters, Charles Dickens. (Great cheering.) We did not need, sir, that he should tell us how
much that name was cherished by the lovers of humanity
all the world over, wherever the English tongue was
spoken or read; but he never said one word in praise
of that name that did not meet with as hearty a response
here as human words ever brought from human hearts.
He told us then, what was true then, and what has
been growing more and more true ever since, that the
writings of that illustrious brother of his in the world
of letters had done more than any other event or occur-
rence—more than any other service, which he could call
to mind—to make the men of the world feel that they
were brothers, that they had common interests, that

they were all sons of one father, striving and mounting toward one end, and that each deserved and ought to have the love, the sympathy, the cordial good offices and kindly feeling of every other. (Applause.) These, sir, are among the felicities of the New York Press. The Press of other parts of the country have enjoyed them also to a greater or less extent, and I know they have all sympathized with the feelings which pervaded our hearts at our good fortune in meeting such men, and hearing them speak such words of brotherly kindness and love. The president, the honourable, the distinguished and honoured president on this occasion has spoken in words which I know came from his heart, as they reached all our hearts, of the service rendered the causes of humanity by our guest this evening. We are all labouring in a common cause. I think it may be truly said that the Press, the free Press, all over the world, has but one common mission—to elevate humanity. It takes the side of the humble, the lowly and the poor—always of necessity, a necessity of its own existence—as against those who from mere position and power hold in their hands the destinies of the lowly and the poor for whom the Press is instituted. We are all of us more or less directly, more or less exclusively, connected with the movements of governments—governments of various forms in different parts of the world, and through different agencies and ways in that common effort to elevate the great mass of our fellow-men, to improve their material condition, and give them a higher ground to stand upon and a stronger foot to go through the weary task that all of us, in some degree, have to undergo before we fulfil our pilgrimage here on earth. But it often strikes me when I think of the labours of governments and the labours of those who try to aid governments, and when I contrast them with the fruits of the efforts and the machinery through which literary men labour for the same common end—it often strikes me how coarse and crude and ineffective is the whole machinery of government to accomplish the great end of elevating humanity. It is not through machinery, it is not through organizations, through forms, through constraints, through laws, that we touch the real strings of human action. (Applause.) It is not through those agencies that we learn what it is that elevates humanity, what it is that purifies it, what it is that brings all men to think themselves brothers and act toward each other as brothers. It is those who deal with the secret springs of actions, who through the channels of fiction or of congenial and sympathetic history touch the springs of the human heart, and make us feel, as well as convince our intellect; it is those who do most who carry the world on to what we all believe to be its ultimate destination. (Applause.) And certainly in the Press, or out of the Press, in government or out of government, nowhere on the face of the earth, in any form or in any shape, or through any agency, have there lived many men—I might make it stronger if I did not dislike to appear extravagant—have there lived many men who have touched so nearly the secret springs of action and of character of the human heart, and have done so much in that way to bring about that unanimity of human feeling, that cordiality of human brotherhood, as the distinguished guest whom we have here to-night. Everything that he has ever written—I say it without the slightest exception of a single book, a single page, or a single word that has ever proceeded from his pen— has been calculated to infuse into every human heart the feeling that every man was his brother and that the highest duty he could do to the world, and the highest pleasure he could confer upon himself, and the greatest service he could render to humanity was to bring that other heart, whether high or low, as close to his own as possible. (Applause.) What he has accomplished in that way, how many human hearts he has thus brought together, how much of kind feeling he has infused throughout society, among all men, of all classes, high and low, rich and poor, powerful and weak —how much he has done to infuse into them all the spirit of brotherhood, I know too well the poverty of any language I could use to attempt to describe. (Applause.) But I know there is not a man here, and there is not a man who has known any man here, who knows anything of his writings, who has made himself familiar with their spirit, or has yielded to their influence, who has not been made thereby a better as well as a wiser and prouder and kinder, nobler man. (Loud cheering.) Excuse the prolixity into which I seem to be running. I will not prolong my remarks. I only desire to return thanks, on behalf of the New York Press, for the compliment which has been paid it by the assembled Press of the United States. ("Go, go on.") I think I may fairly claim that the New York Press—and I know no higher claim that I could put in for it here to-night than this—that the New York Press from the very beginning, from the time when words first dropped from the pen of our illustrious guest, the New York Press has appreciated them, and, I may add, appropriated them—(laughter); and that the fruits thereof are apparent in some of the changes, the improvements, the advances which he has been good enough to speak of here to-night. We all know his characters. They seem like persons. We cherish them as friends. I feel as well acquainted with some of them— yes, a great deal better acquainted with some of them —than I do with many of the men whom I meet here on the streets every day of my life. I know I have derived more good from some of them than from any, or at least many, of the friends whom I meet every day. They do everybody good, for they are always cheerful, always hopeful, always earnest, always kind to every one; and, in spite of all we may claim for our republican institutions and our equality of rights, humanity in this country—I say it fearlessly—owes more of its substantial advances to the writings of Mr. Dickens than even to the Press of New York. (Laughter and applause.) His is a kind of public service, which is done without consciousness and sometimes without intent. Such a man writes what he knows of men, and what he writes addresses itself to all men. It reaches their hearts, and through their hearts governs their conduct; and that is the only government of conduct worth a straw anywhere. (Applause.) I think often of these things in connection with the noble lines of

one of our own poets, speaking of the unconscious work
done by the great architect of Rome in the building of
St. Peter's; and if you will allow me to quote those
lines (and I am sure you will thank me for substituting
them for anything that I could say myself), I will close
therewith. I mean that beautiful passage in Emerson
where he says—

> " The hand that rounded Peter's dome
> And groined the aisles of Christian Rome,
> Wrought with a sad sincerity.
> Himself from God he could not free,
> He builded better than he knew ;
> The conscious stone to beauty grew."

The band here gave the "Star-spangled Banner," and
the audience joined in the chorus.

The President then said : Gentlemen, when we speak
of the Press of New York we are too apt—we gentlemen
of the daily journals are too apt—to monopolize the
phrase as peculiarly, if not exclusively, our own. The
Daily Press has a certain conspicuous position in the
public eye. By means of the telegraph and its con-
nections it seems more directly related to the leading
minds of the country than any other portion of the
Press; but we must remember that where one man
reads a daily journal there are several who read a weekly
journal—(laughter)—and that the position of the Daily
Press, though important, is certainly not solitary. I
propose the "Weekly Press," and I call upon George
William Curtis to respond. (Great applause.)

Speech of Mr. George William Curtis

Mr. President and Gentlemen, as I now look around
upon this cheerful company, I like to think that this
pleasant feast is not merely a tribute to an author whose
books have made all his readers his friends, but is a
fraternal greeting of welcome and farewell from us who
are all, in various ways, reporters, to our comrade, a
late reporter of the London *Morning Chronicle*, who

T

shall here and now, and at no other time, and nowhere else in the world, be nameless. He has ceased, indeed, to write for the *Morning Chronicle,* but he has not ceased to be a reporter. He is a famous story-teller, but I ask this table of experts whether that shows him to be no longer a reporter? (Laughter.) He is a great novelist, but what are novelists? They are men commissioned by Nature to see human life and the infinite play of human character and write reports upon them. So a certain Spaniard inspected the grotesque aspect of decaying chivalry and wrote his famous report *Don Quixote.* (Applause.) So a certain Scotchman beheld the romantic splendour of the Crusader and called his report *Ivanhoe.* So a sad-eyed countryman of ours saw a tragic aspect in early New England life and called his marvellous report *The Scarlet Letter.* And so our nameless friend of the *Morning Chronicle,* with the same commission as that of Cervantes, of Scott, of Hawthorne, observing the various aspects of life in his own time, has written his prodigious series of reports, which have become "household words" "all the year round." (Loud cheering.) They have not only revealed wrongs, but have greatly helped to right them. One he called, for instance, *Nicholas Nickleby,* and with hilarious indignation Dotheboys Hall was laughed and cried away. Perhaps he called another *Oliver Twist,* and the cold poorhouse was turned inside out and warmed with the sun of human charity. Upon another I read *Bleak House;* and as I turn the pages, the long, bitter winter of the law's delay lies exposed. He turns his eye backward, and it seems to me nobody truly understands the terrible form and spirit of the French Revolution, although you may have read all the historians, if he has not read that wonderful report, *The Tale of Two Cities.* (Applause.) And, thank Heaven, the good work still goes on. (Renewed applause.) The eye and the heart and the hands are untiring. The eager world reads and reads and reads; and the reporter's genial magic makes it a great good-natured Oliver asking for more. (Cheers.) If in the pursuit of his calling he came to us who loved and

honoured him, he still faithfully and frankly reported
his observations. The old proverb says nobility
obliges. But genius obliges still more. (Applause.)
Fidelity through his own observations is all we can
ask of any reporter. However grateful he may be for
our hospitality, we cannot insist that he shall pour our
champagne into his eyes so that he cannot see—(great
laughter)—nor stuff our pudding into his ears so that
he cannot hear. (Laughter, applause.) He was obliged
to hear and see and report many things that were not
pleasant nor flattering. It is the fate of all reporters.
I do not remember that those very competent observers,
Mr. Emerson and Mr. Hawthorne, whom we sent to
England, represented that country as altogether a paradise and John Bull as a saint without blemish.
(Laughter.) They told a great deal of truth about
England, as it seems to me our friend told a great many
and valuable truths about us. Naturally we did not find
every part of his report very entertaining; but neither,
I suppose, did Sir Leicester Dedlock find *Bleak House*
very amusing, and I am sure to this day neither
Serjeant Buzfuz nor Mr. Justice Stareleigh have ever
been able to find the least fun in *Pickwick*. (Bursts
of laughter and cheers.) For my undivided thirty-
millionth part of the population I thank the reporter
with all my heart, and I do not forget that if his touch,
like the ray of a detective's lantern, sparkled for a
moment upon some of our defects, the full splendour
of its light has always been turned upon the sins and
follies of his own country. (Applause.) If I seem to
have wandered from my text, Mr. Chairman, it only
seems so. (Cheers.) The members of the Weekly Press,
for whom I have the honour of speaking, pursue literature as a profession; and I know not where we could
study the fidelity, the industry, the conscience, the care,
and the enthusiasm which are essential to success in
our profession, more fitly than in the example of the
editor of *All the Year Round*. M. Thiers, in a recent
speech, says "that the world now needs every day a
new book, written every day." Hence the newspaper.
The responsibility of the authors of that book is enor-

T 2

mous. The world is governed by public opinion, and
nothing moulds that opinion more powerfully than the
Press. Its great divisions are two—the literary and the
political. The paramount duty of the literary Press is
purity; of the political Press, honesty. Our Copyright
Law, as you are aware, Mr. Chairman, inflicts a fine
for every repetition of the offence, so that the fine is
multiplied as many times as there are copies of the book
printed. So the man who, as a writer for the Press,
says what he does not believe, or defends a policy that
he does not approve, or panders to a base passion or
a mean prejudice for a party purpose, is so many times
a traitor to the fact represented at this table as there
are copies of his newspaper printed; and, as honest
or dishonest difference of opinion is entirely compatible
with courtesy, as even denunciation is a thousandfold
more stinging and effective when it is not vituperation,
decency of manner no less becomes the Press than
decency of matter. (Applause.) When the manners
of the Press become those of Tombs pettifoggers or
Old Bailey shysters, or the *Eatanswill Gazette*—
(laughter)—its influence will have to be revealed by a
coarse and brutal opinion. While we boast of the
tremendous power of the Press, let us remember that
the foundations of that power as a truly civilizing
influence are, first, purity, then honesty, then sagacity
and industry. It may sometimes seem otherwise; but
it is an illusion. A man may build up a great journal
as he may amass any other great fortune, and seem to
be a shining miracle of prosperity, but if he have neither
love, nor honour, nor troops of friends, his prosperity
is a fair orchard bearing only apples of Sodom. It is
a curious and interesting fact that at an official
investigation made a few years since in England, a newspaper dealer, in reply to a question of Mr. Cobden,
gave it as the result of twenty years' experience that
objectionable newspapers, daily or weekly, were short-
lived; while the publications of the highest intellectual
and moral quality constantly increased in circulation. It
is impossible to determine the limits or the merits of
individual agency, but there is no doubt that among

the most vigorous forces in the elevation of the character of the Weekly Press have been *Household Words* and *All the Year Round*, and since the beginning of the publication of *Household Words* the periodical literature of England has been born again. Mr. Chairman, the obligation that, in the name of the Weekly Press, I wish to express to our guest is for his example of high fidelity and of honourable pride in his profession of letters. His career illustrates what Charles Lamb called the sanity of true genius. He has never debased it to unworthy ends. He has shown us that it is not a denizen of Bohemia only, but a citizen of the world. He has always honoured his profession by asserting its dignity in his own person. If Dr. Johnson was content to wait humbly, hat in hand, in Lord Chesterfield's ante-room; if Sir Walter Scott—he of all men !— was proud to preserve the glass out of which George Fourth drank his toddy; the late reporter of *The Morning Chronicle*, when the Queen invites him to the palace to amuse her company, respectfully replies that he cannot come as an actor where he is not welcome as a guest. (Great applause.) In that spirit of common respect for a noble calling upon whose roll are written the best beloved names in history, a calling of which the technical Press, whether daily or weekly or monthly or quarterly, is but a department, let us take the hand of our friend at parting. Wherever he may be, whatever fate befall, his name will be a kind of good tidings. It will always have a pleasant Christmas sound. Old Ocean, bear him safely over ! English hedges, welcome him with the blossoms of May ! English hearts, he is ours as he is yours ! We stand upon the shore; we say farewell; and, as he sails away, we pray with love and gratitude, May God bless him !

The President :—Gentlemen, our friend who spoke for the Press of New York, remarked that the writings of our guest had not merely been appreciated but appropriated here. (Laughter.) That is true, to some extent, of the Daily Press, to a greater extent of the Weekly Press. (Laughter.) But a very large section of the Press still remains. I have already stated that his writings which caught the attention of the western hemisphere appeared in a monthly periodical, and the monthly periodicals of both continents printed in the English tongue have for thirty years been largely sustained and commended to support by his contributions. I, therefore, propose the sentiment of the "Monthly Press," and require William Henry Hulbert to respond. (Cheers.)

Speech of William Henry Hulbert

Mr. Chairman and Gentlemen, the Emperor Gallienus once gave a prize to a marksman because he had never hit a mark. I can't help thinking that this wily prince must have been in the minds of the committee when they asked me to respond to the toast which has just been read. For I have certainly not written, and I don't think I have read, a magazine article for seven years past. (Laughter and applause.) But if there be no special fitness in my responding to the toast, there certainly is a special fitness in the toast itself. For all who find comfort and value in monthly literature owe a great debt, both directly and indirectly, to our illustrious guest. There were magazines, we all know, long before Boz took up his formidable pen to sketch the manners and customs of his fellow-creatures. But it is certain the range of English serial literature has been greatly widened and its quality greatly enriched by his influence. (Applause.) To those of us who were boys when Mr. Dickens first visited America, serial literature must always seem to have been in a manner his invention. We counted time in our boyhood by dear *Old Master Humphrey's Clock*, we knew the first day of the month by a new number of *Oliver Twist* or *Nicholas Nickleby*, just as we knew the last day of the week by a holiday. Insatiable urchins that we were, we had no sooner devoured this new number which we got than, like Oliver, we clamoured for "more." (Laughter.) But unlike Oliver, we got more. We have been getting more ever since—and I am sure I speak for all who hear me when I say that we are as far off now as

we were then from getting enough. And that we hope
we may keep on getting more, not for months, but for
years to come. (Immense applause.) Perhaps it would
hardly be fair to say that we owe Mr. Dickens to
monthly literature, as we owe Shakespeare to the theatre.
And yet I like to believe of Mr. Dickens, as I am sure
I believe it of Shakespeare, that he would never have
given himself the trouble of being an author if he had
not been tempted by opportunity. (Cheers.) The
theatre was the opportunity of Shakespeare, and
monthly literature of Mr. Dickens. But if monthly
literature played the witch with Mr. Dickens, he has
returned the compliment by playing the dickens with
monthly literature. (Cheers.) The traces of his
influence are over it all since first he touched its hem,
always for good, shall I say?—no, not always for good,
since the best of styles seduces simpletons into imitations
which do the author more discredit than his own worst
foibles (and the cleverest of men have their foibles)
deserve. But by enlarging the scope, by elevating the
range of literature in its relations with life, Mr. Dickens
has wrought a real and positive good to English letters,
and for this, monthly literature has rewarded him by
miscellaneously and mercilessly cribbing, at least on
this side of the Atlantic, all that he has written. Now
this, speaking as I do, by warrant of this committee,
for monthly literature, I hold to be a wrong demanding
redress. If I had no other audience than the editors
and publishers of monthly magazines, I might, I suppose, appeal in vain. (Laughter.) But I see before me
the most complete representation which has for years
past been assembled, or which for years to come may
be assembled, of the real working men of the American
Press, of the men who make, night after night and day
after day, the broad sheets which are reeled off from the
hundred armed giants who do our work in caves, go
forth to all the world bearing their mingled messages
of truth and falsehood, of the probable and improbable.
These at best know, I am sure, and will testify, that the
"labourer is worthy of his hire." I appeal to them
henceforth to see to it that in season and out of season

they lose no occasion of supporting that just and righteous and reasonable cause of an International Copyright, of which our distinguished guest has for years been so faithful a defender—(immense applause)—and by the arrested, I will not say the defeated, progress of which not he alone has been a sufferer, but every man in England and America, whom his example might else have stimulated to authorship. (Cheers.) If the monthly magazines did not mean to plead for this cause, so much the worse for them that I am their spokesman. If they did, let them be grateful. And so I yield my place not to a worthier sentiment, but to more eloquent men. (Cheers.)

The President:—Gentlemen, there is a place on the eastern border of our continent which a high authority among us would probably describe as "hanging on the verge" of the continent—(laughter)—called "The Hub." (Laughter and cheers.) That town is known to some of you by description, or possibly by observation. It is the place where our friend and guest had the bad taste to land when he came here. In deference to our guest and his taste I propose "The Boston Press," and require Mr. Charles Eliot Norton to respond to it. (Applause.)

SPEECH OF CHARLES ELIOT NORTON

Mr. President and Gentlemen, I feel as embarrassed as the last speaker said he felt when he rose, in responding to a toast to which I have little claim to answer. I am only indirectly connected with the Boston Press, and therefore I cannot speak for it as one of its members, who are engaged night and day in the work of preparing those newspapers which send out the ideas which are generally understood to be the governing ideas of America. I know that many of our notions are derisively called "Boston notions"; but I find that after a time a good many of those notions become embedded in the civilization of the country, through what may be called the common schools, and also through the churches which everywhere mark the first springs of

American civilization. (Applause.) I am not worthy
to speak for the Boston Press except in one regard, and
that is in the cordial unanimity with which that Press
would join you to-night, will join you always, in doing
honour not only personally to our guest, but to the
principles which he has represented and which, in their
real essence, I claim to be "Boston notions." There
is one notion wrought into the very nature of every true
New Englander and Bostonian, which is, the equal rights
of man—the claim of man upon man—the broad claim
of humanity; and I know not any one, either in America
or England, who has done more to secure respect for
that "notion" than the guest whom we honour in our
heart of hearts to-night. We claim him as by right a
citizen of Boston, a citizen of the world—(applause); the
Hub of the Universe depends on him for inspiration.
There was a humorous friend of mine who said the
other day that if Mr. Dickens started with ten cents in
his pocket from Cambridgeport—and Cambridgeport,
you know, is hardly allowed to be "hanging upon the
verge" of the United States—it is to Boston the "abom-
ination of desolation"—this friend of mine said that
Mr. Dickens might start from Cambridgeport with ten
cents in his pocket, and travel round the world, and he
would come back no richer than when he started.
(Laughter.) But there is something I would desire to
say for New England, if I may consider Boston a part
of New England, and so gain a right to speak for it.
And what I desire to say is this, that we are glad and
proud to bear the name of the old land which gave birth
to Charles Dickens. (Repeated cheers.) There are two
Englands. There is the actual England; there is the
England of *The Times* newspaper; the England of
Thackeray's *Book of Snobs;* well, the England which
we do not like. And there is the real England; the
England of the imagination and of the heart; the England to which no American can go without feeling a
rapture in his heart as he thinks of the old and glorious
memories of our race. And when he wakes in the
morning and with keen ears hears the lark singing at
heaven's gate, and when he takes a walk in the fields

he sees the very haystack under which "Little Boy
Blue" laid down to sleep, and the very meadows, too,
where he ought to have sounded his horn but forgot to
sound it; he will see the England which he has believed
in and dreamed of; and it will seem to him that it is
some old, old place where he has been in his boyhood.
It is as familiar to him as his grandmother's garden?
There he will see the daisies and the cowslips which he
has never seen since he grew up, but which belonged
to the dreams of his youth. He will see the old, the
real, the dear England—(great cheering)—transmuted
in "the light that never was on sea or land, the con-
secration, and the poet's dream." He will see the
England of Chaucer, of Shakespeare, of Milton, of
Dickens. (Cheering.) He will recognize that there is
a responsive drop in his heart which beats quicker and
warmer because the life which is in him springs from
the dear old England, mother of us all. (Great
applause.) He will return home the better, the more
patriotic, for having seen the home of all his ancestors.
He will return home with more faith in America, because
he will have seen where America started; because he
will be able to appreciate the solid foundation of right,
the impregnable rock of justice on which all that is
glorious in the real England of the imagination rests.
He will come here with fresher convictions in his own
heart, prepared to do his best for his own part, and for
those who work with him, in carrying out those glorious
principles which England hides in her heart, places first
in her faith, first in her religion—the principles of
justice, of liberty, of humanity. I will not attempt to
repeat the sentiments which we have heard from the
eloquent lips which have preceded me, in saying how
deeply, how earnestly, how hopefully he feels that
between England and America is a bond which no
earthly catastrophe can sever; but I will say that the
idea of war between the old mother and the young,
promising, vigorous man-child of the future is an idea
which is enough to raze all the foundation of reason
from its throne; and we hope it is one that he will
never permit himself, or permit others in his presence

to speak of. And this because of his love, not for England, but for humanity. There is but one more word to say, and it is this: that as a representative of one of the oldest journals of the country, I have the pleasure of believing that it has been during the whole of its career a supporter of those ideas which are most essentially American, and in that journal five-and-twenty years ago appeared one of the earliest criticisms upon that great genius which was to make our generation happy. (Applause.) And it was on that account I felt willing to speak at all to-night; and that I might be able to add the tribute of New England, of gratitude, of constant love to him who, while binding this generation to him by affectionate respect, has had a success beyond that which ordinarily falls to the literary man—a success which is not limited to England, but which binds the New World to him by cords that are stronger and have a subtler magnetism than the electric cable by feelings as delicate and as powerful as those which belong to the inmost domesticity of home. And when he returns to his own country he may carry back the assurance that the faith with which he came upon this voyage, the faith that he should be able to lay one chain more to bind those two dear lands together—has been thoroughly fulfilled.

The band here played "We are a Band of Brothers."

The President:—Boston is conceded to be in New England, and yet there is a considerable portion of New England outside of Boston. (Laughter.) In deference, therefore, to that portion, I am instructed by your Committee to propose as a sentiment "The New England Press," and require General Joseph R. Hawley, of the *Connecticut Courant,* to respond.

REMARKS OF GENERAL J. R. HAWLEY

Mr. Chairman, it is but a few hours, comparatively, since I received warning that I should be called upon, and as I was obliged to work diligently upon other matters in order to have the pleasure of being here at all, I had hoped to be "off duty" this evening. I feel somewhat as might a very respectable and very courteous old bachelor if he should kindly consent to hold a small bundle for a few minutes while the lady stepped round the corner, and should then find himself the responsible holder of a strange baby growing to be a very big elephant on his hands. This chair just vacated by my side, belongs to the gentleman who should have responded for the New England Press— our excellent friend Sam Bowles of the *Springfield Republican*, the model newspaper of the Provincial Press. But there will be one merit—brevity—in what I shall have to say. One still July afternoon the city items man of the journal upon which I work, in despair of matter for his column, sat meditatively observing a small boy climbing up to and upon the figure of Madame Justice upon the state-house cupola. Said he, "If that boy should fall he would make about so much" —measuring a "stickful" on his finger. (Great laughter.) If I were to speak of and not for the New England Press, perhaps I may claim New England has spoken already, and speaks for herself through her newspapers everywhere. The honoured chairman (Mr. Greeley) is one of our New England boys, and so also is the gentleman who has just spoken so eloquently upon the right of our distinguished guest [*Mr. Raymond shook his head*]. Well, we certainly educated him, and I thought, from his versatile and characteristic ability, that he must be one of our own Yankees. The venerated senior of the *Post*, whose absence we all regret, went from us, and the able editors of the *World* and the *Journal of Commerce*, and the other eloquent gentleman upon my left (Mr. Curtis) were ours. There is then little necessity that I should continue. But I am right glad and proud to have an opportunity of gratefully acknowledging our indebtedness to Mr. Dickens. Twenty-five years ago, as a school-boy, I hung upon the timbers of a bridge that I might have a fair opportunity to look upon the man whose books were my delight above all others, and I could not have dreamed that after such a lapse of time I should have the happi-

ness of thanking him. It is sometimes said that there
is something rigid and severe in the traditional New
England character, that we have been unable to see it
as clearly as our critics outside. Whether it be so or
not, I do most heartily thank him on behalf of many
thousands of Yankee boys who have grown up his
devoted readers and admirers, and whom he has for a
generation wonderfully delighted and greatly instructed;
whom he has taught to look tenderly upon the weaker
side of humanity; whom he has taught that it is not
unmanly to cry, and certainly not to laugh heartily.
Those who have preceded me have spoken of the debt
we owe him. Newspaper men owe no small share of it.
What a deal of trouble it saves us, for example, to say
of an opponent that he is Pecksniffian! You anticipate
me by seeing at a glance the numberless instances in
which a word upon Dickens by a sort of stenographic
system of allusions and characterizations well compre-
hended by a universal public saves you whole columns
of writing. Yes, the whole people owe him a debt that
we shall never be able to discharge. Sir Walter Scott,
dismounting at an inn, and being unable to find in his
pocket the customary sixpence, threw to the ostler a
shilling. "There," said he, "you will owe me a sixpence." "May your honour," was the response, "live
and prosper until I pay it." Our guest, when he goes
back to his own home, will, I am very sure from what
we have seen and heard, bear with him a kindly remembrance of this country. We have not the assurance to
ask him to say of us anything so hearty, enthusiastic,
and complimentary as we say of ourselves. (Laughter.)
If he will even considerably moderate our own terms we
shall be abundantly satisfied. And when, if ever, he
shall undertake to satirize us, permit me to entreat him
not to say anything as severe as we are often saying
of each other. Gentlemen, I most cordially join in the
sentiments here expressed of goodwill, fairplay, and
justice in the profession, in your wishes for the advancement of our common humanity, and in the desire for
permanent peace, friendship and co-operation with our
cousins across the water. (Cheers.)

The President:—Gentlemen, New York is flanked by great cities, one of which, if not older, was long larger, more popular, more important than herself, was the city of the Declaration of Independence and of the first Government of the Federal Union. I am asked to propose next "The Press of Philadelphia," and request Mr. George H. Boker to respond to the sentiment. (Applause.)

Speech of George H. Boker

Mr. Chairman, I am astounded at being called upon to reply to any toast. The Committee of Arrangements were under bond not to require me to speak for any purpose whatever. I am therefore entirely unprepared to speak on any subject. As responding to the toast "The Press of Philadelphia," gentlemen who have preceded me have disowned connection with the Daily, and with the Weekly, and with the Monthly, and with the Quarterly Press. I am connected with no Press whatever—(laughter)—and how I am to represent the Philadelphia Press it is impossible for me to say. (Renewed laughter.) However, I have no doubt the Philadelphia Press owes Mr. Dickens the same debt of gratitude that the Press of our country generally seems to owe him. (Laughter.) I represent a class of the community without which the members of the Press could hardly exist. I am a subscriber—(cheers and laughter)—and I am happy to be able to say, with my hand upon my heart, that I have always paid my bills—(applause)—generally in advance—(cheers); not that my credit was not good, but because that seemed to be the requirement. I do not know whether it was a lack of capital on their part or a suspicion of me. (Laughter.) I am an American curiosity in another way. I never read a book of Mr. Dickens's except in the original English editions. (Cheers.) I will not go into the subject of an International Copyright Law lest I should get heated and say something injudicious, but I think such a law would be a justice to the American author

as much as to the English author. The writings of
Mr. Dickens have affected and softened the heart
wherever they have been read, and more especially
where they have been heard through the magic medium
of his voice. (Cheers.) We have lately had the pleasure
of hearing him interpret his own works throughout these
United States, and after that interpretation of them he
will go home to his own country, if possible, more
beloved than ever. (Cheers.) It has been said by many
of our critical writers that Mr. Dickens, in *Martin
Chuzzlewit* and *The American Notes*, was not altogether
just to us. That may be. Mr. Dickens saw with his
own eyes and from one point of view. However, we
know that this tour of his through our country has been
one continued triumphal progress; he has overcome all
prejudice, and his audiences have listened to him with
delight. Different views of these entertainments have
been taken in our different cities, but all of them have
agreed in being favourable. I can only say that I thank
him in behalf of Philadelphia. We shall be delighted
to see him again in any capacity whether as an ambassador of England to the United States—(great applause)
—or as an ambassador from his literary brethren sent to
conclude the great International Copyright Treaty of the
future, which we all hope to see. (Applause.) Whenever he comes, and however he comes, we will welcome
him to Philadelphia. (Cheers.)

The President:—Gentlemen, our Committee have
rather limited notions, I think, with regard to geo-
graphy. They propose as the next sentiment, "The
Northern Press"—very appropriately—and they ask me
to call upon our friend Mr. George W. Demers of the
Albany Evening Journal to respond, which he will do
worthily—however, I think not so far north as we might
probably have called into service on this occasion.

Mr. Demers said that his dearest recollections were
connected with the man whom they had met to honour.
He remembered his characters not as fictions, but as
living beings, as men and women whom he had met
face to face. He knew them in their entities, in their
ambitions and in their degradations, in their rags, in

their sufferings. He had stood by the bedside of little
Paul dying. He had triumphed in the triumph of virtue
which the story of Nicholas Nickleby portrayed. He
owed Mr. Dickens a debt of gratitude for the delight
and instruction which he had derived from the perusal
of his works. He remembered that a year ago, when
travelling in a mountainous region of the great wilderness in the northern part of New York, finding in a rude
cabin where he stopped all night, five miles removed
from any other habitation, where no one would expect
to find any evidences of intellectual culture, a complete
edition of Charles Dickens, and his rough-handed host
had told him that next to his Bible he valued the works
of Charles Dickens. ("Good!" and applause.) This
little incident was but an illustration in miniature of
the sentiment which prevailed among the people of the
United States, who recognized in the writings of Charles
Dickens the ideas and principles which, if carried into
the great common life of a community, were calculated
to make it wiser, purer and happier. (Applause.)

The president then announced that in consequence of
the exceedingly bad health of their guest, who was suffering great pain, he had excused him; and he would pass
out of the room as he preferred to do, unnoticed. The
audience then rose and gave Mr. Dickens three hearty
cheers as he retired.

The President:—We have present among us representatives of the Press from the far valley of the Ohio,
who have come to-night to join with us in doing honour
to our guest. I, therefore, in behalf of the committee,
have great pleasure in recognizing their generous attendance, and asking you to join in the sentiment "The
Western Press," to which Mr. Halstead, of the *Cincinnati Commercial*, is expected to respond.

SPEECH OF MR. MURAT HALSTEAD

Mr. President and Gentlemen, if I should protract
my remarks in proportion to the geographical extravagance of the part of the country from which I come, I

fear we should break the Sabbath. There is some mistake here, sir. My home is not "in the bright setting sun." I think it is an antagonism—if it were not for offending the august majesty of New York—a provincialism—(laughter)—to speak of anything this side of the Mississippi as the West. Why, sir, I live five hundred miles this side of the mouth of the Ohio river, and when we have ascended the Missouri river five hundred miles to the city of Omaha, there is a railroad yet six hundred miles west of that, so that I only live at one-third of the distance from New York to the western terminus to our railway system. Our honoured guest this evening flatters himself that he has seen the United States. He has seen that portion of it which "hangs on the verge" of the Atlantic, a very small portion of the country. We have regretted exceedingly that we could not have him with us in the West for a time. But our country was so unfortunately large that it was impossible for him to get over the breadth of it. (Laughter.) We had prepared for it; we had read up everything, including *American Notes*—(renewed laughter)—and we were astonished to find what an exceedingly clever, good-natured and true book it was. (Laughter.) And we are intensely grateful to him for the many omissions in it he has made in recording the exceedingly disagreeable things that he saw when he was in this country twenty-five years ago. We would be very happy to welcome him at any time. We hope he may visit us every quarter of a century, for all the centuries that we may wish he may live. (Laughter.) It has been said of the British dominions that upon them the sun never sets. It may certainly be said of the sentiment of Charles Dickens, that the sun never sets upon it, that it goes round the world. We hope that in his next visit to this country he may be able to approach it by the golden gates of the Pacific—the western pillar of Hercules. The only fear we have is that he would be so much attracted by our Pacific shores that—as in the case of his visit to the Atlantic coast—he could not penetrate to the valley of the Mississippi. (Cheers.)

U

The President:—Gentlemen, we will not forget that there is a south in our country, and a southern Press, as well as a northern and eastern and a western. And as I propose the sentiment "The Southern Press," I shall call upon a gentleman to respond to it who is probably not now connected with that Press, but who represents its spirit, and genealogically may be held its representative. I propose, then, "The Southern Press," and require Mr. Edwin de Leon to respond.

Mr. de Leon's Response

Mr. de Leon said that all had read with wonder in childhood that story in the *Arabian Nights* of the prince who, on his magic carpet, could transport himself to the remotest corners of the earth. What our childhood had doubted, our manhood had realized; for into what remote nook or diversity of land and language had not the magic woof woven from his own brain transported Charles Dickens? The Southern Press had paid their tribute to him. He had fed this generation with the most wholesome food of literature, and among those who would welcome him on his return to his own land there would be found no hearts that would throb for him with a more genuine warmth than those that sent a "Godspeed" after him from Maine to Louisiana. (Cheers.)

The President then proposed the sentiment, "The Southwestern Press," and called upon Mr. T. S. Thorpe to respond.

Speech of Mr. Thorpe

Mr. Thorpe spoke of the future in store for a section so large in extent and so rich in its resources as that which was known as "The Southwest." Twenty-eight years ago he saw a flat-boat coming down the Missis-

sippi with the name painted in large letters on its side,
Samuel Keller. On his asking the captain of the craft
whose name it bore, he replied that he thought probably
it was that of the new candidate for Congress in the
then new territory of Indiana.

The President:—Gentlemen: The last sentiment is
"The Scientific Press," to which Mr. Edward L.
Youmans is expected to respond.

REMARKS OF PROFESSOR YOUMANS

Mr. Chairman and Gentlemen, I appreciate the honour
of being called upon on this occasion to represent the
Scientific Press, although very incompetent to do justice
to its interests.   But if any subject can afford to be
careless to its mouthpiece it is Science.   The daily,
weekly, and the monthly Press, and the Press east, west,
north and south have to-night paid the tribute of their
sincere and profound respect to the genius and the
labours of Charles Dickens.   Time and space have been
thus exhausted; where is the room for science?   But
though allowed no geographic or periodic opportunity,
the Scientific Press is nevertheless a power not only
through its own organs, but in its influence upon
thought, through all the multitudinous channels of publication.   It is a common belief that science consists of
mere curious inquiries about rare and extraordinary
things, remote from the interests of common life.   This
is a grave mistake.   Science is entirely an affair of
thought—of the correct action of the human mind.
Knowledge grows in the individual and in the race—
grows from vagueness into certainty, from looseness
into precision, and in its highest or perfect form we
call it Science.   It is simply a bringing of the human
mind into better harmony with the truth of things, and
it matters not what are its objects—stones or stars,
human souls or the social relations of men.   It is not
the material triumphs of science, splendid as they are,
to which I would call attention on this occasion, but

U 2

to its influence in widening and elevating human thought, by which it must become a new power in literature and all renovating influence in education. Action and reaction are equal and opposite as well in the mental as in the material world. The forces of thought cannot reconstruct our civilization as they are now doing without a profound reflex effect upon the mind itself. It is much to have gained the mastery of the powers of Nature for a thousand purposes of usefulness; it is far more to have gained an intellectual insight into her mysteries. No agency of the Press is more salutary than its influence in diffusing the results of scientific discovery and ministering to the universal extension of the principles deduced and the views that are based upon them; and the claims of science to be represented here to-night as a distinctive power, having a Press of its own, and pressing all others into its service, is, that it is the most methodical and irresistible of all the agencies which are co-operating to work out the progress and elevation of humanity. There is another misconception of the character and influence of science which it seems pertinent to notice on this occasion. It is the notion that it is unfavourable to the finer faculties of the mind—the enemy of the imagination. That growing science has acted as a check upon the wild and lawless play of the imagination is unquestionable, for its function is to lead men into the dispensation of the true. The history of imaginative literature in the department of poetry and fiction shows that coeval with the advance of science there has been a steady repression of its more wayward and volatile flights—a steady subordination of it to the limits of the truth of Nature. The imaginative faculty has been stripped of its old prerogative of unbounded licence, and its highest praise now is that it does not transcend the verities of nature and experience. But if science may thus seem to have invaded the ancient domain of the imagination, has it not made munificent amends by revealing a wealth of thought—resources which infinitely enlarge the scope of imaginative combinations. So far, indeed, from science being unfavourable to the imagination, it is the very faculty on which she most relies for the accomplishment of her special work—the discovery of truth. From the time of Bacon the attempt has been made to formulate the mental processes of discovery in terms of pure logical procedure, but the thing is impossible. The imagination here comes into play in a manner so subtle and elusive of all rules as to nonplus the keenest psychology. I am afraid Mr. Gradgrind, with all his "facts," will never make a discovery for the lack of this mental quality. The scientific attainment of truth is, after all, mainly a matter of fervour of imagination—a phantasy, and is just as truly an inspiration of genius as a successful stroke of poetry or fiction. Thus all the lines of intellectual labour harmonize at last. Our illustrious guest has devoted his wondrous powers of imagination and description to the noble end of ameliorating the condition of his fellow-beings. Science bids him Godspeed with the fullest sympathy, for she too has for her inspiring aim that understanding of Nature which is indispensable to the "bettering of man's estate."

Mr. Dolby's name was then loudly called, but he had retired from the hall.

The following are among the letters received upon the occasion—

From Thurlow Weed

New York, April 18, 1868.

My dear Sir,

When you informed me that the honoured privilege of responding to a sentiment this evening had been assigned by the Committee of Arrangements to me, you will remember that I expressed my deep regret that the power of utterance on such occasions disqualified me for duty. In a subsequent conversation the desire to speak was so strong that I allowed you to infer that I would make the attempt. But as the hour approaches I find my courage "oozing out" so rapidly that I have reached Falstaff's conclusion that "discretion is the better part of valour." With a theme so bright and beautiful, so eloquent and touching—a theme that almost speaks itself—it is hard indeed to be capable of consecutive utterances, to be unable to find words for thought or to fashion inspiration into sentences—such, however, is my painful lot. Under obligation to Mr. Dickens for infinitely more intellectual instruction and enjoyment than I have derived from all other sources—Shakespeare and Scott included—with no power to make either just or equitable compensation, I am too poor to express in fitly chosen words an adequate sense of the gratitude which my reading of his glorious works awakens and intensifies. If, like an ancestor in very early times similarly situated, I had a trusty friend to speak for me, I might venture to take my seat at your festive board, but as I have no right to hope for miraculous assistance, I must submit to a great disappointment by denying myself that pleasure. I am, however, consoled by the reflection that what I lose others will gain, for time, to-night, is too precious to be wasted. For the mental chaff which I should offer there are waving fields of fully ripe wheat ready for the intellectual sickle. Mr. Dickens may not be aware of this, but most of the offspring of his brain, real creations with flesh and blood and immortal spirits, now reside in America. In a sense easier understood than explained, they have been inmates, welcome inmates, of my own household—I know them familiarly, pass hours almost every day of my life in quiet but cheering communion with them. For many of them I cherish the warmest affection. Little Nell, at the age of two years, came an orphan into my home and heart, bringing Heaven's brightest sunshine and choicest gifts with her, to be darkened and shrouded only when, at fourteen, the spirit of that slight spark, resting on the bosom it loved best, drifted away into the wide ocean of eternity. Even Mr. Micawber, whom Mr. Dickens left in Australia prosperous and popular, has been several years in New York, subjected again to his earlier pecuniary embarrassments, negotiating bills on which payment is inconveniently demanded at maturity, being "took" occasionally, but ever looking about for "something to turn up." Just now he is inquiring whether "coals are likely to be remunerative." I have received several letters from him which Mr. Dickens would instantly recognize. Those legitimate sons and daughters of Thespis, the Crummleses, as Mr. Dickens knows, came to America. One has not forgotten the ostentatious leave-taking between Crummles and Nicholas. Their various and brilliant dramatic merits have been appreciated. The "Phenomenon," though no longer an "infant," is secure of a double encore; and that incomparable woman, "Mrs. Crummles," while balancing her head upon a fourteen-foot pole with a brilliant display of fireworks at her heels, never fails to bring down the house. The "Veneerings" scattered throughout our city are doing much to improve, adorn and varnish society. Mark Tapley, who honoured us with a visit, found so much to be "jolly" over, met with so much that was congenial in Jefferson Brick, Colonel Diver, and Mr. Julius Washington Merryweather Bib there, but for the remembrance of Mrs. Lupin, with an anticipation of "ten more," and then just "fifteen more" because the last was not fair and "must be done over again," would have settled down permanently on a charming "corner lot" that he fished out of the pond in the very attractive and imaginative city of Eden. Boarding schools constructed upon the Squeers, Creakle and Blimber plans, however admirable, have not, I regret to inform my patron, Mr. Dickens, been as flourishing as they were formerly. The discipline, though, is not quite popular. There is a prejudice indeed, I may say, unreasonable, but nevertheless a prejudice against such memorable institutions as "Dotheboys Hall." This will not, I hope, dishearten Mr. Dickens or diminish his praiseworthy efforts in behalf of education. Nor while "modern prisons" have fairly accomplished all the reforms he anticipated should his labours in that direction be intermitted. Here, as in London, visitors are delighted with the wonders we read in numbers "twenty-seven" and "twenty-eight." A prison system which produces so perfect a change of habit and heart as Uriah Heep and Littimer experienced may be fairly expected in due time to reclaim Traddles and Copperfield. Mr. Bumble and Mrs. Corney, who come out to give us the benefit of their experience, are placing our workhouses in a palmy condition. Our beadles and matrons have already learned that the health of sick paupers can be improved by eating the toast and drinking the tea provided for patients themselves. And we have lots of excellent waiters who know how to beguile young travellers of their beer and chops. The Circumlocution Office and Family are happily adapted to our own circumstances and begin to harmonize with our business habits. But it is my duty to apprise Mr. Dickens that his first chapter of *Bleak House*, whatever of merit the succeeding chapters may possess, has impaired the working and destroyed the charm of our court of chancery. Before that ingenious chapter was written and read, we too could boast of our Jarndyce and Jarndyce. Our courts were enlivened with occasional vehements of Gridley, the man from Shropshire; and we had little Miss Flights expecting judgments. But now, with the solitary exception—that of Broden against Corning—we have not a single chancery suit that has outlived a generation, into which children have been born, or out of which they had died. Madam Mantalini retrieved her fortune in New York, but was brought a second time to grief by her spendthrift Italian husband, whom I saw to-day through a basement window in 14th Street turning a mangle. When Mr. Dickens arrived in New York I attempted to pay by small instalments some fractional part of the large debt of which he has been defrauded by our refusal to enact an International Copyright Law. I applied to my friend Roberts, the host of Westminster, to further my scheme, but either from its bundle, conception or by accidental discovery it collapsed. Instead of receiving my check and sending two tickets, Mr. Dolby returned the check along with the tickets for the course; not to speak irreverently, I experienced the surprise that awaited the sermons of the patriots who went to Egypt for corn, but on their return found their money with the corn in the mouth of their sacks. But while moved for its affection

for Mr. Dickens, my mind possesses the motive power
of the cork leg. I must "stop her."

Permit me therefore to offer a brief sentiment—

Charles Dickens—The philanthropist who has con-
ferred the greatest happiness upon the greatest number.

Yours truly,

THURLOW WEED.

FROM DONALD G. MITCHELL

Mr. H. E. SWEETSER.

Edgewood, March 13, 1868.

MY DEAR SIR—I delayed replying to the circular of
Mr. Young to the very last, hoping that I might be able
to participate in your festal supper to Mr. Dickens.
Saturday night, however, is an awkward one for me,
and other engagements will compel me to decline.
Believe me, however, when I say that there will not be
one among you more sensible of the debt you all owe to
your honoured guest than your obedient servant,

DONALD G. MITCHELL.

LETTER FROM OLIVER WENDELL HOLMES

Boston, April 9, 1868.

DEAR SIR,

I am very sorry that it will not be in my power
to attend the dinner to be given to Mr. Dickens on the
18th of April. All of us delight to honour him, and
our hearts will all be with you as you speak the kind
words of farewell to your and our illustrious guest. No
invader ever astonished these Western shores with so
complete a triumph. He has subdued and rendered
tributary to himself the mighty multitudes of our great
cities more rapidly and more universally than Cortez
overcame the thronging Aztecs. He has taught his
gracious lessons of sympathy with all it suffers, of
delight in all joyous life, to a larger class of enraptured
scholars than Marco Polo found among the docile

Peruvians. He belongs to us and to all that breathes
the vital air as a true defender of the faith—faith in this
divinely human race, the congenial creed of its nobler
natures in the face of all its false priests and prophets.
His writings, fresh as they are in fame, are one in spirit
with the smiles and the sighs of the little family circle
of Eden before the firstborn of our mothers interfered
with its harmony. The language of true feeling is of
all time. The pleasant humour of *Pickwick* might have
been traced in the original character of an antediluvian
palimpsest, and the sweet humanity of *David Copperfield*
might have been deciphered from a manuscript thrown
overboard (in a bottle) by Father Noah. In varying
phrases we all strive to express the same wish : peace,
prosperity and happiness be with our parting guest, on
the land and on the deep, now and always; the man
who has been as a brother to more of his fellow-creatures
than any other of his time, and who all over the English
world is the companion of every age and condition, and
the welcome guest in every household.

Yours very truly,

O. W. HOLMES.

To Mr. John Russell W. Young, for the Committee
of Invitation.—Amen.

THE DICKENS BANQUET

The dinner given on Saturday evening by the Press
of the United States to Mr. Charles Dickens was something more than an ordinary compliment from the
members of the profession to the foremost man of their
craft. To those who sat round those brilliant tables it
seemed not so much a testimonial to the genius of a
successful author as a tribute of personal regard for the
characters with which that genius has improved and
delighted us. When Charles Dickens took his place
at the board, many a dear old friend sat down with us
unseen ; and it was hard not to imagine we were cheering Sam Weller, or hobnobbing with Tom Pinch, or

laughing with Mark Tapley, or gazing into the beaming spectacles of Mr. Pickwick. The cordial greetings were interchanged not only between Mr. Dickens and the two hundred of his admirers whose invitation he had accepted, but troops of those delightful people who live only in his books seemed to be there with him, and the hand-shaking, the toasting, the waving of handkerchiefs, were quite as much for them as for their genial creator. And so, amid lights and flowers, and the breathings of delicate music, and the laughter of many voices, the evening passed merrily away, as if in the society of friends whom we had long known in fancy, but never met in the flesh.

The admirable speech in which Mr. Dickens acknowledged the compliment paid him will undoubtedly add a great deal to his personal popularity in America, for it was just such a speech as Americans particularly like to hear. It was frank, it was cordial, it was generous; and as for those old darts of offence which have rankled so long in the wounds of a few of us, he drew them out with a deft and tender hand, and salved the injury with the unction of a little national flattery. We do not know that he was under any obligation to do this, but we are glad that he has done it, for we would have him leave none but warm friends here, and we trust that when the ship bears him away, the American people will wish him with entire unanimity Godspeed and long life and happiness.—*From the* NEW YORK TRIBUNE *of April 20, 1868.*

CHARLES DICKENS'S FAREWELL READING

Mr. Dickens has read for the last time in America. As we write these words the tones of his voice have scarcely died away. The living presence of his genius still warmly enkindles the hearts of his hearers. At such a moment joy and sorrow naturally blend—joy in the fullness of his splendid success; sorrow in the thought that the loved and admired artist will be seen and heard no more. Such a moment is naturally one of extreme emotion. Happily the voice of criticism may be silent. Its claims have been satisfied, its duty has been done. Only the voice of honest admiration need now be heard. Mr. Dickens has endeared himself to us in every possible way. As an author by his humanity, integrity and goodness, directing the use of great natural gifts; as a reader by his perfect honesty and simplicity in conveying to us the comic and pathetic creations of his art; and as a man by his frankness, his gentleness, his modesty, and his whole-hearted response to our sympathetic greeting. Henceforward the great humorist is entirely understood in America. Before he came here to give these readings there were some among us who remembered only his old-time strictures on the young republic, and some who doubted whether he would be welcome. But there was never real reason to doubt. The bare fact that these strictures were so clearly remembered after so many years was the best possible proof that Charles Dickens had always and from the outset of his career been beloved in this country. The heart remembers longer than the head. The great poet has told us what it is to be wroth with one we love. Charles Dickens's coming, however, was needful to disperse every cloud and every doubt and to place his name undimmed in the silver sunshine of American admiration. After the revelation of his inner nature that he has given to us in the readings now ended, and after the noble words he has spoken on the occasion of the recent banquet, we cannot help knowing that the creator of Little Nell and Peggotty and Sidney Carton and all the other friends, is as true in his heart as he is great in mind. Not to know this, indeed, would be to have heard him in vain. The delicious reading of the *Christmas Carol* and the "Trial of Pickwick"—with which Mr. Dickens last evening closed his series of entertainments in this country—should have won the heart of even the most inveterate bigot. The humane spirit of the man lit it up with a beautiful light. His fine fancy played over it like sunbeams on the water. His humour, his pathos, his direct and forcible portraiture of character, his poetic temperament, his unerring intuition as to motive and emotion, his simplicity of style in reading and of method in delivery—found illustration in this reading. What we said at the outset indeed remains true at the close—that the keynote of his genius is sounded in the *Christmas Carol* and the "Trial of Pickwick." That note found an echo in every bosom last night, and awoke the response of a tumultuous applause. The audience which crowded Steinway Hall in every part was, in truth, profoundly moved. By laughter and by weeping it testified its sympathy with the humour of Bob Cratchit and the pathos of Tiny Tim, and the fine lesson of humanity that was once more enforced by its honoured teacher. By its cheers it told him how deeply its feelings had been moved, and summoned him to say farewell. What he said is hereto appended, and we have only to add that his beautiful words were said with equal grace and tenderness.

"Ladies and Gentlemen : The shadow of one word has impended over me all this evening, and the time has come at last when the shadow must fall. It is but a very short one, but the weight of such things is not measured by their length : and two much shorter words express the whole realm of our human existence. When I was reading *David Copperfield* here last Thursday night, I felt that there was more than usual significance for me in the declaration of Mr. Peggotty : ' My future life lies over the sea.' And when I closed this book just now I felt keenly that I was shortly to establish such an alibi as would have satisfied even the elder Mr. Weller himself. (Laughter.) The relations that have been set up between us in this place—relations sustained, on my side at least, by the most earnest devotion to my task; sustained by yourselves, on your side, by the readiest sympathy and kindliest acknowledgment—must now be broken for ever. But I entreat you to believe that in passing from my sight you will not pass from my memory. I shall often recall you as I see you now, equally by my winter fire and in the green English summer weather. I shall never recall you as a mere public audience, but rather as a host of personal friends, and ever with the greatest gratitude, tenderness and consideration. Ladies and gentlemen, I beg to bid you farewell. And I pray God bless you, and God bless the land in which I have met you." (Great applause, the audience with waving handkerchiefs and loud voices cheering the distinguished author as he passed from the room.)

We should add that Mr. Dickens was last evening suffering from illness, which, though it did not in the least mar the fervency and the thorough art of his reading, evidently caused him great personal inconvenience. The following certificate—which speaks for itself—was distributed in the hall—

"I certify that Mr. Dickens is suffering from neuralgic affection of the right foot, probably occasioned by great fatigue in a severe winter. But I believe that he can read to-night without much pain or inconvenience (his mind being set on not disappointing his audience), with the aid of a slight mechanical addition to his usual arrangements.—FORDYCE BARKER, M.D."

The reading stand was beautiful with flowers—the gifts of friends. One wreath came from Boston, arriving in the course of the reading. It was fit that Nature's best adornments should embellish a scene of which every element was lovely, and of which every remembrance will be for ever sweet and gracious.—*Copied from the* NEW YORK TRIBUNE *of April* 21, 1868.

APPENDIX I

ITINERARY OF CHARLES DICKENS'S AMERICAN TRIP IN 1842

JANUARY

Saturday	22nd	Arrived in Boston 4 p.m. At Tremont Hotel
Sunday	23rd	In Boston
Monday	24th	Visited Massachusetts Legislature at Springfield
Tuesday	25th	In Boston
Wednesday	26th	,, ,,
Thursday	27th	,, ,,
Friday	28th	,, ,,
Saturday	29th	,, ,,
Sunday	30th	,, ,,
Monday	31st	,, ,,

FEBRUARY

Tuesday	1st	Dinner at Papinti's Restaurant, Boston
Wednesday	2nd	In Boston
Thursday	3rd	Visited mills at Lowell (Mass.)
Friday	4th	,, Harvard College, Cambridge (Mass.)
Saturday	5th	Left Boston for Worcester (Mass.)
Sunday	6th	Spent day in Worcester as guest of Governor Davis
Monday	7th	Left Worcester in morning via Springfield for Hartford (Conn.)
Tuesday	8th	Dinner at City Hotel, Hartford
Wednesday	9th	,, with Colonel Grant, Hartford
Thursday	10th	Visited Public Institution of Hartford

Friday	11th	Left Hartford 5 p.m.; arrived New Haven 8 p.m. Public reception at Tontine Hotel
Saturday	12th	Left New Haven in morning by boat for New York
Sunday	13th	Arrived in New York in morning
Monday	14th	"Boz" Ball at Park Theatre. Dined with Charles A. Davis, 365 Broadway
Tuesday	15th	Dined with David C. Colden, 28 Laight St.
Wednesday	16th	Confined to Hotel with bad cold
Thursday	17th	„ „ „ „ „
Friday	18th	Complimentary Dinner at City Hotel
Saturday	19th	In New York
Sunday	20th	At St. John's Church with ex-Prest. Van Buren
Monday	21st	In New York
Tuesday	22nd	„ „
Wednesday	23rd	„ „
Thursday	24th	„ „ Private Dinner at Astor House
Friday	25th	„ „
Saturday	26th	„ „
Sunday	27th	„ „
Monday	28th	„ „

MARCH

Tuesday	1st	In New York
Wednesday	2nd	Visited Tombs Prison and Public Department
Thursday	3rd	In New York
Friday	4th	In New York
Saturday	5th	„ „
Sunday	6th	Left New York in morning; arrived Philadelphia in evening. At United States Hotel
Monday	7th	In Philadelphia
Tuesday	8th	Reception at U.S. Hotel in morning. At Penitentiary in afternoon.
Wednesday	9th	Left Philadelphia in morning; arrived Washington in evening. At Fuller's Hotel
Thursday	10th	Visited Capitol and White House
Friday	11th	
Saturday	12th	Visited various public buildings
Sunday	13th	Dinner at White House 2.30. Dinner at Robt. Greenhow's 5.30
Monday	14th	Private Dinner at Boulanger's Restaurant
Tuesday	15th	Attended Levée at White House

Wednesday	16th	Left Washington for Richmond
Thursday	17th	Arrived at Richmond in evening. At Exchange Hotel
Friday	18th	Private Supper at Exchange Hotel
Saturday	19th	Visited Capitol in morning. Held reception at hotel 12 till 2
Sunday	20th	Left Richmond in morning for Baltimore
Monday	21st	Arrived at Baltimore in evening. Put up at Barnum's Hotel
Tuesday	22nd	Visited Hospital and Penitentiary in morning. Reception in evening
Wednesday	23rd	Left Baltimore in morning; arrived Harrisburg 6.30 p.m.
Thursday	24th	In Harrisburg till 3 p.m. Left for Pittsburgh
Friday	25th	by canal boat
Saturday	26th	En route to Pittsburgh
Sunday	27th	,, ,,
Monday	28th	,, ,,
Tuesday	29th	Arrived in Pittsburgh 9.30 p.m. Went to Exchange Hotel
Wednesday	30th	In Pittsburgh
Thursday	31st	,, ,,

APRIL

Friday	1st	Left Pittsburgh on Steamer *Messenger* for Cincinnati
Saturday	2nd	En route to Cincinnati
Sunday	3rd	,, ,, ,, ,,
Monday	4th	Arrived at Cincinnati in morning. Went to Broadway Hotel
Tuesday	5th	Ball at Judge Timothy Walker's residence
Wednesday	6th	Left Cincinnati in morning; arrived at Louisville (Ky.) midnight. Went to Galt House
Thursday	7th	Left Louisville 1 p.m.
Friday	8th	En route to St. Louis
Saturday	9th	Do. Passed Cairo (Ill.) in morning
Sunday	10th	Arrived at St. Louis (Mo.) at 9 p.m. Went to Planter's House
Monday	11th	Spent day viewing St. Louis
Tuesday	12th	Left for Prairie in morning; stayed in hotel in Lebanon (Ill.)
Wednesday	13th	Back at St. Louis at noon. Soirée in Planter's House in evening

x

Thursday	14th	Left St. Louis for Cincinnati
Friday	15th	En route to Cincinnati
Saturday	16th	,, ,, ,, ,,
Sunday	17th	Arrived at Louisville ; stayed overnight at Galt House
Monday	18th	Left in morning for Cincinnati on Steamer *Ben Franklin*
Tuesday	19th	Arrived in Cincinnati at 1 p.m.
Wednesday	20th	Left Cincinnati by stage at 8 a.m. for Columbus (Ohio)
Thursday	21st	Arrived Columbus 7 a.m. Reception at Neil House in evening
Friday	22nd	Left Columbus by stage 7 a.m. ; arrived Lower Sandusky 10 p.m.
Saturday	23rd	Left Lower Sandusky 7.30 a.m. ; arrived Sandusky 6 p.m.
Sunday	24th	Left Sandusky by boat in afternoon ; arrived at Cleveland in evening
Monday	25th	Left Cleveland in morning for Buffalo (N.Y.)
Tuesday	26th	Arrived Buffalo 6 a.m. Left for Niagara Falls at 9 a.m.
Wednesday	27th	Niagara Falls
Thursday	28th	,, ,,
Friday	29th	,, ,,
Saturday	30th	,, ,,

MAY

Sunday	1st	At Niagara Falls
Monday	2nd	,, ,,
Tuesday	3rd	,, ,,
Wednesday to Sunday	4th 29th	In Canada
Monday	30th	Left Montreal for New York
Tuesday	31st	Arrived Albany 5 p.m. Left by boat for New York at 7 p.m.

JUNE

Wednesday	1st	Arrived in New York at 4 a.m.
Thursday	2nd	Left New York in morning for Lebanon ; arrived there 10 p.m.

Friday	3rd	At Lebanon (Shaker Village)
Saturday	4th	Left Lebanon in morning; arrived at West Point in afternoon
Sunday	5th	At West Point Military Academy
Monday	6th	Left West Point for New York; arrived there in afternoon
Tuesday	7th	Left New York for England

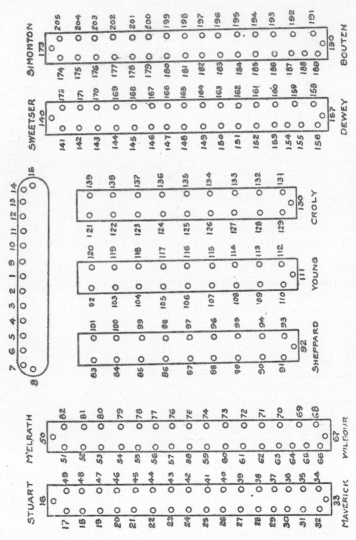

DIAGRAM OF SEATS AND TABLES AT THE DICKENS DINNER.

APPENDIX II

SINCE the account of the Dinner given to Dickens in New York in 1868 was put in type, the following complete list of the guests and the diagram showing the seating of the guests at the tables have been discovered in the New York *World* of April 29, 1868. While this list may not be of interest to British readers, it is believed that it will be especially interesting to readers in the United States, containing as it does the names of so many famous editors and literary writers of the "sixties," most of whom, like the great author in whose honour the dinner was given, have passed away.

LIST OF THOSE PRESENT AT THE DICKENS DINNER

1. Horace Greeley, *Tribune*, New York.
2. Charles Dickens, *All the Year Round*, England.
3. Thurlow Weed, *Commercial Advertiser*, New York.
4. Henry J. Raymond, *Times*, New York.
5. Manton Marble, *World*, New York.
6. Wm. Henry Hurlbert, *World*, New York.
7. Murat Halstead, *Commercial*, Cincinnati.
8. George W. Demers, *Evening Journal*, Albany.
9. Robert Hoe, New York.
10. Samuel Bowles, *Republican*, Springfield, Mass.
11. Jos. R. Hawley, *Courant*, Hartford, Conn.
12. George Wm. Curtis, *Harper's Monthly*, New York.
13. Robert Bonner, *Ledger*, New York.
14. James Parton, Author, New York.
15. Chas. Eliot Norton, *North American*, Boston.
16. William Stuart, New York.
17. Mr. Lester Wallack, New York.
18. Mr. Lamb, Scotland.
19. Henry D. Palmer, New York.
20. George Dolby, England.
21. Wm. D. Morgan, New York.

22. R. B. Roosevelt, *Citizen*, N.Y.
23. Isaac H. Bailey, New York.
24. James A. Whitney, *American Artisan*, N.Y.
25. J. B. F. Walker, *Evening Mail*, New York.
26. E. H. Clements, *Tribune*, N.Y.
27. Franklin Philip, Washington, D.C.
28. H. A. Dike, *Evening Post*, New York.
29. R. S. Chilton, Dept. of State, Washington, D.C.
30. C. T. Lewis, *Evening Post*, New York.
31. C. F. Briggs, *Putnam's Magazine*, New York.
32. Charles Nordhoff, *Evening Post*, New York.
33. Aug. Maverick, *Evening Post*, New York.
34. Thomas W. Knox, *Herald*, New York.
35. R. T. Colborn, Cor., *St. Louis Republican*, New York.
36. J. H. Browne, *Galaxy*, New York.
37. James M. Scovel, *New Republic*, Camden, N.J.
38. Chark Waggoner, *Commercial*, Toledo, Ohio.
39. J. H. Bates, New York.
40. James H. Benedict, New York.
41. Robert Sewell, New York.
42. T. B. Thorpe, Author, New York.
43. J. H. Hackett, New York.
44. H. Clapp, Jr., *Leader*, New York.
45. C. Fulton, *Mercury*, New York.
46. C. B. Seymour, *Times*, New York.
47. Mr. Osborn, Scotland.
48. L. W. Jerome, New York.
49. Thomas N. Rooker, *Tribune*, New York.
50. Thomas McElrath, *Tribune*, New York.
51. C. A. Runkle, *Tribune*, New York.
52. J. N. Balestier, *Tribune*, New York.
53. R. W. McAlpine, *Tribune*, New York.
54. James B. Mix, *Tribune*, New York.
55. James McConnell, *Tribune*, New York.
56. H. S. Olcott, *Tribune*, New York.
57. J. F. Cleveland, *Tribune*, New York.
58. S. Cobb, New York.
59. A. C. Armstrong, New York.
60. Peter S. Hoe, New York.
61. Richard M. Hoe, New York.
62. Charles Scribner, Publisher, New York.
63. Rev. H. M. Field, Evangelist, New York.
64. A. H. Green, New York.
65. Wm. Orton, *Western Union Telegraph*, N.Y.

66. A. J. Vanderpoel, New York.
67. Charles E. Wilbour, *Transcript*, New York.
68. C. Corson, *Transcript*, New York.
69. A. J. Peabody, Publisher, New York.
70. Ddl Ouymour, *Hours at Home*, New York.
71. J. D. Sherwood, Author, New York.
72. D. O'C. Townley, *Times*, New York.
73. D. A. Casserly, *Round Table*, New York.
74. Aug. Snow, *Times*, New York.
75. J. E. Munson, *Times*, New York.
76. R. Lexow, *German Press*, New York.
77. A. J. Schem, *Tribune*, New York.
78. J. F. de Conto, *Spanish Press*, New York.
79. W. W. Harding, *Inquirer*, Philadelphia.
80. J. F. Graiff, *Press*, Philadelphia, Pa.
81. R. E. Selmes, *Transcript*, New York.
82. Andrew Devine, *Times*, New York.
83. S. S. Conant, *Times*, New York.
84. Augustine Daly, *Times*, New York.
85. F. J. Ottarson, *Tribune*, New York.
86. R. D. Benedict, *Times*, New York.
87. H. J. Winser, *Times*, New York.
88. John Ireland, *Times*, New York.
89. Thos. Nast, *Harper's Weekly*, New York.
90. A. M. Stewart, *Scottish American*, N.Y.
91. Edwin de Leon, *Citizen*, New York.
92. George Sheppard, *Times*, New York.
93. Sheppard Homans, *Bankers' Magazine*, N.Y.
94. J. Smith Homans, *Bankers' Magazine*, N.Y.
95. C. C. Norvell, *Times*, New York.
96. Gaston Fau, *Galaxy*, New York.
97. George E. Pond, *Army and Navy Journal*, New York.
98. John Swinton, *Times*, New York.
99. Isaac Butts, *Union*, Rochester, N.Y.
100. D. C. McEwen, *Tribune*, New York.
101. Edmund T. Davis, *Mercury*, New York.
102. A. D. Richardson, *Tribune*, New York.
103. R. B. Kimball, Author, New York.
104. J. T. Fields, Publisher, Boston, Mass.
105. Samuel Sinclair, *Tribune*, New York.
106. M. C. Hart, *Chronicle*, Washington, D.C.
107. E. C. Stedman, *Galaxy*, New York.
108. George H. Boker, Author, Philadelphia.
109. Whitelaw Reid, *Gazette*, Cincinnati.

110. J. R. G. Hassard, *Tribune*, New York.
111. John Russell Young, *Tribune*, New York.
112. A. K. McClure, *Repository*, Chambersburg, Pa.
113. J. W. Dowling, *Times*, New York.
114. T. M. Davis, Keokuk, Iowa.
115. T. B. Carpenter, Author, New York.
116. Oliver Johnston, *Independent*, New York.
117. E. L. Youmans, Author, New York.
118. J. B. Sheridan, *Tribune*, New York.
119. Alfred Ford, *World*, New York.
120. W. L. Ormsby, Jr., *World*, New York.
121. W. W. Vaughan, *World*, New York.
122. Frederick Creighton, *World*, New York.
123. George W. Childs, *Ledger*, Philadelphia.
124. Paul Du Chaillu, Author.
125. E. L. Godkin, *Nation*, New York.
126. Edward Carey, *Union*, Brooklyn.
127. C. W. Sweet, *Real Estate Record*, N.Y.
128. Oscar Sawyer, *Herald*, New York.
129. Douglass Taylor, *Courier*, New York.
130. D. G. Croly, *World*, New York.
131. W. L. Stone, Author, New York.
132. W. J. Demorest, *Demorest's Monthly*, New York.
133. L. Israels, *World*, New York.
134. A. C. Wheeler, *World*, New York.
135. L. J. Bigelow, Watertown, New York.
136. George Wakeman, *World*, New York.
137. Steven Hayes, *Herald*, New York.
138. Ed. J. Holden, *Post*, Detroit.
139. Wm. N. Armstrong, New York.
140. Henry E. Sweetser, *World*, New York.
141. Henry Holt, Publisher, New York.
142. F. H. Houston, Mercantile Library, New York.
143. A. B. Crandall, *Tribune*, New York.
144. Joseph B. Lyman, *World*, New York.
145. Ellis H. Roberts, *Herald*, Utica, N.Y.
146. John Gamgee, London, England.
147. George Thurber, *Agriculturist*, New York.
148. Orange Judd, *Agriculturist*, New York.
149. A. J. Drexel, *Ledger*, Philadelphia.
150. D. Mellis, *World*, New York.
151. J. G. Floyd, Jr., *Commercial Chronicle*, N.Y.
152. John Bonner, Author, New York.
153. J. Ely, New York.

154. J. R. Osgood, Publisher, New York.
155. W. McClintock, *Post*, Philadelphia, Pa.
156. D. W. Judd, *Commercial Advertiser*, N.Y.
157. C. P. Dewey, *Commercial Advertiser*, N.Y.
158. I. E. Leeds, New York.
159. Samuel Barton, New York.
160. A. H. Almy, *Sun*, New York.
161. Dr. Marsden, *Evening Post*, New York.
162. Dr. Wilder, *Evening Post*, New York.
163. Thos. J. Ham, *Herald*, Honesdale, Pa.
164. Isaac Dayton, New York.
165. S. S. Packard, *Business Monthly*, New York.
166. Mr. Drayton, *Phrenological Journal*, N.Y.
167. Bronson C. Howard, *Evening Mail*, New York.
168. Dr. C. F. Heywood, New York.
169. Chas. H. Sweetser, *Evening Mail*, New York.
170. A. D. F. Randolph, Publisher, New York.
171. Dr. Wm. A. Hammond, *Medical Magazine*, N.Y.
172. A. D. Munson, *Our Young Folks*, New York.
173. J. A. Simonton, Associated Press, New York.
174. H. T. Lee, New York.
175. J. E. Spear, New York.
176. Wm. E. Marshall, New York.
177. Z. E. White, *Tribune*, New York.
178. John R. Walker, *Citizen*, N.Y.
179. B. Gallagher, *Tribune*, New York.
180. S. T. Clark, *Tribune*, New York.
181. W. B. McKean, *Ledger*, Philadelphia.
182. C. H. Webb, *Citizen*, New York.
183. Chas. E. Fitch, *Journal*, Syracuse, N.Y.
184. Leroy Shear, New York.
185. Thomas A. Acton, New York.
186. J. M. Francis, *Times*, Troy, N.Y.
187. C. E. Smith, *Express*, Albany, N.Y.
188. E. K. Olmstead, *Journal of Commerce*, New York.
189. C. S. Groot, New York.
190. J. B. Bouten, *Journal of Commerce*, New York.
191. L. A. Hunt, *World*, New York.
192. H. M. Wyncoop, Publisher, New York.
193. Joel Benton, *Times*, Amenia, N.Y.
194. F. G. Fairfield, *Herald*, New York.
195. George O. Glavis, *German Press*, N.J.
196. J. M. Winchell, *Public Spirit*, New York.
197. W. W. Warden, *Inquirer*, Philadelphia.

198. M. H. Northrup, *Express*, New York.
199. W. S. Chase, *Herald*, New York.
200. J. R. Thompson, *Southern Press.*
201. J. B. Lippincott, Publisher, Philadelphia.
202. Wm. Young, Publisher, New York.
203. R. K. Potter, Boston.
204. H. M. Ticknor, Publisher, Boston.

Among those present at the dinner was Mr. D. O'C. Townley, of the New York *Times.* Mr. Townley evidently enjoyed the dinner to the uttermost, as shown by the following account in rhyme, of which he was the author, which was published in the *World* on the Monday following the dinner. Mr. Townley sent a copy of his effusion to Mr. Dickens, and received the following characteristic letter in acknowledgment :—

" *Gad's Hill Place, Higham by Rochester, Kent.*
" *Monday, May 25,* 1868.

" MY DEAR SIR,
    " I am truly obliged to you for your note enclosing ' Alderman Rooney's ' account of a dinner never to be forgotten by me. You are very hard upon the ' Alderman,' I think, in your depreciation of his work ! For playfulness and earnestness combined, and for a special ease in versification, the ' Alderman ' seems to me to be rather remarkable. I cannot claim to be a disinterested judge of his production, certainly, for it has touched me in a tender place ; but if you can, by any means, convey my appreciation and thanks to him, pray do.

" My dear Sir,
    " Very faithfully yours,
        " CHARLES DICKENS.

" D. O'C. TOWNLEY, ESQ."

THAT WONDERFUL DINNER WID BOZ

BY ALDERMAN ROONEY

OH Goddess ov Song ! in whose honor
    Bow lowly the fair and the brave,
From the glory crown'd pake ov Parnassus
    Look down to the foot on your slave !
Look down on your Rooney, bewildhered—
    Wid poethry brimmin' his sowl ;
And you, great Apollo ! whose singin'
    Deludhered the nymphs of the strame,

Till widout any clothes but their blushes,
    They crept to your feet in a dhrame;
Look down, oh great bard! on your Rooney,
    His sowl wid your janius inspire,
And, if its iithely convaynient,
    Oh lind him the loan of your lyre!
He'd sing as he never before sung,
    Since first he wove music and thought
Into words, by that wonderful magic
    Your spirit, not Rooney's had wrought!
Oh breathe on your slave but a minnit,
    Then who shall refuse his applause
To him who put nately in verses,
    That wonderful dinner wid Boz!

The North, on whose cloud-kissin' summits,
    The snow-wreath rests "all the year round,"
Whose valleys are fertile as Ayden
    Ere Adam and Eve got aground!
The South, on whose slopes the banana
    Grows ripe with the glad gooldin corn,
Where the sheep that strayed off from the shepherd
    Were fearfully, fearfully shorn!
The East, land ov Pilgrims and praychers,
    Or janius that blossoms in books,
Providers ov mental provision,
    Ov which half the world are the cooks!
The West, land of produce and prairies,
    Ov cities that rise in the night,
Like palaces built by the fairies
    Ov which the bold Pagan did write.
All these to the dinner to Dickens,
    Sent on the first fruits of the soil—
The tireless brained thinkers who labor
    To smooth out the roughness of toil,
The oily-tongued, ready-penned writers,
    Great moulders of people and laws!
Aye, all of these came and were at it—
    That wonderful dinner wid Boz!

Delmonico troubled in sperit,
    Had slept ne'er a wink for a week;
"The fat boy!" he knew he was comin',
    He knew who would drink and who'd speak.

Good Lord! how he laid out the tables,
    In twinty most elegant rows!
And spread them all over wid damask,
    As white as the wind-driven snows.
And how he bedeck'd them wid flowers,
    And sugar-built Temples of Fame!
Wid great piles of shivverin' jellies,
    And icebergs ov beautiful crame!
Wid real silver spoons near the forks too,
    And regiments of plates in a line,
And cut crystal jugs and decanters,
    Brimful wid red tears ov the vine!
And how he hung up on the walls too,
    Right over the President's chair,
Our flag and the flag ov ould England—
    A little the worse ov the wear.
But agra he forgot the Green Island,
    Mayhap left her out for a cause,
Yet Dickens saw Irish who love him,
    Aye worship him, wonderful Boz!

Right under the banners stood Charley
    Wid joy in his heart and his eye,
As again and again from two hundred
    Rose up the wild welcomin' cry!
Down under the banners sat Dickens,
    Beside him great Greeley sat down
Wid spring in his face of good nature,
    And winter's snow-white on his crown.
And Raymond the thinker, and Parton,
    And Curtis the graceful, and Hoe,
And Hurlbert, a man worth a million,
    And Marble that makes the "World" go.
And there too, sat others, brave fellows
    Who fear not to shortin life's span
If robbin' their own they can lengthin
    And brightin the life-time ov man;
And down the long tables sat many,
    Whose names are well known to you all,
Hard workers, grate thinkers, fine spaykers
    Well primed for the work ov the Fall;
And wits too, your Rooney among them,
    Good fellows of stories and saws,

All blessin' wid brotherly kindness
    That wonderful dinner wid Boz.

'Tis useless to talk ov the aytin',
    Unless you're acquainted wid French,
If you're not, thin by dad, you should larn it,
    'Tis useful sometimes in a pinch.
If you *are*, then get hould ov a paper,
    You'll see thim set there in a row—
Most wonderful scholarly dishes,
    Invintions ov Swinton and Blow!
Wid the names ov Kings, Queens and great authors,
    For the fish and the flesh and the frog;
'Tis comfort to know, whin you're aytin',
    That larnin' goes down with the prog.
But enough of this faystin' and drinkin',
    Tis hardly good natured in troth,
Wid this I stop, least you get hungry—
    There was lashin's and lavin's ov both.
Wid the jokes that wint round there's no tellin',
    How half ov us ever got through,
Wid the fun thay spill'd soup on shirt bosoms,
    Or scalded our throats with Burgoo!
Wid the tales that passed over the glasses,
    The wit that slipped in at each pause—
And made like a faste at Olimpus,
    That wonderful dinner wid Boz!

The speeches? no, no, I won't try them;
    Not even your Rooney could tell
How sowls were uplifted with rapture,
    Whose tongues held our hearts wid a spell!
Enough that I wept and I shouted,
    I laughed and I cried in a breath—
If Dickens had spoke any longer,
    You'd surely been " in at a death."
For I swear, no I won't, yes, by Jabers!
    He played on my feelings so much,
That I felt my poor heart a piano
    That throbbed to his exquisite touch!
I blissed him in silence, and after
    I blissed them that followed him, too,
Who spoke ov the man who had ever
    Been faithful and valiant and true;

Who spoke as I felt ov that janius—
  Our brightest, our greatest, our own—
The wave of whose wand has uplifted
  The Press that o'ershadows the Throne!
Farewell, Great Reporter, may Heaven
  Preserve you, more stories to tell,
And God be as pleased wid your labors,
  As we are, who bid you farewell!
Our children will read in the future,
  Ov brothers who fought the good cause,
And met the Great Taycher to thank him.
  Good-bye! and God bless you, dear Boz!